A Guide to Letter-Writing

GEDDES & GROSSET

Published 2007 by Geddes & Grosset
David Dale House
New Lanark
ML11 9DJ
First published 2005, reprinted 2007

© Geddes & Grosset 2005

All rights reserved. No part of this publication may be reproduced, stored in a retrieval system, or transmitted, in any form or by any means, electronic, mechanical, photocopying, recording or otherwise, without the prior permission of the copyright holder

ISBN 1 84205 334 5

Printed and bound in Poland

Contents

Introduction   5
Part 1
Chapter 1
A Potted History of Letters and Their Delivery   9
  The Communication Boom   9
  Delivery Methods Down the Ages   10
  Establishing the Modern Method of Postal Delivery   12
  Stamps   13
  Postal Codes   14
  Writing Surfaces   15
  Writing Instruments   16
Chapter 2
Now and Into the Future   18
  Telephone   19
  Fax   20
  Word Processing   21
  Email   23
  Messaging   25
Chapter 3
Getting Organized   34
  Social Letters   35
  Business and Personal Letters   37
  Handwritten or Typed/Word Processed?   37
  Writing Tools   41
  Writing Paper   41
  Cards   45
  Envelopes   47
Chapter 4
Presentation and Layout   49
  Blocked, Indented and Semi-blocked Style   50
  Pre-printed Stationery   51

Formatting Continuation Sheets	52
Overall Appearance	52
The Individual Elements of a Formal or Business Letter	62
Addressing Envelopes	82
Fax	89
CV	90

Chapter 5
Finding the Word 92
Style	92
Usage	99
Grammar	116
Punctuation	150
Word Formation and Spelling	173
British English and American English	199
Words That Are Difficult to Spell	212
Words That Can Be Confused	230

Part 2
Sample Letters 307
Employment	307
Business and Financial	329
Personal and Social	340

Appendices
Appendix 1
Some Special Forms of Address 359
Appendix 2
United States Guidance on Addressing Mail 367
Appendix 3
Abbreviations for English and Welsh Postal Counties 372
Appendix 4
Irregular Verbs 373
Appendix 5
Some Abbreviations, Acronyms and Short Forms Used in Text Messaging and Email 379

Introduction

Though some may question the need to write letters nowadays, to use the telephone, fax and email is not necessarily as effective – nor is it as lasting – as a letter. Phone calls may, on the face of it, be quick and easy, but who has not been kept on hold for extended periods listening to a maddening tinny tune, until they can stand it no longer and ring off in disgust. Neither a phone call nor an email message provides the formal documentation you may need to substantiate facts or follow something up at a later date. In other situations, such as thanking someone or offering your sympathy, there really is no substitute for a note or letter written in your own hand.

Therefore, most of us will need to write letters at some time, whether we are making a complaint, writing to our bank or building society, accepting or rejecting a job offer, or offering condolences. Writing a letter allows you to consider carefully what you want to say, to express your feelings, to put things in a logical order, to revise and fine tune, and so produce an impressive and effective result.

The aim of this book is to set you firmly on the path of being a confident letter-writer.

In the first section, there is a brief history of letter-writing, guidance on the tools and equipment you may need, advice on presentation and layout, and on grammar, spelling and correct usage. There are also some pointers on how to make best use of the new technologies of word processing, emailing and text messaging.

The second section is made up sample letters. These letters provide templates for business letters of various types, including the all-important covering letter for a CV, as well as social and personal letters for many occasions. These templates should help you compose the letters that will bring you the results you are looking for. *These sample letters are designed as outlines only, and any letter you write should be in your own words.* All names and addresses used in the sample letters are fictitious.

In the Appendices at the end of the book there are various lists for quick reference, including correct forms of address, as well as a guide to irregular verbs, and a selection of text messaging abbreviations.

Part 1

Chapter 1
A Potted History of Letters and Their Delivery

A letter – according to the *Shorter Oxford English Dictionary* – is 'a written, typed or printed communication, addressed to a person, organization, etc., and usually sent by post or messenger.' Expanding this definition a little, a letter is a written message delivered – by a variety of means – to an addressee located at some distance geographically from its sender.

Letters were, and still are, written for a variety of reasons: people may be too distant from each other to allow face-to-face discussion; they may not be able to communicate by any other means; one person may wish to communicate private or sensitive information to another; or it may be desirable to have a written record of an exchange which can be retained for future reference.

The Communication Boom

In ancient Egypt, Persia and Greece, the earliest recorded letters were written by the political and military elite, the only section of society able to write themselves, or to pay for the services of a scribe, and also with the means to organize, in a reliable and consistent way, the delivery of their messages.

In the Hellenistic period after the death of Alexander the Great, personal letter-writing seems to have become almost commonplace. Letters were being written by a wide range of people in many different situations for a variety of purposes. These purposes included maintaining contact during long separations, reporting news, expressing thanks or condolences, and making requests or giving advice. Certain conventions in letters of this period – especially the formulaic greetings and endings used – seem to suggest that basic letter-writing, or at least the basic structure of a letter, was taught in schools.

Because letters are often essentially substitutes for conversations between friends and acquaintances and because human beings are insatiably curious and social animals, the habit of letter-writing between private individuals became more and more popular and widespread. It was not even absolutely essential to be literate; those without the skill to write could dictate to a scribe, who, for a fee, would write the letter for the sender.

Once people began to write to each other regularly, they also started to put some time and effort into what they had to say and how it was said. The conventional greetings and endings of letters evolved and polite wishes for good health, etc., were included. Correspondents often vied to outdo each other in witty written exchanges. Especially amongst the educated classes and literati, letter-writing was elevated to an art form and began to be used as a literary device.

It is widely known that some of the New Testament of the Bible is in the form of letters, such as the 'Epistles of St Paul'. Some novels are also written in the form of letters, early examples being *Pamela* (1749) by Samuel Richardson and *The Expedition of Humphrey Clinker* (1771) by Tobias Smollett. Fiction in this style, known as the epistolary novel – though comparatively rare – is classed as a literary genre. Poetry has also been written in epistolary verses; a notable example is 'An Epistle to Dr Arbuthnot' (1735) by Alexander Pope.

Delivery Methods Down the Ages

Before letters, news and information travelled very slowly between communities. When it was absolutely necessary to convey information over a distance, the message would have to be communicated orally and carried by a messenger or courier. The most frequent senders of messages were the powerful:

rulers, government officials and military commanders. Their messengers were usually a trusted servant or slave, or a soldier of their army.

A Persian queen, Atossa, is credited with being the person who 'invented' the letter. Whether this is historical fact or myth, it is known that one of the earliest known postal systems was set up in the ancient Persian Empire. Royal dispatches and other official documents were carried to the furthest points of the empire by a relay system of riders. A rider carried the message to a given point on the road where a fresh rider was stationed, waiting to carry the messages over the next stage to the next rider. This fast and efficient method of communication allowed the Persian rulers to maintain power and control over their empire. Similar relay systems were used in ancient Greece and Roman, mainly for military and official purposes. Letters written by private citizens were generally not carried by these early carrier systems.

As education brought literacy to greater numbers, letter-writing gave private citizens new opportunities to communicate over long distances. Although more and more people took to letter-writing, the difficulties of travel meant that delivery remained, for many centuries, very expensive or uncertain, with correspondents dependant, not on the cheap and reliable international postal system we have today, but on paid messengers, or any ships, traders, and merchants who might be travelling in the right direction and who reached their destination safely.

Even in more modern times – before the establishment of a railway network – delivery of letters was a slow and expensive business. It was not until the early sixteenth century that the faster and more efficient post-horse system, a relay system of horsemen similar to that first used in the ancient Persian Empire, replaced the personal messenger.

In the United States, too, there was the famous Pony Express relay system over some 2,000 miles from St Joseph, Missouri to

Sacramento, California. An advertisement for riders in a California newspaper of the time read: 'Wanted. Young, skinny, wiry fellows. Not over 18. Must be expert riders. Willing to risk death daily. Orphans preferred.' Set up in part as a publicity stunt to try to secure a lucrative government mail contract, it operated for only 18 months between 1860 and 1861, before the first telegraph link was made with California. Despite its short life, the Pony Express is firmly fixed in the history of the American West; it provided the fastest communication between east and west before the telegraph, and captured the imagination of people all around the world.

Establishing the Modern System of Postal Delivery

In Britain in 1626, the postal service which up until that time had been used only for royal dispatches and official messages was extended to run between London and Plymouth. Soon, a more extensive postal network grew up between the main cities of the United Kingdom. On 31 July 1635, King Charles I issued a proclamation extending the use of the Royal Mail to the public.

The British Post Office was reorganized in 1660; Henry Bishop was made Postmaster General, and, in 1661, he introduced the first postmark. This so-called 'Bishop mark' showed only the day and month of the posting, its principal purpose being to ensure that the letter carriers did not delay the mail. Also around this time, all letters were distributed around the country via one of the main post roads, to the cities of London, Edinburgh and Dublin, before being sent on to their specific destinations. Each of these three cities had individual Bishop marks. Similar postmarks were being used in America, notably in Philadelphia and New York. These early American postmarks are often referred to as 'Franklin marks', after Benjamin Franklin, who at one time was Deputy Postmaster General.

The network of post roads around London and the roads to Edinburgh and Dublin were soon added to with a series of additional routes: cross posts ran between two post roads and by-posts ran between a post road and a town some distance from it. A way-letter went between two towns on the same post road. Instructions for delivery were put on the bottom left corner of letters.

Before the invention of the prepaid penny postal system, the addressee – not the sender – usually had to pay the carrier. The letter carrier received payment on delivery, with the amount of the delivery charge calculated according to the distance travelled and the number of sheets of paper included in the letter. The whole process was very time-consuming and expensive, so that only the wealthy could afford to send letters regularly.

A special local penny-post was introduced in London in 1680 by William Dockwra. This cheap local post was soon used in other major cities and later adopted in many provincial towns.

Rowland Hill (1795–1879) was probably the greatest reformer of the postal service in Britain. He advocated a cheap and efficient postal system that everybody could afford to use, and a convenient method of prepaying the postage. He demonstrated that it was better to charge by the weight of a letter rather than by the number of sheets, suggesting a uniform charge of one penny per half ounce on all letters delivered within the United Kingdom, and recommending that postage should be prepaid using a stamp or special stationary. These innovations were eventually approved and a uniform penny post introduced on 10 January 1840.

Stamps

On 6 May 1840, the famous Penny Black stamps went on sale at post offices. After the issue of these first stamps, many countries, which at that time were British colonies, wanted to have their own stamps. However, the GPO (General Post Office) in

London would permit only a red-coloured hand-stamp to be applied to letters from countries within the British Empire. This stamp showed a crown on top of a circle with the words 'paid at' and the name of the city or country. The GPO's justification for refusing to allow country-specific stamps within the British Empire was that a plethora of designs might confuse the people whose job it was to sort the mail, and so lead to delays and errors.

Beyond the power and influence of Britain's General Post Office, other countries started to introduce their own postage stamps. Brazil introduced its famous 'Bull's Eye' stamps on 1 August 1843, followed in 1843 and 1845 by the first issue of stamps from the cantons of Switzerland. In 1847, stamps were issued by the United States and Mauritius and, in 1849, by France, Belgium and Bavaria.

Postal Codes

The earliest form of postcode was introduced in London in 1857. Sir Rowland Hill, the inventor of the penny post, divided London into districts using compass points, 'N' for north, 'SW' for south-west and so on. In 1916, numbers were added to the London postal districts to divide them up more specifically into NW1, SW2, etc. In 1864, Liverpool was the first provincial city to be divided into postal districts.

The modern British postcode, with its mixture of six letters and digits, was first used in Norwich in October 1959. Designed to facilitate sorting of the mail by machine, this was the world's first use of alphanumerical postal address codes. By 1974, the postcode system had been adopted throughout Britain.

In the United States, the ZIP code system using a five-digit code was introduced in 1963. The first digit designated a broad geographical area of the United States, from zero to nine. This was followed by two digits that pinpointed more closely population concentrations and those centres accessible to transportation networks. The final two digits designated small post offices or postal zones in larger cities. An expanded ZIP Code was introduced in 1983. This ZIP + 4 code added a hyphen and four digits to the existing five-digit ZIP code. The first five numbers continue to identify an area of the country and delivery office. The sixth and seventh numbers denote a delivery sector, which might be several blocks, a group of streets or Post Office boxes, several office buildings or a single high-rise office building, a large apartment building or a small geographic area. The last two numbers denote a delivery segment, which might be a single floor of an office building, one side of a street between intersecting streets, specific departments in a firm, or specific Post Office boxes.

Writing Surfaces

The earliest letters were written on tablets made of clay or wood, or, more rarely, metal or ivory. Often the writing surface would have a layer of wax into which the message was inscribed using a sharp pointed writing instrument, or stylus. Writing in a layer of wax meant that the message in the wax could be easily erased using the blunt end of the stylus, the wax surface made smooth again, and the tablet reused for another message.

Later, the materials on which letters were written were papyrus, followed by parchment, and then paper.

Paper was comparatively expensive until fairly recently. In the 18th and 19th centuries, writers sometimes tried to make a single sheet work overtime by writing on both sides of the sheet of paper, then turning the sheet sideways and writing across what they had already written. This was known as 'crossing' and made their letters messy and difficult to read. Irritation with the practice is expressed in many novels and journals of the time and is dealt with in one of the rules of Lewis Carroll's light-hearted 'Eight or Nine Wise Words About Letter Writing' (written under his real name of Charles Dodgson):

My ninth Rule. When you get to the end of a notesheet, and find you have more to say, take another piece of paper – a whole sheet, or a scrap, as the case may demand: but whatever you do, *don't cross!* Remember the old proverb *'Cross-writing makes cross reading.'* 'The *old* proverb?' you say, inquiringly. *'How* old?' Well, not so *very* ancient, I must confess. In fact, I'm afraid I invented it while writing this paragraph!

Writing Instruments

Using a quill pen and inkwell too often must have made writing a laborious and messy business, and had very little to recommend it. Considerable practice and skill was needed for a good standard of penmanship. There was also the continual trimming of nibs, filling of inkwells, blotting and sealing of letters – all in all, a time-consuming and bothersome process which most modern writers couldn't imagine having time for. An innovation that swept away the quill pen, and at the same time encouraged more people to write, was the modern fountain pen, invented by Lewis Edson Waterman around 1883. Waterman's version perfected earlier fountain pens – so called from having a reservoir of ink attached – by adding a device that slowed down the rate at which the ink got to the nib, and so stopped the pen leaking.

Next came the ballpoint pen, invented and named after Hungarian-born Laszlo Biro, who patented the design in 1943. His design had a tiny ball that rotated inside the tip of the pen and delivered quick-drying ink to the writing surface, further reducing the risk of leaking.

Where next for letter-writing? Have the gains we have made in the last thirty years in convenience and efficiency been worth the cost? Should it be a cause for regret that skills, and aesthetic and decorative qualities, evolved over the whole history of letter-writing before the introduction of the computer, may quickly disappear? Does it matter that fewer and fewer people will want to learn and use the beautiful copperplate handwriting so often seen in old letters; and that collections of letters written on handmade paper and tied with ribbon may be seen only in museums?

Chapter 2

Now and Into the Future

People of an older generation, who remember the pleasure of writing and reading long, newsy letters sent to and received from friends and family, may lament the fact that letter-writing seems to be something of a dying art. However, on a more positive note, it could be argued that we communicate much more now than we did in the past. It is the means of communication that has changed, not the inclination to communicate. But it is certainly true that, for most of us, for most of the time, the pen is far from being mightier than the phone, and when we do write it is more and more likely to be via electronic mail or text message than by the traditional method.

It is undisputedly the case that there has been a steep decline in the number of personal letters written in the traditional way, with pen on paper. Pace of life and lack of time have conspired with the rapider methods of communication – telephone, fax, email and text messaging – against personal letter-writing. Or looked at another way, the rapider methods of communication have freed up time, time which people are now less inclined to fill by writing personal letters.

Whether this is also true of all types of formal and business correspondence is not quite so clear. Certainly there is a marked increase in certain types of letter; we all receive piles of letters – junk mail – from companies who are trying to drum up business, and keep shredders and paper recycling plants busy disposing of it all. But a fair amount of business correspondence is generated as a result of increasing affluence: think of all those letters from credit card and insurance companies, and the sometimes protracted exchanges associated with buying and selling property. Despite predictions of the 'paperless office' that computers would bring, the opposite seems to have happened. The very ease with which material can be produced with word processing software has meant the overall amount of printed material – which includes letters – has increased enormously.

There will be some fairly predictable consequences of the changes brought about by the new technologies, which will have an impact on certain types of research. In future, the decrease in social letter-writing may well deprive family historians and social historians of a valuable source of information. The content of personal letters is often an accurate record of events at the time of writing, within a family and in a wider social context. Amateur and professional genealogists hold great store by old family letters, which can be extremely informative and illuminating. The more ephemeral nature of communication via the new technologies will leave very little material for such researches: telephone calls are routinely recorded only by big financial institutions and government agencies, faxes fade, not many people take the trouble to save, archive or print emails, and text messages are deleted to make room for more.

Biographers too are likely to have cause to regret the falling from favour of letter-writing; letters, both from and to their subjects, can give an extremely valuable insight into an individual's character, temperament, relationships and circumstances. In the past, letters were often kept as precious mementoes by the recipient, or even returned to the sender where he or she had some inkling that the content might be of historical interest. In these ways much material was preserved for posterity.

Telephone

By the second part of the twentieth century most households in Britain had a telephone. Those who did not have a telephone in the home usually had access to a public telephone.

The telephone – and the more recent innovations, fax, email and texting – are in many ways more convenient forms of communication than letter-writing, because information is transferred almost instantaneously. With letters, time has to be allowed for the letter to reach the person written to, and for a reply to return.

The telephone has a further advantage over the letter in that you can be absolutely certain that your message has reached the person for whom it is intended. The telephone has a more informal, personal advantage too. If the person at the other end of the telephone line is a lover, good friend or family member, there is the pleasure of hearing his or her voice – a pleasure that is particularly welcome when the person is far away. If a face-to-face chat is not possible, the next best thing is a phone-to-phone one.

What was, and still is, appreciated about the telephone is that it saves a good deal of time and effort, even when some time has to be spent thinking out what we are going to say. It is, of course, an invaluable business tool.

Fax

Fax machines can send and receive handwritten notes, printed text, drawings, diagrams and photographs quickly along a telephone line from anywhere in the world. The fax machine gives the speed of delivery of the telephone while allowing the sender to consider and then write the information that they wish to convey. A fax has the immediacy of the telephone but also some of the permanence of the letter.

Most fax machines now use plain paper but you may still come across older type fax machines which use thermal paper. Thermal paper is supplied on a roll and is flimsier than standard photocopying grade paper. Messages printed on thermal paper tend to fade over time, so if you want a more permanent record of the fax you will need to copy it onto standard paper.

Most fax machines can store incoming faxes in their memory and print them out later. Many machines are now multi-functional, combining printer, scanner, photocopier, and fax machine. Other multi-function fax machines have mobile handsets and even offer SMS text messaging.

Faxes should always get to the person to whom they are directed, but lack of confidentiality can be a problem because the fax machine in an office is often shared. The basic message is: if you want to keep information confidential, avoid the fax machine.

Faxes have some other disadvantages. Fax is a shortened version of the word 'facsimile' and faxes are sent using a system called 'facsimile transmission'. The document with the printed text or image to be faxed is scanned and converted into digital code by the fax machine at the sending end and then transmitted down a telephone line to the fax machine at the receiving end. The receiving machine reconstitutes the information and produces a copy of the original. Very often the information comes out as clear at the receiving end as it went in at the sending end, but this is not always the case, especially where the document includes fine detail. Although it is usually possible to change the resolution to improve the readability and clarity of the image, high resolution faxes take much longer to transmit.

Many individuals and businesses – especially before emailing became widespread in the 1990s – abandoned all other forms of communication in favour of the fax. Now that more and more information is stored on computer and can be sent via broadband Internet connection between computers, the fax is being used less and less.

Word Processing

The word processor has probably had a greater effect on the production of letters and other documents than any technological advance since the invention of paper.

Before the word processor, if someone needed a letter typed, they usually had to write out what they wanted to say, hand this to a secretary, check it, check it again if there were any mistakes the first time round, and sign it. Or, letters would be dictated to a secretary, taken down in shorthand, typed, and finally presented for checking, correcting and signing. All this took up a great deal of time and effort and used a great many man and woman hours. Nor was it a very satisfactory way of dealing with highly confidential or personal information.

Now that there is a word processor in every office (and most homes too), gone are the shorthand notebooks, the heavy typewriters, the serried ranks of typists in typing pools, the tedious process of checking and rechecking, the correcting fluid ... the boss has even learned to type his or her own letters!

The keyboard on the average word processor is relatively easy to use even by those who have never had a typing lesson. Using a word processor, it is a matter of a moment to correct an error or reword a sentence, and nearly all word processing programs will check your spelling, and even your grammar. If you suddenly realize you have used the words 'good' and 'nice' fifteen times in the same paragraph, your word processing program will almost certainly have an inbuilt thesaurus to offer suggestions for synonyms that will add a bit of variety and interest to leaden prose!

You can create documents that contain formatted text, columns, tables, and graphics.

You can add links to websites, and import and export data from your electronic files, the Web, and other programs.

If you want to send out a standard letter to a thousand different people, but you want to personalize each one, word processing packages have a facility called mail merge, which will print, from a database or electronic address book, each individual's details onto a copy of the standard letter.

Is there anything negative that can be said about this modern

Now and Into the Future

wonder? Well, yes, and mostly about the personal letters produced on word processors.

They may be personal letters but all that print with only the signature in handwriting doesn't seem very personal, does it? Was that word processed letter you got from your great-uncle Augustus at Christmas also sent to all his other friends and relations, as you suspect it might have been? Can your grandson write with that nice fountain pen you gave him last year? You're pretty sure you haven't seen anything he's written, using a pen on paper, since he was 11.

You found out the hard and embarrassing way when you wrote that letter to Mr Nolan, the bank manager, that the spellchecker on your word processor has to be configured not to 'correct' automatically the spellings of words it thinks might be wrong, especially when the words are proper names. You've also found out the hard way that the spellchecker couldn't tell that there was something wrong when you typed 'the affect of this change' instead of 'the effect of this change'. You have stubbornly resisted taking a course in word processing and have thus spent a frightening percentage of your spare time trying to discover how to create columns and increase from the size of a pinhead the piece of clipart you've added to your document!

Email

No sooner had people come to grips with the fax and the word processor, when along came electronic mail (more usually known by its abbreviated name email, or e-mail). The advantages of email over fax and the traditional postal system, or 'snail mail', are its ease of use, its cheapness, and its speed of transmission from one computer to another. You can even keep or print out copies. In the first few years of its use, many people found email so convenient it encouraged them to communicate much more that they would otherwise have done.

More recently, broadband Internet services have increased the speed of transmission even further, but unfortunately, it is also now fairly commonplace to get huge volumes of unsolicited email or 'spam', and emails can carry viruses that will damage your computer. They can also be the means by which identity thieves gain access to your personal details. However, as long as you are aware of the precautions that are necessary to guard against these nuisance and criminal activities by reviewing and updating your security systems regularly, email is a great way to communicate!

The business community has embraced email with enthusiasm because of its speed and convenience and because it made it possible to send any type of computer file over the Internet: pictures, sounds, video clips and text files. An email can be sent to hundreds, even thousands, of email addresses simultaneously and very cheaply. Email addresses are made up of two parts:

everest@highestmountain.co.uk.

The first part of the name – the part before the @ symbol – is the user name (often a personal name or any nickname the user chooses to be known by); and the second part – the part after the @ symbol – is the domain name or host name (the Internet server through which the mail is sent and received). The domain name is often further subdivided into the subdomain (immediately after the @ sign), followed by the domain type (the type of organization, such as a business company, a government department, or an academic institution), followed by a country code (this last is omitted for many of the larger host names, like AOL). Elements in the domain name are separated by dots.

An email message is also made up of two parts: the header information and the message you type. The header information, written by the email software when the message is sent, includes the sender's name or email address, and the date and time of sending and receipt.

Although email is a fairly informal medium, there is a code of conduct (sometimes called Netiquette) designed to ensure that users do not give offence. It is bad form to SHOUT by typing whole words in capital letters; don't show anger or be intentionally rude in emails (this is called 'flaming'); always try to put something in the Subject line to give the recipient some idea of what your email is about; check email addresses have been typed correctly; and don't send anything confidential via email.

Messaging

Text messaging has also proved to be an extremely popular method of communication, especially amongst young people. The younger people are, the more likely they are to text. One study in the UK showed that 80% of those under the age of 25 are more likely to send a text message than make a phone call, while only 14% of people over 55 preferred texting to making a phone call. Other studies list the most popular reasons for social messaging: sending someone a birthday greeting, cancelling or arranging a meeting, receiving news updates and sporting news, contacting a partner, and flirting.

Of course, texting also has less frivolous purposes; increasingly businesses are using it as a standard method of sending messages.

Texting has many advantages: it can be relatively cheap compared to a phone call; a text message can be sent in situations where it is not practical to talk or when the recipient is not able to answer a normal voice call; information can be sent to someone's phone which they would otherwise have to write down; and, like email, the same message can be sent to a large number of people.

With increasing technological sophistication, mobile phones are now becoming a one-stop communication tool, incorporating digital cameras and lots of other features. But texting doesn't have to be limited to mobile phones. Special software programs are available which allow you to send text messages from your PC to a mobile phone, and get replies via your email program. Also, with a text-compatible handset, you can send and receive texts from your traditional phone or landline.

At the time of writing, there are three main messaging technologies: SMS (Short Message Service); (EMS) Enhanced Message Service; and MMS (Multimedia Messaging Service).

SMS (Short Message Service)

SMS was the first messaging system to appear. It began as a fairly basic person-to-person text messaging system, using the GSM communication system.

GSM (Global System for Mobile Communications) is a digital mobile phone system and is one of the world's main second generation (2G) wireless standards used on mobile phone networks. GSM is very well established in Europe and many other countries of the world, and operates in three frequency bands: 900 megahertz, 1800 megahertz, and 1900 megahertz. The United States equivalent of GSM is PCS (Personal Communication Service), operating in the 1900 megahertz frequency band.

SMS allows alphanumeric text messages of up to 160 characters to be sent and received on a digital mobile phone. The SMS system works in a similar way to a paging service, with messages routed through the network's SMSC (Short Message Service Centre). This is a computer which stores the message until it can be delivered to the recipient. SMS text messages can be sent from a mobile phone, or via a dial-up connection using a modem and a computer.

The SMSC will store messages when the recipient's mobile phone is turned off. When their phone comes back into service, stored messages will then be delivered automatically. Messages can have an expiry time set, with the message being deleted if not delivered at the end of the expiry period.

When a message is received, it is stored in the SIM (Subscriber Identity Module) smart card chip, where it will be available to be read whenever needed, and saved until deleted. The SIM card, when inserted into a mobile phone handset, creates a mobile station. Without the SIM card, the mobile phone cannot make or receive calls (except emergency calls). Information stored on the SIM card includes the International Mobile Subscriber Identity (IMSI), the number used by the mobile phone network to track calls made and assign call charges.

Most mobile phones can be set to beep when a message is received, or have an indicator light on the display panel for situations where the sound of a beep would be inappropriate. Depending upon the phone and the SIM card, you can store between 5 and 15 messages.

Because SMS limits each message to 160 characters, a whole new language of abbreviations and shortened forms has developed. People, especially young people, are communicating by shortening words, using phonetic spellings, missing out letters, or using symbols to represent words, letter combinations, and syllables.

Messaging, with its informal style and abbreviated forms, is now so ubiquitous that some parents and educators are worried that text talk is affecting children's ability to spell and use English correctly. However, children and young people seem to be just as literate as they were before the texting boom. Concerns about standards of literacy have been around for decades, even centuries, and there was a move towards greater informality long before chat rooms, email or texting existed. It's a moot point whether loss of formality is a bad thing, but the reality is that things are changing and will go on changing. Our language is always in a state of subtle change. New words find their way into English all the time: coming from other languages; giving names to scientific, technical, and technological discoveries and innovations; reflecting social change; or adopted from street slang. The spelling and shortening system used in texting is very unlikely to be used much outside the specific context for which it evolved. And, anyway, texting does have its own rules, however loose and informal. To shorten words and expressions in a meaningful way you first have to know something of the basic rules of English usage. In other words, you have to know the rules before you can break them. The anxious observers may just be anxious because they aren't particularly comfortable with the new technology, or perhaps it's because young people are busy with something that they haven't had to learn from their 'elders and betters'.

Many mobile phones now include a software application called Predictive Text Messaging, designed to make writing SMS text messages quicker and easier. Instead of the message writer having to perform multiple key strokes to scroll laboriously through letters, predictive text systems make the most of the limited number of keys found on phone keypads. Each key (usually one of nine) is allocated 3 or 4 letters of the alphabet. A dictionary database with the most commonly used words, abbreviations, emoticons, and punctuation comes as part of the predictive text messaging package. As the writer begins to key words in, the software reads the keystrokes and scans the dictionary for matching words. Where it finds a match, it will 'predict' what the word being typed is going to be and complete it. Where its prediction is wrong, changes can be made manually. Words that the software does not recognize can be entered into the dictionary and stored for future use. Like the spellcheckers used with word processing software, predictive text can sometimes get it very wrong, causing, at best, amusement and, at worst, irritation.

EMS (Enhanced Messaging Service)

EMS (Enhanced Messaging Service) adds a few more bells and whistles to SMS. It is what it says it is – an improved message system, which allows you to send and receive formatted text messages, simple pictures, sounds and animations. An EMS message may contain one or all of these elements. If messages exceed the length of a single SMS message then they will be made up of a number of concatenated (linked) SMS messages. However, the phone receiving an EMS message must also have EMS capability; otherwise the received message will be displayed without formatting, like a plain SMS text message.

MMS (Multimedia Messaging Service)

MMS (Multimedia Messaging Service) represents a significant advance from the fairly basic SMS. With MMS a message can include images, graphics, text and audio clips. Photo messaging is a popular use of MMS, with an inbuilt camera in the mobile photo used to take a photograph and the photograph then being sent as a message or an email. MMS offers unlimited text with formatting. Where a full third generation (3G) network is available, video clips can also added to messages. MMS will support graphs, tables, charts, diagrams, animated GIFs, image editing and sound streaming.

MMS messages can sent via web sites. For receiving MMS messages, if the device does not support MMS, the user gets an SMS message pointing to a URL where the message is stored. MMS messages can also be sent to an email address.

The steps in the delivery of MMS messages are slightly different from SMS. An MMS message is sent to a MMSC (Multi-Media Service Centre). When the MMSC receives the message, this is indicated on the sender's phone by 'Message Sent'. The MMSC sends the receiver a notification that a new message is waiting. The receiver can then download the message immediately, or download it later. When the receiver has successfully downloaded the message, the sender gets a 'Message Delivered' message.

For MMS to become fully functional network operators need

A Guide to Letter-Writing

to upgrade their infrastructure to the 3G standard. Devices supporting MMS must also be available. However, if the speed of change in the last 30 years is matched, MMS will very soon be the norm.

Texting hints

Here are a few suggestions to make your text life more exciting.

- Shorten words by missing out vowels:

  | weekend | wknd |
  | message | msg |

- Use numbers if they sound like a word:

wonder	1der
to	2
for	4
ate	8

- Why use more than one letter when one will do?

see	C
tea	T
you	U

- You can substitute a single letter for combinations of letters when they sound the same:

phone	fone
some	sum
night	nite

Now and Into the Future

- A capital letter can be used as a substitute for a double letter that comes in the middle or at the end of a word:

  middle   miDle
  tell   teL

- A capital letter can be used as a substitute for a long vowel:

  phone   fOn
  broke   brOk

- A capital letter in a string of text can mean a new word starts here:

  Jenny broke my phone   JeNyBrOkMyFOn

- The dollar sign ($) can be used for 'double S':

  Tell me some gossip!   TeLMeSumGo$ip!

- The percentage symbol (%) can mean 'double O' or the 'oo' sound:

  could   c%d
  would   w%d
  wood   w%d

Smileys

Why type 'I'm happy today' when you can use a smiley :-)? have you ever sent a text or email to someone and they took it completely the wrong way? Sometimes it's hard to tell whether someone is serious, joking, sarcastic, or boiling with rage, because you can't get any verbal cues from the words alone.

That's where smileys come in (also known as emoticons because they represent emotions). Adding a smiley to a statement can qualify it and indicate to the reader your feelings and mood.

In Internet folklore, the person supposed to have produced the first online smiley was Scott Fahlman of the Carnegie-Mellon University, Pittsburgh, Pennsylvania on the university's bulletin board in the early 1980s. There are, of course, rival claims.

Most smileys are viewed sideways and some are a lot more obvious than others. A selection of emoticons or smileys used in email and text messaging (viewed sideways) is shown below.

:,-(	crying
:-(	sad
:-)	happy
:-D	wide smile
:-/)	not funny
:-0	yelling
:-@	screaming
:-O	shocked
:-y	said with a smile
(:-&	angry
}:-[	angry, frustrated
:-|	serious
|:-|	frowning
;-)	winking
:-x	kiss
:x	silent
|-o	bored, snoring
:>	cheeky
:">	embarrassed
:-e	disappointed
%-)	confused

:-/	sceptical
#:-o	shocked
{}	no comment
`:-)	raised eyebrow
:-&	tongue tied
:-)...	drooling
8)	wearing sunglasses

For other abbreviations, acronyms and short forms used in text messaging and email see Appendix 5 on page 379.

Chapter 3

Getting Organized

While nowadays there may be many new effective ways of communicating and some of these may be quicker and more convenient than writing a letter, none has, so far, wholly or satisfactorily replaced letter-writing.

The traditional method of writing/typing and posting a letter will have a place for the foreseeable future, and there are still many situations when nothing else will serve your purpose so well as to write a letter.

But – and especially if you are a novice letter-writer – how do you decide when it is appropriate to write a letter and, once the decision to write is made, what do you need to make a start?

Here are a few pointers that might help you decide whether or not to write a letter:

- What is your purpose? If your purpose can be fitted into one of the following broad categories, you should consider writing a letter: requesting information or action; providing information or a detailed description; acknowledging information or an event; persuading someone to take action or demanding they take action; giving someone bad news or saying 'no'.
- Do you and the person with whom you want to communicate have a professional/business relationship? If the relationship is, or will be, a professional/business one, it is usually better to write a letter, at least for the first contact.
- If this is the first contact, how can you be sure that the person you want to get in touch will be free to talk on the phone, or that they read faxes and pick up emails? A letter

gives the recipient – especially someone who is busy and stressed – the opportunity to read your letter, digest the contents, and answer in their own way, and in their own time.
- Does the person or organization require a letter or form with your signature before they will take action to deal with an issue? If this is the case, there is very little point in phoning or emailing them.
- Is the matter in hand important, but not particularly urgent? If there is enough time to put it in a letter and send it by post, this is often the best way to ensure it is properly dealt with.
- Is the information complicated and lengthy? If you don't spend the time considering layout and marshalling the information in a letter, is there a risk it may be misunderstood? Could it be communicated satisfactorily and in its entirety in a single phone call? If not, write it down in a letter.
- Is the information confidential? Confidential material should be sent in a sealed envelope. Fax and email are not guaranteed to be secure.
- Do you want to convey seriousness, formality or great depth of feeling? A well-written letter allows you to express yourself with the care and clarity, and in the tone, which best achieves these aims. Can this be done adequately in a phone call or by dashing off an email or fax? Probably not.

Social Letters

For social correspondence, be guided by the context, the attitudes and personality of your reader, and your relationship (if any) with them. Remember that despite society's increasing tendency to informality, and the convenience of the telephone, fax and email, there are still situations where courtesy demands a more 'old-fashioned' approach. For example, many people would consider it impolite to receive a 'thank you' message by any other means than a letter or card, and unless you are very close to a bereaved person, condolences are best conveyed in writing.

Before making the decision to write a social letter ask yourself these questions:

- What is generally considered to be good manners in the circumstances?
- Is the matter to be dealt with one that you and/or the recipient are more comfortable writing/reading about than talking about? A letter is a good way of dealing with things that you find hard to talk about.
- Are you sure you want to leave a permanent record of your feelings, whatever they may be? It is not really a very good idea to write a letter when you are angry or in a state of high emotion. You may live to regret it! On the other hand, a written message of love, thanks, congratulation or sympathy is often appreciated much more than an ephemeral phone call, and may be treasured for a long time to come.
- Does the individual concerned enjoy receiving, reading and writing letters? Will he or she value the effort you have made and see that your letter of several pages is a labour of love and a work of art? Or, will the pearls of your composition be cast before indifferent or unappreciative swine? Know your audience and try to communicate in a way that does not cause embarrassment or feelings of inadequacy.
- Consider the recipient's physical and mental state. There is no point in writing a letter to a sight-impaired person unless you would be happy about someone else reading your letter to him or her, and this can be easily arranged. Remember that a very elderly person may find it a struggle to get through a long-winded letter.

Business and Personal Business Letters

In the business and professional world, letter-writing plays a crucial role in communication with clients, negotiations, administration, marketing, recruitment and employment, and many other everyday situations.

On a personal level, legal, financial and insurance matters, complaints, requests for service, and job applications are just some of the business matters you will probably have to deal with by letter at some time in your life.

A well-crafted business letter makes a strong impression, so the ability to produce such a letter is an important skill.

Here are a few examples of circumstances in which it is recommended you write a letter – and keep a copy – rather than communicate by any of the other available means:

- when you need to keep a permanent record of an exchange (writing the information down and keeping a copy means you can refer to it later if necessary, and track any subsequent correspondence on the subject);
- when giving or confirming information, especially to institutions like banks and building societies, and government departments like the Inland Revenue;
- when sending several documents in a single envelope (it is good practice to include a covering letter listing the documents being sent);
- when the information is confidential;
- when applying for a job;
- when making or responding to a complaint;
- when a written reply is requested.

Handwritten or Typed/Word Processed?

You have now decided to write a letter. The next decision is whether the letter should be handwritten or typed/ word processed.

In the past, most letters were handwritten because not many people could type and few had access to a typewriter. Nowadays, the widespread ownership of personal computers with their word processing software and printers has made the decision rather more difficult.

If this choice is available to you, first take into consideration the likely reaction and attitude of the letter's recipient. Despite the fact that word processing skills are something that nearly everyone aims to acquire, there is a lingering feeling, especially among older people, that a handwritten letter is more personal and somehow more caring. So unless you are certain that the other person will not object to a typed letter, it is still advisable to write your most personal letters.

There are some specific situations where one method or the other is strongly recommended. Letters (or cards) that should, ideally, be handwritten include:

- love letters
- thank you letters
- letters of congratulation
- messages of condolence.

Letters that should, ideally, be typed or word processed include:

- all professional and business letters
- CV and covering letter (unless handwriting is specified by the prospective employer).

It is not only desirable, but increasingly necessary, to type all business letters. Handwritten ones create a less professional image and are therefore likely to receive less serious attention than those laid out and printed in the standard printed business format. If a letter is of particular importance and you cannot type it yourself, it is worthwhile getting someone to type it for you.

Before the word processor, most job applicants would have submitted a handwritten application. Nowadays, a letter of application should always be typed, as should the CV and its covering letter. Very occasionally, a job advert will stipulate that applicants should apply only in their own handwriting. Reasons for making such a stipulation vary. It may be that the job is one in which legible handwriting matters, or the employer may feel that the neatness or otherwise of the handwriting gives a clue to the applicant's likely approach to the job. Amongst larger firms with human resources departments to vet and analyse applications, a handwritten application may even be scrutinized by a trained graphologist. Recruiting new staff is a time-consuming and costly business and appointing the wrong person to a job is even more costly. By using graphological analysis, the firm can get some insight into applicants' characters, personalities and suitability for the job.

Handwriting

Another important consideration when making the choice to write or type your letter is the legibility or otherwise of your handwriting. Most of us tend to be view our own handwriting through somewhat rose-tinted glasses. Because we can (usually) read our own handwriting we tend to assume that others will be able to read it too. Be self-critical and, above all, realistic. Is your handwriting really a thing of beauty, with clear well-formed letters that any child can read without the least difficulty? People whose handwriting is impossible to read should think about typing even their most personal letters.

> Here is a golden Rule to begin with. *Write legibly*. The average temper of the human race would be perceptibly sweetened, if everybody obeyed this Rule! A great deal of the bad writing in the world comes simply from writing *too quickly*. Of course you reply, 'I do it to save *time*.'

A Guide to Letter-Writing

A very good object, no doubt: but what right have you to do it at your friend's expense? Isn't *his* time as valuable as yours? Years ago, I used to receive letters from a friend – and very interesting letters too – written in one of the most atrocious hands ever invented. It generally took me about a *week* to read one of his letters. I used to carry it about in my pocket, and take it out at leisure times, to puzzle over the riddles which composed it – holding it in different positions, and at different distances, till at last the meaning of some hopeless scrawl would flash upon me, when I at once wrote down the English under it; and, when several had been thus guessed, the context would help with the others, till at last the whole series of hieroglyphics was deciphered. If *all* one's friends wrote like that, Life would be entirely spent in reading their letters!

Charles Dodgson (Lewis Carroll) 'Eight or Nine Wise Words About Letter Writing'

When your handwriting is an execrable, illegible, spidery, blotchy scrawl you cannot expect plaudits from your readers. They are likely to display the same sort of impatience as Lewis Carroll does here. But even if your handwriting is difficult to decipher, there are times when you should make a real effort to write neatly and when the recipient will probably exercise a little tolerance if your effort doesn't quite come off. Letters of condolence to the bereaved, love letters, and other letters of a particularly personal nature should be handwritten, however illegible your handwriting.

> Remember that the overall appearance of your letter is almost as important as the content. A neat, well-laid-out letter is a courtesy to the person you are writing to and will create a good impression.

Writing Tools

It is important to choose a pen that will make your handwriting as neat and attractive-looking as possible.

Some people derive great pleasure from using a good fountain pen and feel that their handwriting is at its best when they use one. There are very handsome fountain pens around, ranging from the modestly priced to the extremely expensive. Disadvantages of the fountain pen are that it is less forgiving and requires more skill to use than a ballpoint pen, it needs to be refilled with ink, and it can sometimes leak.

The ballpoint pen, or biro, is considerably cheaper and on the whole is easier and quicker to use. Check before writing your letter that the pen you intend to use does not leak and ink flows smoothly from the ballpoint. Otherwise, your writing may end up being blotchy, messy and difficult to read.

Other modern pen options which produce good results include fibre tip pens, some of which have very fine points, and roller ball pens. The use of thicker felt tip pens should be confined to marking uneven surfaces, such as the outside of bulky envelopes or packages.

Next give some thought to ink colour. As a general rule, stick to dark blue or black ink. They are unobtrusive and contrast best with white or pale cream paper. Vermilion or violet ink with silvery flecks are all very well if you are writing a very informal letter to a close friend but should always be avoided in more formal letters.

> Never write a business letter in pencil.

Writing Paper

The process of writing can be made more pleasurable if you use good quality paper that doesn't crease or tear and takes ink without smudging or blotching.

It is obviously not a good idea to tear a piece of paper from one of your child's school exercise books and start writing. This is going to look both scrappy and sloppy – and will be treated as such.

It really is worth investing in good quality writing paper. Cheap flimsy paper gets you off to a bad start and is a false economy. As a rule it is best to opt for plain paper, white or off-white without ornament or fussy edgings. Avoid coloured paper unless you are absolutely certain that the recipient shares your taste for luminous violet or turquoise. Pale cream, pale blue or pale grey may look rather tasteful and will usually do very well for social letters, but for formal business letters it really is best to stick to white.

Because letters that are sent by airmail cost more in postage, there is nothing wrong with writing personal letters on the special thin (and light) writing paper produced for this purpose or you can use airmail letters (specially printed sheets that function as both writing paper and envelope, with the postage pre-paid and guide lines printed on the sheet indicating how it should be folded before sealing). Formal business letters should still be written on normal white writing paper.

Never use lined paper, even if your handwriting is of the kind that slopes ever more upwards or ever more downwards with every word you write. Lined paper has an uneducated look about it, perhaps because it carries memories of the schoolroom with it. If you find it difficult to write in even-spaced horizontal lines, try using a ruled backing sheet under your unlined paper.

Anything in the way of fancy illustration should not appear on a business letter or on a formal personal letter. Writing paper dappled with tea roses, or with whistling bluebirds and cute cavorting teddy bears round the edges should be kept for your closest and most intimate friends.

If you are thinking about having your address and telephone

Getting Organized

number pre-printed or engraved on your personal writing paper, it is important to avoid anything too fancy. Better instead to have something simple and understated if you want to make a serious impression. If you are starting up your own business, and are not of an artistic bent, it is worth consulting a good designer to help you select something that is eye-catching and memorable but not too overwhelming. Ideally, your headed notepaper should be printed by a professional printer. Even if you have the most advanced design software on your computer and are practised in its use, for the smartest results it is usually still best to leave the printing of your design to a professional.

These days in the UK, Europe and many other places, nearly all commercially produced paper for writing, printing and photocopying is supplied in one of the 'A' sizes. The A sizing system is an international standard for paper. The main advantage of this standardization — from the paper manufacturers' and their customers' points of view — is that each A size is half the area of the previous one, in a descending scale from A0 to A7. Thus, an A1 sheet folded and cut in half will produce two A2 sheets, an A2 sheet will produce two A3 sheets, and so on. The dimensions of each A size are:

A0 = 841 mm x 1189 mm
A1 = 594 mm x 841 mm
A2 = 420 mm x 594 mm
A3 = 297 mm x 420 mm
A4 = 210 mm x 297 mm
A5 = 148 mm x 210 mm
A6 = 105 mm x 148 mm
A7 = 74 mm x 105 mm.

In the United States and Asia, imperial paper sizes may also be used. Their names and dimensions are:

Executive = 7.25 in x 10.5 in (184 mm x 267 mm)
Folio = 8.25 in x 13 in (210 mm x 330 mm)
Foolscap = 8 in x 13 in (203 mm x 330 mm)
Index card = 5 in x 8 in (127 mm x 203 mm)
Ledger = 17 in x 11 in (432 mm x 279 mm)
Legal = 8.5 in x 14 in (216 mm x 356 mm)
Letter = 8.5 in x 11 in (216 mm x 356 mm)
Photo = 4 in x 6 in (102 mm x 152 mm)
Quarto = 8.5 in x $10^{13}/_{16}$ in (216 mm x 275 mm)
Statement/Halfletter = 5.5 in x 8.5 in (140 mm x 216 mm)
Tabloid = 11 in x 17 in (279 mm x 432 mm).

In the A series, the most frequently used paper sizes are A3, A4 and A5. A3 is too large for letters, and is used principally for spreadsheets and large printouts. A4 is the standard size used in business. It will fit into a standard file and filing system, and into the hoppers of printers and photocopying machines. A5 is mostly used for memos or shorter personal letters.

If your letter is to a business or other organization you should always use A4 paper. However, for personal letters you do not need to stick to the A4 size. Your main consideration here should be the likely length of your letter and the size of your handwriting. If you are planning to write a very long newsy letter and your handwriting is large and sprawling, then it is clearly sensible to choose a larger page size. On the other hand, if you know that you have very little to say, it would be best to opt for a smaller page size, especially if you also have rather small, cramped writing. A few lines surrounded by huge area of blank paper will simply draw attention to the fact that you don't have much to say.

It is probably best to avoid notelets, especially highly colourful or fancy ones, unless you are writing to a very close friend or a family member. They are not appropriate for formal letters.

The traditional advice was to avoid writing or printing on both sides of a piece of paper, though conservationists will point out that using both sides of the sheet saves paper and we should all be making an effort to avoid wasting precious resources. However, it is probably best to restrict this practice to your personal correspondence.

Business and formal letters should be typed or written on one side only, using continuation sheets for the second and subsequent pages.

Before sending a letter with writing on both sides of the paper, be sure that both sides are legible. If the pen has been pressed down heavily and dark ink has been used, the writing may be very difficult to read. It is unfair to send such a letter; the recipient may have to spend hours trying to decipher what is written, and may even give up in disgust.

If your handwritten letter stretches to more than three sides, it is a good idea to number the second and subsequent sheets. This avoids any muddle on the reader's part, should the individual sheets get out of order.

Cards

Those who do not really like writing letters, or who find them too difficult to write, often send a card instead. The main effort involved is in selecting a card that is suitable to the occasion and to the taste of the sender and intended recipient.

There are many occasions for which greetings cards are perfectly acceptable, whether you choose to send a card with pre-printed message suitable for the occasion, or a 'blank' one in which you write your own greeting.

Christmas and birthdays generate the greatest volume of card-writing. It is quite usual to send a card rather than write a letter when someone passes an exam or a driving test or graduates from university. Likewise, if someone is ill we will send a 'get well' card, and for this and other occasions when people may appreciate a little humour, there are dozens of cards on sale, with humorous illustrations or messages.

Some occasions, on the other hand, can be trickier. If you have been a guest in someone's house, for example, and want to thank your host and hostess, it may be tempting to send a quick card. However, your host or hostess, especially if they are of an older generation, may be sticklers for formality and expect a letter (the kind of letter that used to be called a 'bread and butter letter'), thanking them for their hospitality and saying a few words about how pleasant your stay with them was.

Another difficult choice is whether to send a 'sympathy' card when someone dies. You will probably be able to gauge what is most appropriate in the circumstances, and a card at least lets the bereaved person know that you are thinking of them. However, a card with a short printed message followed by your signature may give the impression that you are just going through the motions. Though they are very difficult letters to write, ask yourself if the bereaved might not be more comforted by a letter which expresses more fully how you feel and offers them your support.

Postcards, unlike greetings cards, usually don't have to be put in an envelope and can be popped into the post-box with a minimum of fuss. However, they obviously shouldn't be used to send private or confidential information.

Here are some situations in which a blank postcard is useful:

- when you are moving house and want to let people know your new address;
- when sending information about an appointment;
- when sending non-personal information suitable for the eyes of the world;
- when entering some competitions.

Some people find it worthwhile to have some postcards

pre-printed with their address and phone number, for use on appropriate occasions.

Of course, the most familiar kind of postcard has a picture on one side and is bought principally by people who are on holiday or on a day trip somewhere to send to friends and family members at home. Their use in this context is absolutely standard and part of convention. At the end of the nineteenth and beginning of the twentieth century, picture postcards were used much more widely, with the pictures printed on them being more typically of some local event or activity or of a national or international event that was in the news. Postcards from that era are historical documents, and are now collectors' items.

Envelopes

When it comes to choosing an envelope it is best to select a good quality, one that matches the colour and weight of your writing paper. Use a size that allows you to insert the letter into the envelope with the minimum of folds. Standard envelope sizes are:

DL = 110 mm x 220 mm
C3 = 324 mm x 458 mm
C4 = 324 mm x 229 mm
C5 = 229 mm x 162 mm
C6 = 162 mm x 114 mm.

If you don't want to fold an A4 sheet, use a C4 size envelope. The C5 size will take an A4 sheet folded once, or an A5 sheet unfolded; the C6 size will take an A4 sheet folded three times, an A5 sheet folded once, or an A6 sheet unfolded.

Many business letters are sent in DL envelopes measuring 110 mm x 220 mm. These take an A4 sheet folded neatly twice, i.e. into thirds. When using this size of envelope, make sure the corners of the sheet of paper are precisely aligned before making the folds. Any refolding or an extra small fold will spoil the appearance of your letter.

Window and aperture envelopes are occasionally used for business letters. A window envelope has a square or oblong panel cut out and covered with a transparent material through which the name and address on the letter can be seen. In an aperture envelope, there is no transparent protective covering over the cut-out section. For both of these types of envelope, the letter inside must be folded and inserted correctly so that the address appears in the correct position under the cut-out panel.

In the UK, the Royal Mail uses electronic sorting for letters up to a certain weight and within a certain size range. The envelope sizes coming within this range are known as POP (Post Office Preferred) sizes: they should be no smaller than 90 mm x 140 mm and no larger than 120 mm x 235 mm; and, with contents, should weigh no more than 60 grams.

When the letter is a business communication or a fairly formal letter, especially to someone whose tastes you do not know, avoid decorated envelopes. Some business letters are routinely sent in brown, or manila, envelopes, because it is supposed to be less easy to detect an enclosure in a brown envelope. In the past, small brown envelopes were used for sending out bills. However, this practice is not so widespread now, and many bills today come through the letterbox in plain white envelopes. Airmail envelopes are available for letters going overseas.

Summary

If you are going to take the trouble to write a letter you should aim for as professional a final product as possible. It is worthwhile spending money on good paper, a good quality writing instrument, and putting a little thought into the layout. This will help you to create a good impression.

Chapter 4

Presentation and Layout

The layout and design of a letter will have an impact on the reader before he or she gets around to considering its content. A high standard of presentation is very important, especially in today's highly competitive business and employment environments. (Of course, this applies not just to letters, but to all the communications that may affect an individual's, a company's or an organization's image: emails, faxes, reports, sales literature, advertisements, and brochures.)

You certainly won't want any letter you write to give the impression that it has been produced hastily and carelessly. It should be well designed, properly spaced, and well organized. A well-laid-out letter can also help to highlight any important points you want to make.

Much of this chapter gives advice on how formal and business correspondence is laid out. For personal and social letters, you don't have to stick to a rigid structure, though some of the tips in this and the next chapter should nonetheless be useful for personal and less formal social letters.

> If you use a word processor, a good deal of the formatting can be done automatically. You can also make use of the extra features word processing programs provide such as bullets and numbering, columns, tables and boxes. Most programs include letter templates of various designs and layouts from which to choose.

Blocked, Indented and Semi-blocked Style

There are two main styles for presenting typed letters in the English-speaking world: blocked style and indented style. There is also an intermediate style, semi-blocked style. While all these styles can be individualized in some of their elements they are broadly as described below.

Fully blocked style

The most popular format for typed or printed formal and business letters is the fully blocked style with open punctuation, i.e. minimum punctuation (see also the Punctuation section in Chapter 5.)

An example of a letter laid out in fully blocked style is given on page 53. This sample letter also illustrates some of the standard elements of a letter, which are more fully described later in this chapter. The fully blocked format is easy to set out using a typewriter or personal computer and extremely convenient for the increasing numbers of people who word process their own correspondence, but do not necessarily have traditional secretarial skills.

Fully indented style

The fully indented style is the most traditional format, nowadays regarded in business and professional circles as being extremely old-fashioned. It is still occasionally used for personal and handwritten letters, but its popularity is steadily declining as more and more people use word processors at home. The stepped indents for each element of the fully indented format are time-consuming to set up on a word processor. (See the sample fully indented letter on page 54.)

Semi-blocked style

The semi-blocked style has some fully blocked elements and some indented elements. Though this format is thought by some people to be a little old-fashioned, it is quite easy to type on a word processor. It is therefore a useful way of ringing the changes from the seemingly ubiquitous fully blocked style. (See the sample semi-blocked letter on page 55.)

As has been said before, none of these styles needs to be rigidly adhered to in all its details. Where the stationery has been pre-printed with the sender's name, address and other details, it is obviously not necessary to duplicate these details.

Pre-printed Stationery

All letters should include the sender's address. Some people choose to avoid the trouble of laying out their address by having their address pre-printed on their personal notepaper. This is, of course, standard practice for business stationery; most large companies spend quite a lot of time and money on a design that will create the sort of image they want to project.

The pre-printed stationery of businesses, institutions and government agencies will usually include logo, name, full postal address, telephone number, fax number, and often also an email address and URL or website address. These elements usually appear at the top of the page. Private limited companies are legally obliged to show the company's registered number, registered address, and directors' names. This information is often printed along the bottom of the page. Businesses registered for VAT (value added tax) must print their VAT number somewhere on their stationery; often this is under or next to the company name and address.

The pre-printed stationery of a private individual will usually include their name, postal address, telephone number, fax number, and email address.

Graphics and text design tools come as part of nearly all modern word processing and desktop-publishing programs. It is perfectly possible to design your stationery on your personal computer using these tools. However, you should seriously consider paying a professional to print the stationery that will incorporate the design you decide on. Unless you have a very sophisticated printing machine, producing the stationery yourself may be a false economy.

If you do have your stationery printed by a professional printer, it is also a good idea to get a supply of continuation paper, i.e. sheets used for typing second and subsequent pages of a letter. These should match the colour and weight of your letterhead. Continuation sheets are often pre-printed with some element from the main letterhead, such as a company name and logo.

Formatting Continuation Sheets

When typing continuation sheets, it is usual to include a page number, the date, a reference, and/or the name of the addressee. One method of formatting these elements is shown in the sample below. Alternatively, you might prefer to have the page number, the date and the reference on the same line. A word processor can be set up to include automatically page number, date and various other types of references which will be printed as a header or footer on each page of the letter.

You should always leave 3-4 lines blank at the top of the continuation sheet before going on with the body of your letter. (See the sample continuation sheet on page 56.)

Overall Appearance

Use design and formatting to help the reader of your letter.

A good start

Make sure there is enough contrast between the colour of the ink and the paper. For preference, use black or dark blue ink on a white background.

Whether you are writing by hand or using a word processor, it is a good idea to take the time to make a first draft. A draft set

Presentation and Layout

                              Hall Office Management Ltd
                              47 Yarn Street
                              LIVERPOOL
                              M100 XYZ
                              Telephone: +44 (0)1234 5678910
                              Facsimile: +44 (0)1234 5678911

Your ref: AA/Corr01
Our ref: VH/NDEC

7 July 2005

Mr Albert Appleby
Manager
Havestock Mill
101 Walpole Street
LIVERPOOL
M100 XXZ

Dear Mr Appleby

FULLY BLOCKED STYLE

This is an example of the style my company uses to present our business letters. It is nowadays the standard layout for nearly all business correspondence.

Blocked style's most obvious feature is that all the elements of the letter are aligned to the left. In the main body of the letter, the first line of each paragraph and all subsequent lines within a paragraph are also aligned to the left.

There is no punctuation in addresses or after the salutation or complimentary closing. Headings are in block capitals without underlining.

Notice that, in this layout, there is a single line space between the paragraphs and between all the other elements. This is the usual method of spacing in blocked style.

I enclose further examples of reports, faxes and memos in blocked style.

Yours sincerely

Victoria Hall

Victoria Hall
Director

ENC x 3

A GUIDE TO LETTER-WRITING

                                                       45 Yarn Street,
                                                        LIVERPOOL,
                                                          M100 XYZ.

                                                           7 July 2005

Messrs. Smith & Gemmell,
  101 Walpole Street,
    LIVERPOOL,
      Merseyside,
        M100 XXZ.

Dear Sirs,

FULLY INDENTED STYLE

  I have pleasure in providing you with an example of a letter written in fully indented style, and a description of the main characteristics of this style.
  The sender's address is on the right hand side of the sheet with the second and subsequent lines of the address beginning one or two characters to the right of the first letter or number on the preceding line. The date is to the right below the sender's address.
  If the recipient's address is included the first line is aligned to the left with the second and subsequent lines beginning one or two characters to the right of the first letter on the preceding line.
  There is a full stop following the last line of the address. Commas follow all other address lines, and the salutation and complimentary close. Generally, there is more punctuation in indented style than in fully blocked style.
  The salutation or opening greeting is aligned to the left-hand margin, any heading following the salutation is centred above the main text of the letter and may be underlined, and the first line of each paragraph of the main text is indented.
  Line spaces between the paragraphs of the main text are optional in indented style. While the indent is often sufficient to distinguish the paragraphs, no line spacing between paragraphs can give a dense appearance to the page.
  The complimentary close and signature can be indented from the left margin, centred under the main text, or (as here) placed near the right hand margin of the page.

                                                                  Yours sincerely,

                                                             Alicia Amberhurst

                                                            Alicia Amberhurst

45 Yarn Street,
LIVERPOOL,
M100 XYZ

7 July 2005

Messrs. Smith & Gemmell,
101 Walpole Street,
LIVERPOOL,
Merseyside,
M100 XXZ

Dear Sirs,

SEMI-BLOCKED STYLE

  I have pleasure in providing you with an example of a letter written in semi-blocked style, which illustrates how blocking and indentation can be combined to vary the layout.

  The sender's address is on the right hand side of the sheet with the second and subsequent lines of the address aligned with the first letter of the first line. The date is under, and aligned with, the sender's address. All lines of the recipient's address are aligned to the left of the page, as is the salutation.

  Commas and full stops have been used in the addresses, with a comma following the salutation and complimentary close.

  The salutation or opening greeting is aligned to the left hand margin, and the heading is centred and may be underlined. The first line of each paragraph of the main text is indented, and there are line spaces between the paragraphs.

  The complimentary close and signature are centred under the main text.

Yours sincerely,

Alicia Amberhurst

Alicia Amberhurst

Page 2 of 2

7 July 2005

Mr Albert Appleby

Notice that, in this layout, there is a single line space between the paragraphs and between all the other elements. This is the usual method of spacing in blocked style, though line spacing is sometimes varied to suit the extent of the letter.

I enclose further examples of reports, faxes and memos in blocked style.

I hope you will agree that this style has a pleasing and business-like appearance.

Yours sincerely

Victoria Hall

Victoria Hall
Director

ENC x 3

out in paragraphs will give an idea of the length, and therefore how the lines ought to be spaced on the page. A draft will also make it easier to refine and correct the content. Aim to make the final version of the letter as professional-looking and free of corrections and errors as possible.

Spacing and line length

Leave generous margins. Try to allow a margin of about 25 mm at the top and bottom, and at both sides, of each page.

For the main body of the letter, the space between lines should always be greater than the space between words. Otherwise, the reader's eye can jump down the lines. The usual (default) line spacing in a word processing program for 10–12 point type size will be 12 point, or about 120% of the type size.

Very long and very short lines make people read more slowly. A full line of body text should have about 10 to 12 words. The size of the type you use depends on the length of the line. Longer lines need larger type.

If your letter is short, the text should not be pushed up to the top of the sheet with a large area left blank at the bottom.

It does not look good if the first page is densely printed and closely spaced with only one or two lines appearing on a second page. Try to alter the spacing so that more text appears on the second page, or try to fit the letter into a single page. A second page, or continuation sheet, should have at least three or four lines of text, excluding the complimentary close and signature.

Alignment

Using a word processor, text can be aligned in various ways: justified, with the column of text aligned on both left and right; ranged left, also called ragged right; ranged right, also called ragged left; and centred.

A GUIDE TO LETTER-WRITING

This is an example of *justified text*. The spaces between the words are different lengths so that full lines of text align to the left and to the right.

This is an example of text *ranged left*. The spaces between the words are the same length. The text is aligned at the left side of the page but not at the right side, hence the informal name 'ragged right'.

This is an example of text *ranged right*. The spaces between the words are the same length. The text is aligned at the right side of the page but not at the left side, hence the informal name 'ragged left'.

This text is *centred* and has equal spaces between words.

It is best to avoid justifying the body text of your letter. Though it gives a neat appearance some people find it more difficult to read than body text aligned on the left side. To avoid the long spaces between words that justified text can create, it may be a temptation to try to fit more into a gappy line by splitting a word at the end of a line and inserting a hyphen at the split. While this is a common technique in newspaper, magazine and reference-book publishing, it is not recommended for letter-writing, simply because anything that might inhibit the recipient's reading should be avoided. End of line splits can make the reader hesitate. In any event, there is not absolute agreement about where words should be split, and it is quite likely you will irritate your reader by using a method of splitting that he or she does not agree with.

The standard alignment for letter-writing is to range the text to the left. Text ranged to the right is only used for specialist purposes or in certain languages. Centring the text can sometimes be useful for making some part of the letter stand out, but it is not used routinely.

Presentation and Layout

Which typeface should be used when word processing a letter?

Fonts can be divided into two groups: serif fonts, which have little curls (serifs) on the letters, and sans serif (meaning 'without serif') fonts, which are plain.

There are many different fonts available to users of word processing and email programs and more are being designed every day. You may imagine having so many different font styles available to you gives you a great opportunity to express your individuality. Up to a point this is true, but don't get carried away.

For formal letters, business letters, and especially for job applications, care should be taken when selecting a font. Always consider readability and the appropriateness of the font for the task. After all, you would probably be rather taken aback to receive a letter from the tax office or the bank manager in a font that communicates a sense of playfulness or light-hearted simplicity, such as the following:

formal application or *business methods*

Researchers in the field of CV-writing have found that the font can be an important factor in determining if a CV and its covering letter is rejected early in the vetting process, or given further attention. Keep in mind that an employer is likely to receive many CVs in response to a job advertisement, and while making the first selection of suitable candidates he or she may spend no more that a minute or so on each CV. If your CV and its covering letter are badly presented or difficult to read, your application is quite likely to fall at this first hurdle.

For typed CVs and covering letters, and formal correspondence in general, it is probably advisable to stick to more conservative fonts, such as the serif fonts:

Baskerville   Palatino   Times New Roman

or, a clear, elegant and readable sans serif font, such as:

Arial   Trebuchet MS

Avoid using more than two fonts in a letter. With so many different fonts available, you may be tempted to use more than two, but too many changes in font will almost certainly make your letter look cluttered and so reduce its readability. One font for headings and another for the text is usually enough. Alternatively, you could use a single font throughout, and use bold or a larger font size to make headings, reference lines or other elements stand out.

Type size is measured in units called 'points'. The type size most often used for letters is 12 point, though you can go down to 10 point if this is necessary to fit your letter onto a single sheet. Don't go below 10 point because smaller sized type will make your letter difficult to read. Headings are usually 2 point sizes larger than the text size, so if the main text of your letter is in 12 point, you might use 14 point or larger for headings.

Paragraphs

Keep paragraphs short. For formal and business letters, this usually means no more than six to eight lines per paragraph.

Don't leave one line of a paragraph at the bottom of the previous page or at the top of the next page. Try, wherever possible, to start a new page with a new paragraph.

Ideally, a formal letter or business letter should consist of a beginning, a middle and an end. There will usually be a short introductory paragraph, whose purpose is to acknowledge any previous letter received and/or state briefly the purpose or subject of the letter. This is followed by a longer paragraph, or series of paragraphs, making and expanding on various points. The letter should ideally end with a short final paragraph (the conclusion). For more on the content of paragraphs see page 93.

Each paragraph should deal with only one main point or idea. The information should be laid out in a logical sequence, providing relevant details where required, and making sure the information flows smoothly from point to point.

Highlighting and structure

When formatting a letter, take care to get the balance right between style and content. As was mentioned in the previous chapter, take care about the font you use, and don't use more than 2 or 3 different fonts or sizes within the same letter.

The most effective way to highlight a word or phrase is to use bold. Avoid using block capital letters for emphasis in the body of the letter and try not to use underlining in the body of the letter. Italic should be used sparingly and not for long stretches of text, as this can be difficult to read, especially in a smaller font size.

It is becoming increasingly common to find 'bullet points' in business letters. These can give a professional and attractive appearance to a letter or report and allows the reader to extract each point easily. Bullet points, when used within the body of a long letter, can make the letter appear less dense and daunting. A cautionary note: because bullet points are designed to stand out they may be the only thing the reader focuses on, with the surrounding text getting little or no attention, for example:

We require separate estimates for:
- Re-roofing the house with traditional slates.
- Thatching the barn.
- Clearing the old farm equipment and debris from the yard.
- Replacing any missing granite setts in the yard.
- Rebuilding any damaged boundary walls and fences.

The Individual Elements of a Formal or Business Letter

The boxed sample on page 64 shows all the elements likely to be used in a formal or business letter. This sample is intended to show the order in which these elements usually appear in blocked style. It is not necessary to include all of them in every letter. The obligatory elements are shown in bold in the sample.

Return address (sender's address)

Where this is not already in place on pre-printed letterhead, the sender's address must be written or typed on every letter. When typing or keying the address, it should be placed at the top right-hand corner of the sheet of paper. The address must include all the information that will be needed for the fast and safe delivery of any reply. Make sure you include the post town and postcode (or ZIP code). The post town and postcode should be typed in capital letters.

> 23 Park Drive
> SEAFIELD
> RA14 2TY

If a county name is included only its first letter should be in capitals.

> 23 Park Drive
> SEAFIELD
> Blackshire
> RA14 2TY

Inside the letter, the post town and postcode can be typed on the same line, but on the envelope the post town and postcode should always be on separate lines.

Presentation and Layout

In the UK, postcodes are made up of a mixture of letters and numbers (a total of five, six or seven characters). The postcode should be typed with a single space before the group of three numbers/letters at the end of the code.

RA14 2TY

In the US, the Zip code is on the last line with the municipality and the state abbreviation, like this:

CHICAGO IL 85672-4332

Each country has its own formula for postcodes. For international mail, you should refer to your correspondent's letters to ensure you use the correct layout for their address and postcode. Also for international mail, the country name should be on a separate line after the postcode or Zip code and should be written in English.

Herrn
Hermann Gottlieb
Hertzstrasse 12
16935 Leipzig
GERMANY

Punctuation in addresses has now largely been dispensed with, except in letters written by hand or by traditionalists who don't want to change the style they have always used. Of course, it won't cause shudders of horror anywhere if you decide to use blocked style but also opt to use a more conventional, rather than minimum, level of punctuation.

So, you can put commas in after the street number and at the end of each line of the address – in the UK, it's really a matter of choice.

A GUIDE TO LETTER-WRITING

**Return address (sender's address)
including postcode**
Sender's contact information

Reference

Date

Special markings/type of dispatch

Attention line (1)
**Inside address (recipient's address)
including postcode**
Attention line (2)

Salutation (opening greeting)

Subject heading

Body of letter

Complimentary close

Signature

Sender's name
Sender's position and/or personal contact details

Postscript

Enclosures

Copies

Sender's contact information (telephone and fax number, email address and website address)

Nowadays, many individuals, and nearly all businesses, include contact information in their letters. This is likely to include telephone number and fax number, and sometimes also a mobile phone number, email address and website address. The positioning of this information is to some extent a matter of taste, though it is most often placed below the sender's address.

For telephone and fax numbers, it is now standard practice to include the international dialling code. This comes at the beginning of the number and is preceded by a plus sign (+). For example, the international dialling code for the United Kingdom is 44, so a telephone number including this code will look like this:

+44 (0)141 000 1000

Note that the first digit of the area code is bracketed. This is because it is not used when dialling from abroad.

Ideally, and for clarity, there should be a line space between the contact information and the last line of the sender's address. Contact information is often presented like this:

Tel: +44 (0)141 000 1000
Fax: +44 (0)141 000 1001
Email: heman@superrepairs.co.uk
Website: www.superrepairs.co.uk

Or, the words 'telephone' and 'facsimile' can be written out in full. This is, again, a matter of personal preference.

Reference line

Personal letters do not typically include reference lines. In business letters, the reference line is usually placed at the top

A GUIDE TO LETTER-WRITING

left side of the page with a line space between it and the return address above, and a line space between it and the date below.

Reference lines usually include the word 'Reference' or the abbreviation 'Ref'. The abbreviation may or may not have a full stop, nowadays more often not. Conventionally, 'Reference' or 'Ref' is followed by a colon, thus:

Reference: MMM/BR
Ref: MMM/BR
Our ref: MMM/BR

However, those who prefer everything, except the body text, to be punctuation-free may use tab spaces instead of colons, thus:

Reference   MMM/BR
Ref   MMM/BR
Our ref   MMM/BR

References may include the sender's initials followed by the initials of the person who typed the letter. As a rule both the sender's and the typist's initials are in capital letters and separated from each other by a forward slash, for example MMC/CMM. Sometimes the sender's initials are in capitals and the typist's initials are in lower case letters, for example MMC/cmm.

Reference lines frequently show other information, such as a customer account number, or it may include information relating to a company's internal filing system. This information is included in the reference line so that all correspondence on a specific topic or for a specified time period can be easily identified and filed together. A typical formula for such a reference line is:

Our ref: MMC/CMM/05projectX

If you are replying to a letter that has a reference line, you should always quote the other person's or company's reference in your reply. This will speed things up at the other end because the reference will help link your reply to previous correspondence. In business letters, the usual formula for the reference line is as follows:

Your ref   ABC/DR/Accts

If you want to include your own reference as well, the usual formula is:

Your ref   ABC/DR/Accts
Our ref   MMC/CMM/05projectX

Date

The date used to be placed under the postcode (or the contact information) on the right side of the page with a line space between the address and the date. Nowadays, the date is almost invariably placed on the left hand side of the page above the inside address.

Here is another quote from Lewis Carroll's advice on letter-writing which deals with dates in letters. The advice is just as relevant now as it was when it was written:

> . . . put the date in full. It is an aggravating thing, when you wish, years afterwards, to arrange a series of letters, to find them dated 'Feb. 17', 'Aug. 2', without any year to guide you as to which comes first. And never, never . . . put 'Wednesday', simply, as the date! That way madness lies.

There are various ways to write the date:

14 August 2005
or
14th August 2005
or
August 14, 2005

The first and second reflect the usual ordering used in the UK: day, month, and year. The third is the ordering used in the US: month, day, and year. These styles have been variously adopted in other English-speaking countries.

The first style with a cardinal number for the day (for example 1, 2, 3, 14, 31) is now more common than the second with an ordinal number for the day (for example 1st, 2nd, 3rd, 14th, 31st).

In formal and business letters it is better not to use abbreviations for the month names.

In many other contexts, dates are written entirely in numbers, i.e. 14/8/05 or 14/08/2005. However, this is not recommended for letter-writing. Naming the month makes for speed of reference, especially when back correspondence is being consulted. Furthermore, in US style, the month number comes first in dates consisting entirely of numbers, thus the fourteenth of August 2005 is written 08/14/05 in the US. The same date is written 14/08/05 in the UK. This difference in style can cause bewilderment, particularly if the day of the month is in the range 1–12. The potential for confusion adds further weight to the argument that the month should always be written out in full.

Special instructions/despatch type

These are usually typed in capital letters, below the date and above the inside address. However, some special instructions like CONFIDENTIAL and PERSONAL can be typed above the date and reference lines. When a letter is marked PERSONAL, it means that only the addressee should open it; when it is marked CONFIDENTIAL, it means someone deputizing for the addressee can open and read the letter, but that the information should not be made available outside the office or firm to which it is addressed; and PRIVATE & CONFIDENTIAL means no one but the addressee should open or read the letter.

Special instructions like CONFIDENTIAL are not used in personal letters.

Some examples of despatch instructions are RECORDED DELIVERY or CERTIFIED MAIL, SPECIAL DELIVERY, REGISTERED POST, BY COURIER, BY HAND, AIRMAIL and FIRST CLASS.

Special instructions and despatch type should also be printed clearly on the envelope.

Attention line

Attention lines are not used in personal letters. In business letters, an attention line can be in one of two positions on the letter. It is usually duplicated on the envelope.

Where the letter is to be addressed to a company, organization or government department, but you expect the matter to be dealt with by a known individual within the company, the attention line will usually be placed above the inside address, sometimes with a line space between, thus:

For attention of: Jeremy Anderson, Credit Controller

MMM Confectionery Ltd
276 Westwind Avenue
YORK
MM6 6MM

An attention line can also appear at the end of the inside address. This is done when there is a possibility that the person to whom the letter is addressed may not be available to attend to it. This second type of attention line usually names the person, or department, that the letter should be dealt with in the absence of the named addressee.

> Jeremy Anderson, Credit Controller
> MMM Confectionery Ltd
> 276 Westwind Avenue
> YORK
> MM6 6MM
> For attention of: The Accounts Department

There is often a line space between the inside address and the attention line. The wording and format of the attention line can vary, as in the following examples:

> Attention: Jeremy Anderson, Credit Controller
> <u>Attention</u>: Jeremy Anderson, Credit Controller
> <u>Fao</u>: Jeremy Anderson, Credit Controller
> <u>For attention of</u>: Jeremy Anderson, Credit Controller

Inside address (recipient's address)

You should always include the inside (recipient's) address in a formal or business letter. When you are writing a personal or social letter there is no need to include it. The inside address has the same elements as the return address, with the possible addition of a job title, and/or the department in which the recipient works.

> Mrs Angelina Hobson, Principal Librarian
> Special Collections
> The University of Middle England
> 100-146 University Avenue
> Hopehill

SEAFIELD
Blackshire
MM3 3MM

As with the return address, the building number and street name appear on one line; the next line may be used for a locality name, i.e. the name of a village or hamlet or a district of a larger town or city; the next line will be the post town; the next line may be used for a county name, and the last line (provided the letter is not to be sent abroad) for the postcode.

Courtesy titles

The usual courtesy titles are Mr, Miss, Mrs and Ms. It used to be quite common to address a gentleman as Esq. (short for 'Esquire'). However this is becoming rarer. Unlike the other courtesy titles, Esq. or Esq is placed after the surname and is obviously only used when the first name or initial is known. If Esq. is used, the courtesy title Mr is not used before the first name, so the name can be written:

James Barrington-Hume, Esq.
J. Barrington-Hume, Esq.
or
Mr James Barrington-Hume
Mr J Barrington-Hume
Mr Barrington-Hume
but never
Mr James Barrington-Hume, Esq.
Mr J Barrington-Hume, Esq.
Mr Barrington-Hume, Esq.

In common practice, it is now more and more usual to omit the courtesy titles Mr, Mrs, Miss and Ms. Only the name is used, thus:

James Black
Angus Foggert
Hermione Duval

While omitting the gender-specific title may seem somewhat radical, it is a neat way of avoiding faux pas that may arise from not being absolutely certain about the sex or marital status of the recipient. Even if it clear from the name that the correspondent is a woman, there remains the problem of how she should be addressed. People will very often find themselves asking the questions, 'How should I address this woman, whose marital status I do not know? Even if I know her marital status, I don't know how she prefers to be addressed. Does she use her husband's name and the title Mrs, or has she kept her maiden name for business purposes and prefers to be known as Miss or Mrs? Is she divorced, and if she is, has she kept the title Mrs?'

It can all be a bit of a minefield. More and more people, especially in business and the professions, ask why a woman's marital status should be important anyway, and why on earth there should be a different title for each state (Miss and Mrs), with an invented title (the dreadful Ms) for women whose marital status is not known? When addressing a letter to a man, no one would give a moment's thought to whether he was married or not. Doing away with titles altogether in addresses is one way of ensuring there is equality of treatment between the sexes.

While gender-specific titles may be becoming less popular in addresses, professional and academic titles (for example Prof, Dr), hereditary and aristocratic titles (for example Her Royal Highness, His Grace), honorary titles (for example Sir/Dame), and armed forces ranks (for example General, Rear Admiral) are usually still used. For guidance on these and other titles see Appendix 1 on page 359.

If first names are reduced to initials in the address, it used to be the case that each initial was followed by a full stop. Nowadays, full stops and commas in addresses are considered to be unnecessary, so the name in the inside address is more likely to appear in one of the following forms:

Mr J A Black
or
J A Black
or
James Black

In the UK and elsewhere, a company name may be followed by Ltd, short for 'limited' and indicating that it is a limited liability company. Other business names may be followed by plc or PLC, short for 'public limited company'. Again, it is not necessary to use full stops in these abbreviations.

In the US, corporations often have Inc. (short for 'incorporated') after the name. US style is to favour full stops in these and other abbreviations used in addresses.

Salutation (opening greeting)

The opening greeting should align with the inside address on the left-hand side of the page, under the last line of the inside address and with a line left blank, thus:

The Manager
Cosmo Furniture Store
12–15 King Street
SEAFIELD
RA11 6DR

Dear Sir

For personal letters where there is no inside address the opening greeting should go at the left-hand side after the date, usually with a line left blank, thus:

24 May 1966

Dear Mary

The way in which you address the recipient in the opening greeting depends on who the person is and your relationship to that person.

If you know you are writing to a man but you do not know his name, use the opening greeting 'Dear Sir'.

If you know you are writing to a woman but you do not know her name, then the opening greeting is 'Dear Madam'.

If you know you are writing to an individual but you do not know the person's sex or their name, the standard greeting is 'Dear Sir or Madam'.

If you are writing to a firm and you know very little about their set-up, it is common practice to use the opening greeting 'Dear Sirs'.

If you are on first-name terms with the person you are writing to, the greeting is straightforward, for example 'Dear Anwar' or 'Dear Matilda'. Correspondents whose names are known may be addressed as 'Dear Mr Brown' or 'Dear Miss Lee'. Otherwise the opening greeting will be 'Dear Sirs', 'Dear Sir/Madam' or 'Dear Sir or Madam'.

It is sometimes difficult to decide how to address people with titles or who hold certain other elevated positions in public life. Information on special forms of address is given in Appendix 1 on page 359.

For formal and business correspondence, it used to be that the wording of the salutation dictated the wording of the complimentary close, as follows:

Salutation	*Complimentary close*
Dear Sir	Yours faithfully
Dear Sirs	Yours faithfully
Dear Sir or Madam	Yours faithfully
Dear Madam	Yours faithfully
Dear Mr Black	Yours sincerely
Dear Miss Green	Yours sincerely
Dear Mrs White	Yours sincerely
Dear Ms Brown	Yours sincerely
Dear John	Yours sincerely
Dear Mary	Yours sincerely

In other words, when the addressee was not named, the complimentary close was always 'Yours faithfully', and when the addressee was named, the complimentary close was always 'Yours sincerely'. This is no longer so much the case, as is more fully described below in the section on complimentary close.

Subject line

The subject line, if there is one, is typed after the salutation, with a line space between them. A subject line can be useful in letting the recipient of your letter know what it is about at a glance. Subject lines should be typed or written in capital letters to make them stand out. If you are using a word processor, you can also make the subject line bold to make it stand out even more.

Complimentary close

This is placed under the last paragraph – there is often a blank line between the two – and above the signature. The positioning of the complimentary close will depend on the format of the letter: in fully blocked style it must be aligned to the left; otherwise it may be centred or nearer the right hand side of the page

For formal and business correspondence, as mentioned under the heading 'Salutation', it used to be that the wording of the salutation dictated the wording of the complimentary close:

Salutation	**Complimentary close**
Dear Sir	Yours faithfully
Dear Sirs	Yours faithfully
Dear Sir or Madam	Yours faithfully
Dear Madam	Yours faithfully
Dear Mr Black	Yours sincerely
Dear Miss Green	Yours sincerely
Dear Mrs White	Yours sincerely
Dear Ms Brown	Yours sincerely
Dear John	Yours sincerely
Dear Mary	Yours sincerely

When the addressee was not named, the complimentary close was always 'Yours faithfully', and when the addressee was named, the complimentary close was always 'Yours sincerely'. This rule, while still used today, is now not so widely and rigidly adhered to.

The closing greeting can now take various forms. Some feel it is peculiar and rather too obsequious to bring the concept of faithfulness into a letter to someone whom one does not know, and have come to regard 'Yours faithfully' in much the same way as 'Your obedient servant' and other phrases used in letters in the past. We now live in a much less formal, egalitarian age, and like everything else, the conventions used in letter-writing are being affected by this.

If you don't like 'Yours faithfully' but want to keep a slightly formal feel, it is nowadays perfectly acceptable to use 'Yours sincerely' with the salutations 'Dear Sir', 'Dear Sirs', 'Dear Madam' and 'Dear Sir or Madam'. As is shown in the table opposite, when you begin a letter 'Dear Mr Black' or 'Dear Ms Brown' you should close the letter with 'Yours sincerely'. Similarly, with a fairly personal salutation like 'Dear John' or 'Dear Mary' you can use 'Yours sincerely' where you want to maintain a measure of distance between you and the addressee.

Remember that not everyone likes the familiarity conveyed by some of the complimentary closes that are creeping into letters nowadays, probably influenced by email and text messaging.

Of course, there are situations where you may want to use a warmer, less impersonal close, such as 'With best wishes', 'Kind regards', 'Yours affectionately', 'Yours ever', or 'Yours'.

Closing phrases expressing love should be reserved for family members, lovers and very close personal friends, although certain people use these lavishly and loosely, particularly on postcards or greetings cards.

Complimentary closes suitable for business letters

Yours faithfully	formal
Yours sincerely	less formal
Sincerely,	mainly US
Sincerely yours,	mainly US
Cordially,	mainly US
Yours respectfully	very formal
Respectfully yours,	mainly US
Respectfully,	mainly US
Yours truly,	mainly US; informal
Best regards	informal
With kind regards	informal
Kind regards	informal
Warmest regards	informal
Regards	informal

Complimentary closes suitable for personal and social letters

With best wishes
Best wishes
All the best
Fondly,
Yours affectionately
Affectionately,
Love
Much love
With all my love

Never use 'Yours very faithfully' (you are either faithful or you are not). However, there is no technical reason for not using 'Yours very sincerely', though, it is perhaps a little inelegant.

Only the first word in the closing greeting should be given a capital letter; do not write 'Yours Sincerely' or 'Yours Truly'. A comma at the end of the closing greeting is no longer obligatory.

Signature

As has been mentioned above, the signature is placed under the closing greeting, usually with a blank line between them. Since not everyone's signature is legible – indeed some people seem to pride themselves on the illegibility of their signatures – it is important to type or print your name underneath your signature so that people are in no doubt about the identity of the writer and their exact name, thus:

Yours sincerely

James Brown

James Brown

Presentation and Layout

In business letters it is also a good idea to include your position in an organization or firm where this is relevant. This is usually typed on the line immediately following the name, thus:

Yours sincerely

James Brown

James Brown
Club Secretary

Sometimes a letter is signed on behalf of someone else. This usually happens when the person who has dictated the letter is not available to sign it after it has been typed or printed. The signature will then appear something like this:

Yours sincerely

Jane Green

pp James Brown
Chief Executive Officer

The abbreviation p.p. does not stand for 'on behalf of', as is generally assumed, but is an abbreviation of the Latin phrase *per procurationem*, meaning 'by proxy'. Strictly speaking then, pp should precede the name of the person signing the letter and not the name of the person on whose behalf the letter is being signed. However, this is widely ignored.

It is important to remember to sign your letters. If you are in a hurry it is all to easy to type a letter on the word processor, print it out and put it in an envelope without signing it. Provided you have typed your name there will be no problem for the recipient in identifying the sender, but unsigned letters can cause offence because they send a message that you didn't care enough to take the time to check the letter before hastily stuffing it in the envelope.

Personal contact information

An individual writing on behalf of a company or organization may give their personal contact information in addition to the more general company contacts shown at the top of the letter. For example, they may give their individual email address, mobile phone number or telephone extension number. This information is often typed under or near their signature.

> Yours sincerely
>
> *James Brown*
>
> James Brown
> Sales Executive
> Extn: 2073

Enclosures

When other documents are being sent with a letter, the convention is to note this on the covering letter, using the abbreviations Enc and Encs (Enclosure and Enclosures).

The abbreviation Enc or Encs is often followed by a number corresponding to the number of items to be enclosed, for example Encs x 3. This is helpful for checking that you have gathered all the documents before putting them into the envelope, and so that the recipient knows how many documents ought to be enclosed.

If there are enclosures, this is indicated below the signature, thus:

Yours sincerely

James Brown

James Brown

ENCLS x 3

There may be one or two line spaces between the printed signature and the enclosure line.

Copies

When a letter is being copied to others, this is also usually indicated. The standard formula is:

Copies to: Kenneth Barrett
             Delia Jackson
             Sam Trudeau

Notice that the names are in alphabetical order.

Another way of prefixing the names of the people to receive copies is to use the abbreviation CC or cc, meaning 'carbon copies'. This term is inherited from the days when all correspondence was typed and copies were made using carbon paper.

If you don't want the person to whom the letter is addressed to know when other people have been sent copies of the letter, you can use the abbreviation BCC or bcc, meaning 'blind carbon copies'. In this case nothing is printed on the addressee's copy of the letter, and bcc followed by the name of the person or people receiving copies is printed only on the copies.

Postscripts

Postscripts are 'afterthoughts' printed or written after the signature. They are preceded by the abbreviation PS (or P.S.). Try to avoid them in business correspondence as they give the impression you have not formulated your thoughts sufficiently to make all the points you needed to make in the body of the letter.

Addressing Envelopes

Modern style is to align all the lines of the address with no indentation and no punctuation, as in the following example:

Mr James Brown
Flat 3
23 Whitehill Street
SEAFIELD
Blackshire
RA9 5JX

For standard-sized envelopes, the address should be aligned with the longer sides of the envelope, and placed slightly to the left of the mid point between the two shortest sides. The first line of the address should be about two thirds of the way down from the top edge of the envelope. This allows plenty of room for the stamp and postmark.

Legibility is the most important consideration when addressing an envelope. If the mail sorters or reading devices at sorting offices cannot read the address the letter cannot be delivered. Similarly, if there are errors or omissions in the address it may cause delays in delivery.

The conventions for addressing envelopes used to be the same as those for writing addresses within the letter, but nowadays more attention needs to be paid to the increasing automation of postal sorting, and, for international mail, to the conventions of the destination country.

The old style of indenting each line of the address with

commas at the end of each line is now more or less obsolete.

The sender should write or print his or her own name and address on the back of the envelope so that the letter can be returned if it cannot be delivered. Alternatively, the sender's name and address can be printed on the front of the envelope at the top left hand side, provided it is sufficiently distinct and separate from the recipient's address, and is outside the 'reading zone' of mail sorting machines.

Automated Mail Sorting

The optical character reading (OCR) cameras used in many automated systems have a predetermined 'reading zone'. The camera will not read accurately anything that is written or printed outside this zone. To assist automatic sorting the advice is to write or print the address leaving at least 15 mm margins to left and right, with a 40 mm margin at the top edge of the envelope (where the postage information is sited). Address lines should be no longer than 100 mm.

The higher the contrast between ink colour and paper colour, the higher the accurate read rate of the OCR system will be. Black ink on white or cream paper is recommended.

Envelopes should not be too flimsy – the recommended paper weight is 75g/sqm. The paper should also have a high opacity so that the contents cannot be seen through the paper and interfere with the reading of the address.

For window envelopes, the material covering the address window should be shiny not matt and nothing other than the address should appear in the window.

To assist legibility there should be at least one character gap between words; and there should be uniform spacing between address lines, with a recommended gap between lines of 0.5 mm to 12 mm.

While OCR can read most typed upper and lower case characters and numerals, fonts chosen should be clear and sharp, not script, artistic or italic. Some recommended fonts are Arial, Courier, Times New Roman and Century.

Printed addresses should be aligned at the left hand side and parallel to the top edge of the envelope. Adhesive address labels should be at least 80 mm x 25 mm and placed in the 'reading zone' of the envelope. In handwritten addresses, the lines should be horizontal, the individual characters of even size, and characters should not overlap or touch each other.

Addressing guidance for different countries

The conventions for addressing envelopes vary from country to country. A few illustrations are given below.

United Kingdom

For the UK, addresses should include the information as set out in the table on page 85 opposite.

The Royal Mail advises that it is essential to include the post town name in every UK address. To leave it out when addressing an envelope risks a delay in delivery. Although the post town name does not provide any information that is not already contained in the postcode, it is sometimes used to check that the postcode is correct and to aid manual sorting where the postcode is missing or incorrect.

Post towns rarely correspond to political or administrative boundaries. Instead, each post town corresponds to one or more postcodes, and a single post town can cover many individual towns and villages. Thus, for mail sorting purposes, the Isle of Man is a post town, while Douglas, the island's main town, is categorized as a locality within the post town of Isle of Man. A post town may also cover a very large densely populated geographical area, such as Greater London. In large cities or conurbations it is quite usual to give more specific directions by giving a locality name on an additional line above the post town, for example Hampstead or Bethnal Green. However, including

Presentation and Layout

Information	Is this information required?	Address line
Addressee's name	Yes, when applicable	Mr James Brown
Company name or Organization's name	Yes, when applicable	Farington plc
Flat or Apartment number	Yes, when applicable	Flat 3/1
Building name	Yes, except if the building also has a number	Farington House
Number of house, flat, building and name of street, road, etc	Yes	23 Whitehill Street
Name of locality	Yes, but only if there is a similar street or road name within the same post town area	Greenhill
Post town (*PRINT IN CAPITAL LETTERS*)	Yes	SEAFIELD
Postal county, historical county or administrative county/region	No longer necessary provided the post town and postcode are used	BLACKSHIRE
Postcode (*PRINT IN CAPITAL LETTERS*)	Yes	RA9 5JX
Country Name (*PRINT IN CAPITAL LETTERS*)	Only for international mail	UNITED KINGDOM

a locality is only really necessary where there are two or more similar addresses within the post town area.

It is no longer necessary to include a county name, provided the post town and postcode are used. Using the correct post town and postcode and omitting the county name may even avoid the confusion that can arise about county names. Postal counties – used by the Royal Mail internally for organizational purposes – do not necessarily correspond to historical or administrative boundaries. Furthermore, with successive reorganizations of local government, boundaries for administrative counties, districts and regions have been redrawn many times, and areas renamed. Nonetheless, and because counties – historical, administrative, or otherwise – may still be included in addresses (often in abbreviated form), a list of the abbreviations for some UK counties has been given in Appendix 3 at the back of the book.

To check the correct spelling of a city name and/or find a postcode and post town visit the Postcode Finder on the Royal Mail's information and service portal at:

www.royalmail.com/portal/rm

United States

General advice issued by the US Postal Service, including conventional abbreviations used for the individual states, can be found in Appendix 2 on page 367.

The US Postal Service guidance is broadly that the address should have the recipient's name on the first line, the apartment or building number and street name on the second line, and the municipality, state symbol and ZIP code on the third line. When the letter is to a company or organization this basic structure obviously has to be adapted to take in other elements such as the recipient's title, the relevant department and the company name.

Use the two character state abbreviation instead of the full state name and separate the state abbreviation from the municipality by a single space. The ZIP code should be separated from the state abbreviation by two spaces, and if it is a nine digit ZIP code (Zip + 4) there should be a hyphen between the fifth and sixth digits.

Arthur M. Holbrook, Vice President
Public Affairs Department
Ardley, Blackley and Chatley, Inc.
756 Juniper Rd
CHICAGO IL 47657-5675

To check the correct spelling of a city name or to find a ZIP code, visit the United States Postal Service website at:

www.usps.com.

Canada

Canada Post's addressing guide suggests addresses should be written entirely in upper case; postcodes should be in upper case with a space between the first three and the last three elements; and the municipality, province or territory, and the postal code should appear on the same line. For bilingual addressing (French is the first language in some parts of Canada) a solid black line should be drawn between the English and French versions of the address, with a clear space on each side of the black line.

Australia

In Australia, addresses are typically written on three lines, with the recipient's name on the top line, the number and name of the street on the next line, and the place name or post office of delivery + state or territory abbreviation + postcode on the last line. The information on the last line should be printed all in capitals without punctuation or underlining. One or two character spaces should be left between the place name and the state or territory name and the postcode. Some envelopes have pre-printed postcode squares; these are used only when the address is to be written by hand.

France

Madame Bouvier (recipient's name)
36, Rue Olivier (house/building number, street name)
17682 LYONS (postal code + city)
FRANCE (include the country only if posting the letter outside France)

Italy

Sig. Antonio Alberti (recipient's name)
Via Francesco 37 (street name, house/building number)
10000-ROMA RM (postal code-city/ province)
ITALY (include the country only if posting the letter outside Italy)

Spain

Sra. D. Garcia (recipient's name)
Avda de la Libertad 10, 3° B (street name, house/building number, floor number)
28300 MADRID (postal code + city/town/locality)
SPAIN (include the country only if posting the letter outside Spain)

Germany

Herrn (form of address)
Hermann Gottlieb (name)
Hertzstrasse 12 (street name + street number)

16935 Leipzig (postal code + city)
GERMANY (include the country only if posting the letter outside Germany)

Fax

The sample below gives a general idea of the elements that are included in a fax cover page/sheet.

FAX

To	Peter Murray
Company	Peter Murray Garden Structures Ltd
Fax Number	07754 3067 8293
From	Rani Shavir
Date	5 March 2004
Number of Pages	3 (including cover page)

LANDSCAPING AT 275 LIME CRESCENT HEMEL HEMPSTEAD

As we discussed on the phone earlier today, I'm sending the approved drawings and plans for the rear garden, showing the location of the new conservatory and garage block. I'd appreciate if you would let me have your estimate within the next few days.

Regards

Rani Shavir

Some points to remember when sending a fax:

- Always include a cover sheet (handwritten or typed) which shows, at a minimum, the name of the sender, the name of

the recipient, fax number of the sender, date of transmission, and the number of pages sent.
- It is very important to include the number of pages on the cover sheet, and always number the individual pages. It is quite common for pages to become separated during or after transmission.
- Give your message a heading.
- Quote any reference for filing purposes and so that the fax can be linked to previous correspondence.
- There is no necessity to include an opening greeting, such as 'Dear Mr Singh' or 'Dear Britney'.
- Neither do you need to include one of the formal complimentary closes, such as 'Yours sincerely' or 'Yours faithfully'. However, some people do include a closing phrase, such as 'Kind regards' or 'Best wishes'.

CV (Curriculum Vitae)

Because a CV can be such an important first step in gaining the attention of a potential employer, a great deal of care and attention should be devoted to how it is laid out, and, of course, to its content. How to write your CV is not covered in detail in this book, but there is an example of a basic CV (and a US résumé) and information on the sort of covering letter you will need to send with it in the Sample Letters section.. Some brief guidance on how your CV might be laid out, can be seen opposite.

Don't be tempted to use ornamental fonts or brightly coloured ink or paper, unless you are convinced the employer is looking for this sort of originality, and try to get all the information onto one sheet of paper.

> Never hand-write a CV, unless specifically requested to do so by the potential employer.

Name:
Address:

Tel:
Email:

Date of birth:

Nationality:

Marital status:

WORK EXPERIENCE
(List with the most recent first and give date ranges)

EDUCATION
(List, giving the most recent first and including date ranges)

OTHER RELEVANT SKILLS
(List only the most important: be concise)

INTERESTS
(List only the most interesting and relevant; be concise)

REFEREES
(Provide at least two names and addresses)

Chapter 5

Finding the Word

Style

This chapter looks at the content of the letter; it deals with matters of style and usage, grammar, punctuation and spelling.

> Your letter should be easy to read and easy to understand. If it is a business letter it should be obvious what it is about, and all the information the reader needs should be easy to find.

If your letter is not well constructed and clearly written, the point or points you are trying to make will probably be lost. It is not only essential to lay out and present your letter well, but also to consider carefully what you say and how you say it.

This means that the language you use should be understandable, and grammar, punctuation and spelling should be correct. For certain categories of business correspondence, such as applying for a job or making a formal complaint, you will do yourself no favours at all if your letter is misspelled, ungrammatical and badly-punctuated. Such a letter is very likely to be cast aside as not worthy of the reader's attention.

The tone of the letter should be pitched in the appropriate way – not too informal where a degree of formality is expected, and not too formal where it will be better appreciated if you express yourself in a more conversational style.

Decide what you want to say before you begin to write. Marshal all the facts and information you need to include, and discard all that is irrelevant.

> It is always worth doing a rough draft of the letter so that you can check it for errors, or – if you are not confident that you have a complete grasp of grammar, usage and punctuation – ask someone to check it for you.

Standard phrases and expressions that may be useful for quick reference in specific contexts have been grouped under their subjects in the Sample Letters section which follows this chapter.

Vary the length of sentences

Short sentences coming one after the other are fine for special sections of the letter in which you want to list and highlight a number of points (perhaps also using bullets or numbering), but having every sentence short in the body of the letter can produce a rather severe staccato effect.

Long complex sentences should also be avoided, because it is all too easy to get lost, both when you are writing and when you are reading.

Don't pack sentences with too many ideas

If there are too many points or ideas in a single sentence, the reader may very well lose track. The usual advice is that a sentence should contain a single point or idea. Another good rule of thumb is to have only one subordinate clause with each main clause. Too many subordinate clauses in the sentence will reduce readability. A business letter usually has a fairly mundane purpose which will not sit well with complicated structures and rhetorical flourishes.

Paragraphs

Ideally, a paragraph should consist of two or more sentences.

Start each paragraph with a topic sentence and use further sentences, as required, to amplify or expand your point.

Avoid very long paragraphs. If a paragraph is too long, it can look daunting and the reader may skip over important details to get through it. It is better to try to divide your ideas and points up and go for shorter paragraphs. This is especially important in letters.

Writers in general are advised to avoid one-sentence paragraphs. Letter-writers who are aiming for a degree of style in their prose should also follow this advice. However, for a letter whose purpose is simply to provide information, this is probably not worth agonizing over. There is nothing to be gained by padding the letter out just to avoid one-sentence paragraphs.

Register

Register is the name given by linguists to the varieties of language that people use when they interact in speech and writing. Language can vary from the extremely formal to extremely informal, with each variety displaying differences in vocabulary and syntax (i.e. the ways in which words are arranged). For letter-writing, cues about the necessary level of formality can be taken from previous correspondence, but there will also be times when you will have to make an independent judgement about how formal or informal your letter should be. This is quite often a matter of common sense, keeping in mind that the tone you ought to use when writing a letter to a prospective employer is very unlikely to be the tone you are in the habit of using when texting or emailing your bosom buddies.

People who are nervous of writing are frequently told to write as they speak. This is probably quite good advice when the letter is to a friend or family member; the letter will then reflect the writer's personality and be recognizable to the recipient. Any small errors, or idiosyncrasies of style, will almost certainly be overlooked or forgiven by the recipient.

'Write as you speak' is not such good advice for a formal business letter, unless you are adept at changing your tone to suit your audience. In business contexts, too conversational a tone is not likely to suit your purpose or produce the desired effect.

Nonetheless, you should not attempt to use a high-flown formal style because you imagine it is what is expected or it is the only way to impress. When a letter is full of long, pretentious words and outdated expressions, the impression made is much more likely to be a negative one than a positive one. Furthermore, if you use language that you aren't familiar with and don't properly understand,. you risk making yourself look ridiculous, like Mrs. Malaprop in Sheridan's play *The Rivals*. (Mrs. Malaprop peppered her conversation with polysyllabic words so as to sound grand but, having no idea of their meaning, she invariably used them in the wrong context, with laughable results.) Even if these embarrassing extremes are avoided, where the writing style is too formal, the letter may be stiff, stilted and unnatural. The best advice is to try and be yourself as much as possible, without being overly conversational. Try reading the letter aloud to make sure that it sounds unaffected, flows well, and is a true record of what you want to say.

Don't begin every sentence with the same word

It makes for smoother flowing prose if sentences begin in different ways. In particular, avoid beginning every sentence with the first person singular pronoun I or the first person plural pronoun we. One good way to vary sentences is to change the order of main clause and subordinate clause so that the subordinate clause comes before the main clause, for example:

> He won't be able to buy the property unless he can raise a big enough loan.

> can be changed to

Unless he can raise a big enough loan, he won't be able to buy the property.

Brevity not verbosity

For some writers, the urge to use fourteen words when two or three will do seems to be quite irresistible. Although you may be tempted to try to thrill your correspondent with your wide vocabulary and impressive grasp of important-sounding terms, take care! There is a real danger your reader may view your writing style as pompous, or, more seriously, they may not understand what you are trying to say. It is wise to avoid long-windedness and high-falutin' language, and instead stick to clear plain English.

Simplicity and clarity should always be the watchwords for business correspondence. This usual also means aiming for brevity. Nowadays, people do not have the time, inclination or concentration span to read great screeds. When faced with a very long letter they will probably not read it closely, and they may not even begin. A page and a half of A4 paper is about the extent that will be tolerated. While aiming for brevity, though, do ensure that you have included all the points you want to make and all the information that is required.

Various tests have been devised by linguists to assess the readability of texts. One such test is a lexical density test. Here, the number of different words used in the text is divided by the total number of words and the result is multiplied by 100 to give the lexical density. Texts with a lower lexical density are easier to read and understand.

Other tests base readability results on average sentence length and average number of syllables per word. Many modern word processors now provide statistics on readability based on such tests. For example, in Microsoft's® popular word processing program, Word, you are able to select 'readability statistics' in a tick box on the Spelling and Grammar tab (first select Tools, then Options to find the Spelling and Grammar tab). Information on the readability of the document will then be displayed each time a spelling and grammar check is completed on your document.

Avoid humour in formal and business letters

Keep things business-like. Don't try to funny. There is a time and a place for humour and irony – it's fine in personal letters, but not in a letter to your bank manager.

Watch what you say

Take care not to be abusive or libellous, and never tell lies or misrepresent yourself in a letter.

Don't rush to the post with the letter of complaint you have dashed off while upset or angry. Give yourself a bit of time to calm down and then decide if the letter should be sent as written, if it should be revised and toned down, or if it shouldn't be send at all.

Political correctness aims to remove all forms of prejudice in language: sexism, racism, ageism, discrimination against the disabled, religious intolerance, etc. While the motives for promoting political correctness may be wholly admirable (i.e. to achieve a more equal society in which everyone respects each other), some people do carry it to extreme lengths.

It is really a matter of choice whether you observe politically correct rules of language, but even if you don't you should always consider the likely effect of what you write on the feelings of the recipient. Will anything you have written cause irritation or offence?

Remember it costs nothing to be polite.

Avoid saying the same thing twice

Repetition is commonly used in speech for emphasis, or as a means of re-engaging listeners whose attention has momentarily been diverted elsewhere. However, when communication is in writing, the way information is transferred from one person to another is wholly different. In letter-writing, if points are to be emphasized this is usually done by highlighting in some way (for example by underlining, or using italic or bold) not by repeating the point again and again. Where a reader may have suffered a lapse in concentration or had an interruption, he or she can always go back over the text. In any event, if your point is made well enough in the first place, the reader will understand it and will be looking to move on. Repetition can sometimes be interpreted as patronizing, it may irritate or antagonize the reader, or it may even communicate a sense of desperation.

There is another style fault, of a slightly less obvious kind, that involves repetition. This saying in different words something that has been said already, otherwise known as tautology. While using tautological expressions in spoken language is no great sin, they can cause intense irritation to some readers and should be avoided.

Here are some examples of tautology, with the relevant word or phrase in bold and the duplicated meaning in italics:

> Three *additional* sections **have been added** to this year's brochure.
> Our *mutual* respect **for each other** made for an extremely cordial meeting.
> Is a vegan diet **adequate** *enough* for a growing child?
> He lived in *lonely* **isolation**.
> Several letters of complaint arrived **one after the other** *in succession*.
> The heavier particles **sink** *down* to the bottom.

The convoy **progressed** *forward* slowly.
I refer you to the documents **enclosed** *herewith*.
This *new* **innovation** will revolutionize office procedures.
I am *personally* not aware of any such instruction.
Personally, I wouldn't want to be in his position.
the *former* manners of **an earlier time**
The *past* **history** of the village is contained in these dusty volumes.
At this moment *in time*, there seems to be no obvious solution.
The building was **razed** *to the ground*.

Usage

This section deals with more specific questions of correct usage; in other words, which forms are preferred or generally considered to be correct. Language changes as society changes, so it is not always a good idea to be too inflexible about what is, or is not, 'correct' at any one time. Nonetheless, it is helpful to know what is generally considered to be standard or accepted usage, or what might cause the recipient of your letter to conclude that your knowledge of such matters may not be all that it should be.

Entries in this section are in alphabetical order for quick reference.

Also

This adverb should not be used as a replacement for the conjunction and. It is not correct to write:

> Please send me some tile samples, also some carpet samples.

It is correct to write:

Please send me some tile samples, and some carpet samples.

or, more concisely

Please send me some tile and carpet samples.

Apostrophe

It is a common mistake to add an apostrophe in a plural noun where none is required, for example:

This is one of the least densely populated area's of the United Kingdom.

In this sentence, *areas* is a plural so it shouldn't have an apostrophe. It is also a common mistake to omit an apostrophe where one is needed, for example:

He thinks he is the cats pyjamas.

In this sentence, *cat's* is a possessive form, not a plural, and should have an apostrophe. Sometimes an apostrophe is placed wrongly, for example:

The childrens' toys were scattered everywhere.

Here *children* is a plural noun so the possessive form is *children's*.
See also the section on Punctuation (page 150).

As *and* like

In speech and informal contexts, *like* is often used instead of *as* or *as if*. For written work it is probably best to maintain the distinction between the two.

Finding the Word: Usage

Use *like* before a noun or pronoun when a direct comparison is being made, for example:

He's very like his father.
She has eyes like a hawk.
Like you, he cannot stand cruelty to animals.

Where the comparison is more indirect and is contained in a following clause, use *as* or *as if*. Therefore, do not write:

He's behaving exactly like his father did.
You'll never love her like I do.
She felt like she was going to faint.
Like his mother said, he has had to go to hospital.

Use *as*, *as if* or *as though* instead:

He's behaving exactly as his father did.
You'll never love her as I do.
She felt as though she was going to faint.
As his mother said, he has had to go to hospital.

As to whether

This is a clumsy example of circumlocution which should be avoided if possible. Aim to use a more straightforward wording. For example, the following sentence

Will scheduled flights be restored by the end of the week?

gets to the point much more directly than

I'm enquiring as to whether scheduled flights will be restored by the end of the week.

Bored

Someone can be *bored with* or *bored at* something, but if they say they are *bored of it*, they may be bored but they are also using non-standard English!

Dangling participle

A dangling participle is a participle that has been misplaced in a sentence. A participle is often used to introduce a phrase that refers to a subject mentioned in the main clause, as in:

> Worn out by the long walk, she fell to the ground in a faint.

Worn out is the participle and *she* is the subject (i.e. it is she who is *worn out*). It is a common error in constructions such as this for the participle to be related to the wrong subject in the main clause, as in:

> Painting the ceiling, some of the plaster fell on his head.

Here the participle *painting* should refer to *he* but it seems to refer to *some of the plaster*. Sometimes the participle is left dangling because the intended subject is not mentioned in the following main clause, as in:

> Living alone, the days seemed long.

Try to construct sentences so that they say what you mean them to say and they contain all the information the reader needs to comprehend that meaning.

Double negatives

In English, two negative words cancel each other out. Don't

Finding the Word: Usage

be tempted to use a second negative word because you think it makes the first negative more emphatic. It may be a bit obvious to point out that is not correct to say or write double negatives such as:

I didn't have no idea how it happened.
I never saw no one the whole time I was there.

But double negatives can also be rather more subtle. For example, certain words have an element of negativity in their meanings and therefore shouldn't be coupled with a more straightforward negative word such as not or no. These words include the adverbs hardly, barely, scarcely and the verb miss. All the following examples are not correct:

There wasn't hardly a soul to be seen.
You haven't barely touched your breakfast.
We miss not being together.

Where a negative is used in a sentence's main clause and another negative word is used in a subordinate clause or another main clause in the same sentence, be sure that using the second negative doesn't create the opposite meaning to that which is intended, for example:

He said he wouldn't be at all surprised if there wasn't traffic chaos.

If he thought there would be traffic chaos, the sentence should read:

He said he wouldn't be at all surprised if there was traffic chaos.

Equally

Take care not to follow *equally* with *as*. Here are some sentences in which *equally* is used correctly:

> Her brother is an expert player and she is equally talented.
> He is trying hard but his competitors are trying equally hard.

Do not write

> ... she is equally as talented
> ... his competitors are trying equally as hard.

Where the phrase *just as* is used it can be replaced by *as* but not by *equally as*, for example:

> The old dishwasher was just as good as this flashy ultra-modern model.

I *and* me

I should be used as the subject of a sentence, for example:

> You and I have both been invited.
> Why are Jane and I never picked?

Me should be used as the object, for example:

> The cake was made by Mary and me.
> My brother and father played against my mother and me.

People often assume wrongly that *me* is less polite than *I*. This is probably because they have been taught that when asked such questions as Who is there? the grammatically correct reply is *It is I*. In fact *It is me* or *It's me* is much more common now and has gained widespread acceptance.

Should *I* or *me* be used after *between*? Because *between* is followed by an object, *me* is the correct form, so it is quite correct to say:

Just between you and me, I think he is dishonest.

Its *and* it's

As has been pointed out in several other places in this book, *its* and *it's* are very often confused in writing. *Its* is a possessive pronoun meaning 'belonging to it', for example:

The house has lost its charm.
The dog does not like its kennel.

It's is a contracted form of *it is*, for example:

Do you know if it's raining?
It's not fair to expect her to do all the work.

Just

Just is liable to be put in the wrong place in a sentence. It should be placed before the word it refers to, as in:

He has just one book left to sell.

not

He just has one book left to sell.

Just in the sense of 'in the very recent past' is used with the perfect tense, as in:

They have just finished the job.

not

They just finished the job.

Kind

Kind should be used with a singular noun, so the sentence

This kind of accident can be avoided.

is correct but the following is not

These kind of accidents can be avoided.

Similarly

The children do not like that kind of film.

is correct, and should *not* read

The children do not like those kind of films.

A plural noun can be used if the sentence is rephrased, as in:

Children do like not films of that kind.

Less *and* fewer

Less is used to refer to quantity and *fewer* is used to refer to number. The following examples are correct:

less milk/fewer milk bottles
less responsibility/fewer responsibilities
eat less food/eat fewer fattening foods

a score of less than twenty/fewer than a hundred people.

The following examples are ungrammatical and *not* correct:

There were less birds in the garden than in previous years.
Less than a thousand pandas live in the wild.
It's more than fifty but fewer than a hundred.

Negatives

When a sentence made up of two clauses contains a negative word such as *no* or *not* that applies to only one of the clauses, the sentence should be structured so that the negative word does not apply to both clauses. For example, in the sentence:

I don't feel this is your best work and should be looked at again.

don't feel this is appears to apply to *your best work* and also to *should be looked at again*, suggesting that in the writer's opinion the piece of work shouldn't be looked at again. The sentence should be reworded, as in:

I feel this is not your best work and that you should look at it again.

When the sentence includes both *not* and *every* or *all*, it should be constructed so that no uncertainty arises because of the placing of the negative word. For example, the meaning of:

All men are not created equal.

is made clearer when it is rewritten as:

Not all men are created equal.

Neither

When referring to one of two people use *neither*, for example:

We invited Ginny and James, but neither of them came to the party.

When more than two are being referred to use *none* or *no*, for example:

We invited all our neighbours, but none of them came to the party.

In comparisons, *neither* should always be paired with *nor*, for example:

The school had neither swimming pool nor gymnasium.

In informal contexts *neither* may be followed by either a singular or a plural verb. However, a plural verb is frowned on by some, and should be avoided in formal contexts. Thus

Neither of them eats meat.

is considered to be correct and

Neither of them eat meat.

is considered to be incorrect.

For *neither . . . nor* comparisons, when the second subject is singular, use a singular verb, for example:

Neither his children nor his wife has any regard for him.

When the second subject is plural, use a plural verb, for example:

Neither Mr Howard nor his lawyers know anything of this matter.

Nice

This adjective originally meant 'fine, subtle, requiring precision', as in:

There is rather a nice distinction between the two words.

However, nowadays it is much more widely used in the sense of 'pleasant', 'agreeable', as in:

She is a nice person.
We had a nice time at the picnic.

In this second sense, it is overused. Alternative adjectives should be chosen where possible, for example:

amiable   enjoyable
considerate   obliging
courteous   pleasant.
delightful

If you are struggling to find an appropriate synonym for the context, a thesaurus with words divided up into their senses will almost certainly be helpful.

None

When referring to more than two people use *none* or *no*, for example:

We invited all our neighbours, but none of them came to the party.

When referring to one of two people use *neither*, for example:

We invited Ginny and James, but neither came to the party.

When paired with a plural noun *none* can be used with either a singular or plural verb, depending on whether a unit as a whole is being considered, or the individuals making up the unit are being considered, for example:

None of us has been vaccinated.
I've been to some pretty rotten plays, but none were as dreadful as last week's offering.

Not only ... but also

In the sentence that follows, *not only* is in the wrong place:

She not only plays football but also rugby and tennis.

Because the verb *play* applies to both parts, the sentence should read:

She plays not only football but also rugby and tennis.

If there are different verbs, it is correct to place *not only* before the first verb, as in:

She not only plays football but also coaches the rugby team.

On behalf of

It is a mistake to use *on behalf of* as a synonym for *on the part of* or *on his/her/your part*, as in:

> That was an oversight on my behalf.

The phrase *on behalf of* means 'as the representative of' or 'for the benefit of', as in:

> On behalf of all the club members, I'd like to propose a toast to the new chairman and secretary.

Same

Some writers use *same* to avoid repeating a word, for example:

> Pick up the car and deliver same to the owner's residence.

This usage should be avoided at all costs. There is nothing wrong with using *it* or *them* if you don't want to repeat a noun, as in:

> Pick up the car and deliver it to the owner's residence.

Split infinitive

The infinitive is made up the word 'to' and the base form of the verb, for example *to push* and *to leave*. An infinitive is split when a word, usually an adverb, is placed between 'to' and the verb, as in *to rudely push* and *to quietly leave*. This was once considered a great grammatical sin but the split infinitive is not, in reality, a grammatical error in English. Modern thinking is that a split infinitive should be avoided only where it will produce a clumsy or inelegant construction.

Than

Than is used to link two halves of comparisons or contrasts, as in:

> Peter is considerably taller than John is.
> He is older than I am.
> I am more informed about the situation than I was yesterday.

In order to be grammatically correct, the word after *than* should take the subject form when the verb is omitted, as it frequently is, for example:

> She works harder than he (does).

However, this sounds decidedly stilted to modern ears, and the objective form has become the norm, as in:

> She works harder than him.

Where there is no implied verb, the word after *than* is in the objective form, for example:

> Rather you than me!

Their *and* they're

Their is the possessive of *they* and means 'of them, belonging to them', as in:

> their cars
> their attitudes.

They're is a shortened form of they are, as in:

They're not very happy.
They're bound to lose.

Unique

Unique means 'being the only one of its kind', as in:

a unique work of art
Every fingerprint is unique.

Because something is unique or it is not unique, the word cannot be modified by words such as *very, rather, more*, etc. However, something can be *almost unique, nearly unique* or *quite unique*.

Which *and* that

When the information being given is needed in order to decide what item is being discussed, you can use either *which* or *that*, for example:

The train which (or that) leaves at midday does not stop at Glasgow.

However, where the information is supplementary and not essential, only *which* can be used, for example:

This engine, which was built in Glasgow in 1935, was the fastest steam locomotive of its day.

Notice that the supplementary information is enclosed by a pair of commas.

Who *and* whom

Who is the subject of a verb, for example:

Who told you?
It was Janey who told her.
The girls who took part should report to the headmistress's office.

Whom is the object of a verb or preposition, as in:

Whom did he tell?
To whom did you speak?
The people from whom he stole are furious at his release from prison.

In modern usage *whom* is gradually falling into disuse, especially in questions. *Who* is used instead even though it is ungrammatical, for example:

Who did you speak to?

However, *whom* should be retained when it is a relative pronoun, as in:

the person whom you saw
the person to whom you spoke.

Whose *and* who's

Whose means 'of whom' or 'of which', as in:

She's the actress whose brother is my best friend.
Whose bicycle is that?
The firm whose staff went on strike.

Who's is a shortened form of 'who is', as in:

Who's that?

Finding the Word: Usage

Who's first in the queue?
Who's coming to the cinema?

You *and* yourselves, our *and* ourselves

Some writers use *yourselves* or *ourselves* (reflexive pronouns) instead of *you* and *us* (personal pronouns), for example:

We are seeking quotes from various contractors, including yourselves.
Their lawyer has written to ourselves demanding an amount we do not owe.

A reflexive pronoun is so named because its function is to refer back to a noun or a personal pronoun in the same gender, number and case, for example:

He did it himself.
You have always kept to yourselves.

Thus it is not appropriate to use a reflexive pronoun unless it is performing its proper function.

Your *and* you're

Your means 'belonging to you', 'of you', as in:

That's your book and this is mine.
Your attitude is surprising.
It's your own fault.

You're is a shortened form of 'you are', as in:

You're a fool to believe him.
You're going to be sorry.
You're standing on my coat.

Grammar

Grammar is much too complex a subject to cover in depth in this book. However, a basic description of grammatical elements and structures is given here, and a few of the common pitfalls that writers have to avoid.

The various elements of language are words, phrases, clauses and sentences.

There are nine parts of speech: verb, noun, adjective, pronoun, article, adverb, preposition, conjunction and interjection.

The parts of speech

Verb

A verb is often described to children as the 'doing' word in a sentence. This is, of course, a rather simplistic definition. The verb is the word in a main clause or sentence that describes an action or state.

- Verbs function either as *main* verbs or as *auxiliary* verbs. Main verbs are all verbs with independent meaning, for example:

    die   somersault
    fall   talk
    laugh   walk.
    live

Auxiliary verbs are used with main verbs to form tenses, questions and negative statements. Auxiliary verbs include the following:

    can   must
    dare   will.
    may

Finding the Word: Grammar

A small number of verbs function as main verbs and as auxiliary verbs; they are

be
do
have.

- Verbs are classified grammatically in a number of ways. Verbs can be either *transitive* or *intransitive*. Transitive verbs take an object and most can be used in the passive voice (see page 119). In the sentence

The boy broke the window.

window is a direct object and therefore *broke* (past tense of *break*) is a transitive verb. Intransitive verbs do not take an object and cannot be used in the passive voice. The following sentences contain intransitive verbs:

Time will tell.
The situation worsened.
Things improved.

Many verbs can be either transitive or intransitive, according to the context, thus *play* is intransitive in the sentence

The children played in the sand.

but transitive in the sentence

The boy plays the piano.

Likewise, *climb* is intransitive in the sentence

The path climbs steeply.

but transitive in the sentence

The mountaineers climbed Everest.

- Verbs are either *finite* or *non-finite*. A finite verb has a tense. It also has a subject with which it agrees in number and person. For example, *cries* is finite in the sentence

The child cries most of the time.

but *go* is non-finite in the sentence

He wants to go.

because it has no variation of tense and does not have a subject. Similarly, *standing* is non-finite in the sentence

Standing stock-still, the eagle owl surveyed the scene.

- Verbs are further classified as being *strong* or *weak*. A strong verb is an irregular verb with the simple past tense formed by changing the vowel in the base form of the verb, for example:

ride/rode

and whose past participle is formed by altering the vowel and/or having the ending *-en* or *-n*, for example:

stick/stuck
ride/ridden.

A weak verb is any regular verb, and any of the irregular verbs whose past tense and/or past participle ends in -*d* or -*t*, for example:

burn/burned/burnt.

- There are two ways of expressing the action of a verb, based on who or what is doing the action and who or what is receiving the action. This is known in grammar as *voice* and a verb is either in the *active* voice or the *passive* voice. For verbs in the active voice, the subject of the verb performs the action described by the verb. Thus, in the sentence

The bigger boy threw the stone.

the verb *throw* is in the active voice because the subject of the verb (*the bigger boy*) is doing the throwing. If the subject of this sentence was changed to make the verb passive, it would read as follows:

The stone was thrown by the bigger boy.

In verbs in the passive voice, the subject is the recipient of the action of the verb. Thus, in the sentence

Abigail was kicked by the pony.

the subject is *Abigail*, who receives the action described by the verb (*the kick*). If the subject of this sentence is changed to make the verb active, the sentence would read as follows:

The pony kicked Abigail.

> For letter-writing, the usual recommendation is to stick to the active voice as much as possible. This is because the active voice is more direct and concise than the passive voice. Overuse of the passive voice can make your prose seem flat and uninteresting. Of course, this is not a rule that needs to be adhered to slavishly. It sometimes suits the purpose to say things in a less direct way and use the passive.

- Verbs are also said to have *mood*. Mood is not related to tense but instead indicates the attitude or viewpoint expressed by the verb. The three moods are *indicative*, *imperative* and *subjunctive*.

  a) The indicative mood makes a statement of fact, for example:

  He lives in France.
  It's starting to rain.

  b) The imperative mood is used for giving orders or making requests, for example:

  Shut that door!
  Please bring me some coffee.

  c) The subjunctive mood is used for hypothetical statements and certain formal *that* clauses, for example:

  If I were you I would have nothing to do with it.
  Someone suggested that we ask for more money.
  I emailed asking that he send the reference direct to the regional manager.

- English verbs display *aspect*. Without getting too technical about it, aspect is how an action is regarded in terms of time, rather than its actual placing in time. English has only two basic inflecting (that change their form) tenses, the present tense and the past tense. All the other tenses are compound tenses, formed by combining the auxiliary verbs *be*, *have* and *will/shall* with present tense or past tense forms of a main verb. It is these compound tenses that display aspect, namely a) the *perfect aspect* and b) the *progressive* or *continuous aspect*.

a) Essentially, the perfect aspect shows that the action is complete at the time of speaking or writing (*present perfect*), or was complete at the time being referred to (*past perfect*) or will be complete at the time referred to (future perfect).

b) The progressive or continuous aspect shows that the action is in progress or is seen to be in progress at the time of speaking or writing (*present progressive*), it was or was seen to be in progress at the time of speaking or writing (*past progressive*) or it will be in progress or will be seen to be in progress (*future progressive*).

- Most verbs in English are regular verbs and have predictable endings, which derive from the *base form* of the verb. The base form of the verb is, as its name suggests, the form on which inflections of the verb are based. The base form is the same as the *bare infinitive*, for example:

eat
walk
drive
shake.

The *to-infinitive* is the base infinitive with to in front of it, for example:

to eat
to walk
to drive
to shake.

The five forms of regular verbs are:

a) the base form, for example:

laugh, jump, recommend

b) the simple present tense of the third person singular, in which *s* is added to the base form, for example:

laughs, jumps, recommends

c) the present participle, in which *-ing* is added to the base form, for example:

laughing, jumping, recommending

d) the simple past tense, in which *-ed* is added to the base form, for example:

laughed, jumped, recommended

e) the past participle, in which *-ed* is added to the base form, for example:

laughed, jumped, recommended.

Finding the Word: Grammar

- It is important in any piece of writing that the correct part of the verb is used.

  Even though a more relaxed view is taken nowadays about *non-standard* forms used in informal and spoken English, you should not use non-standard forms in formal letters.

  Some people have particular problems with the past tenses and past participles of the verbs *to go*, *to see* and *to do*. These errors are heard in speech more often than they are seen in writing, but it is probably worth illustrating the correct and incorrect forms nonetheless. The following examples are correct:

  She's gone (*or* she went) away.
  He had gone fishing.
  We saw (*or* had seen) our friends the day before.
  All of them have done brilliantly.
  You wouldn't be in trouble now if you'd done what you were told.

  The following examples are *not* correct:

  She's went away.
  He had went fishing.
  We seen our friends the day before.
  All of them done brilliantly.
  You wouldn't be in trouble now if you'd did what you were told.

- English verbs usually change their form so that they agree with their subject in person (first, second or third person) and number (singular or plural):

I walk   you walk
he walks   we walk
they walk.

- English verbs also change their form to indicate tense, for example:

I walk   I walked.

Loosely, *tense* can be defined as the form of the verb that indicates the time the action took place. There are several tenses for past, present and future time.

a) The *simple present* tense describes an action that is going on now or a state that exists now.

| Simple Present Tense |||
| Person | Number ||
	singular	plural
1st person	I walk	we walk
2nd person	you walk	you walk
3rd person	he/she/it walks	they walk

b) The *simple past* tense is used to refer generally to past time.

| Simple Past Tense |||
| Person | Number ||
	singular	plural
1st person	I walked	we walked
2nd person	you walked	you walked
3rd person	he/she/it walked	they walked

Finding the Word: Grammar

c) The *future tense* is formed by combining *will* or *shall* and the base form of the main verb.

Future Tense		
Person	Number	
	singular	plural
1st person	I will walk	we will walk
2nd person	you will walk	you will walk
3rd person	he/she/it will walk	they will walk

d) The *present perfect* tense is used to refer to an action that began at some time in the past and was completed in the recent past.

It is formed by combining the present tense of *have* with the *-ed* form of a main verb.

Present Perfect Tense		
Person	Number	
	singular	plural
1st person	I have walked	we have walked
2nd person	you have walked	you have walked
3rd person	he/she/it has walked	they have walked

e) The *past perfect* tense is used to refer an action that began at some time in the past and was completed at some time in the past.

It is formed by combining *had* and the *-ed* form of a main verb.

Past Perfect Tense

Person	Number	
	singular	plural
1st person	I had walked	we had walked
2nd person	you had walked	you had walked
3rd person	he/she/it had walked	they had walked

f) The *future perfect* tense is used for actions that will be completed at a time in the future. It is formed by combining will and *have* + the *-ed* form of a main verb.

Future Perfect Tense

Person	Number	
	singular	plural
1st person	I will have walked	we will have walked
2nd person	you will have walked	you will have walked
3rd person	he/she/it will have walked	they will have walked

g) The *present progressive* (or *present continuous*) tense is used to refer to something that is in progress now. It is formed by combining forms of the verb *to be* and the *-ing* form of the main verb.

Present Progressive or Continuous Tense

Person	Number	
	singular	plural
1st person	I am walking	we are walking
2nd person	you are walking	you are walking
3rd person	he/she/it is walking	they are walking

h) The *past progressive* (or *past continuous*) tense is used to refer to something that was in progress at some time in the past. It is formed by combining the past tense of the verb *to be* and the *-ing* form of the main verb.

Past Progressive or Continuous Tense		
Person	Number	
	singular	plural
1st person	I was walking	we were walking
2nd person	you were walking	you were walking
3rd person	he/she/it was walking	they were walking

i) The *future progressive* tense is used to refer to something that will be in progress at some unspecified time in the future. It is formed by combining *will* with *be* and the *-ing* form of the main verb. It is often used instead of the future tense to create subtle nuances in tone. For example:

What will you be wearing to the party? (*future progressive*)

is less abrupt than

What will you wear to the party? (*future tense*)

and

I'll be arriving some time tomorrow. (*future progressive*)

sounds less deliberate and decisive than

I'll arrive some time tomorrow. (*future tense*)

Future Progressive Tense		
Person	Number	
	singular	plural
1st person	I will be walking	we will be walking
2nd person	you will be walking	you will be walking
3rd person	he/she/it will be walking	they will be walking

j) The *present perfect progressive* (or *present perfect continuous*) tense is used to refer to actions that began in past time and are continuing in present time. It is also used instead of the present perfect when the action or situation is a temporary one. It is formed by combining the present tense of the *verb* to have with *been* and the *-ing* form of a main verb.

Present Perfect Progressive or Continuous Tense		
Person	Number	
	singular	plural
1st person	I have been walking	we have been walking
2nd person	you have been walking	you have been walking
3rd person	he/she/it has been walking	they have been walking

k) The *past perfect progressive* (or *past perfect continuous*) tense is used to refer to actions or situations that began at a point in the past continued for some time, and ended at another point in the past. It is formed by combining *had* with *been* and the *-ing* form of a main verb.

Finding the Word: Grammar

Past Perfect Progressive or Continuous Tense		
Person	Number	
	singular	plural
1st person	I had been walking	we had been walking
2nd person	you had been walking	you had been walking
3rd person	he/she/it had been walking	they had been walking

l) The *future perfect progressive* (or *future perfect continuous*) tense is used for considering what is in progress now from some point in the future. It is formed by combining *will have been* with the *-ing* form of a main verb.

Future Perfect Progressive or Continuous Tense		
Person	Number	
	singular	plural
1st person	I will have been walking	we will have been walking
2nd person	you will have been walking	you will have been walking
3rd person	he/she/it will have been walking	they will have been walking

- There are some other ways of expressing the future in English. For example, a combination of the verb *to be* and the *to-infinitive* of a main verb is used to talk about an action that has been planned for some time in the future, and often also suggesting an element of obligation or compulsion, as in:

He is to report to the headmaster first thing on Monday morning.
Those who are to die salute you.

A future action is also sometimes expressed in informal English by combining the verb *to be* with *going to* and the base infinitive of a main verb. This structure expresses intention, or predicts what will happen, as in:

I'm going to fly to Paris.
It'sgoing to rain next week.

- A *gerund* is the *-ing* form of a verb when it functions as a noun. It is sometimes known as a *verbal noun*. It has the same form as the present participle but a different function. In the sentence

He was jogging down the road.

jogging is the present participle, but in the sentence

Running is his idea of relaxation.

running is a gerund because it functions as a noun and is the subject of the sentence.

- A *phrasal verb* is a main verb combined with a preposition or adverb (called the *particle*), or both, to convey a meaning that is more than the sum of its parts, for example:

to phase out
to mess about
to sound off.

Finding the Word: Grammar

For more information on regular and irregular verbs see pages 178 and 373.

Noun

A noun is the word which names a person or thing. From the point of view of letter-writing, probably the two things that you most need to know about nouns are whether they are *common* nouns or *proper* nouns and how they form their plurals.

Most nouns are common nouns. Common nouns are simply the names of ordinary, non-specific things, and their first letter is a lower-case letter, for example:

baby   park
car   table.

Proper nouns are the names of specific things or particular people, and their first letter is a capital letter, for example:

Australia   Keith
Everest   President Lincoln
Freya   Rome.
Isabel

For information on forming plurals see page 174 in the Word Formation and Spelling section of this chapter.

Adjective

An adjective is a word that describes or qualifies a noun, for example:

big   long
heavy   tall
light   small.

An adjective usually answers one of the following questions: 'How many?' 'Which one?' 'What kind of?' The simple form of an adjective is known as the *absolute* form, for example:

tiny
enormous.

Most adjectives inflect and have a *comparative* and a *superlative* form. Inflecting adjectives are also known as *gradable* adjectives. Many adjectives take their comparative and superlative forms by adding *-er* and *-est*, for example:

brave/braver/bravest
short/shorter/shortest
mad/madder/maddest

Comparatives and superlatives can also be formed using 'more' and 'most' before the absolute form of the adjective, for example:

more beautiful
more realistic
more suitable

The tendency is for one-syllable adjectives to form their comparatives and superlatives with *-er* and *-est*, and for longer two to three syllable adjectives to form their comparatives and superlatives with 'more' and 'most'.

However, most single-syllable adjectives formed from the past participles of verbs have comparative and superlative forms using the words *more* and *most*, for example:

worn/more worn/most worn.

Finding the Word: Grammar

For many adjectives either is possible, for example:

handsome/handsomer/handsomest
handsome/more handsome/most handsome.

However, do not use both at the same time; in other words, do not use a double comparative, or a double superlative. In everyday speech, especially amongst the young, the use of double comparatives and superlatives is increasingly noticeable, as in:

Nothing could be more clearer.
It was just the most cutest thing I'd ever seen.

Double comparatives and superlatives are also beginning to creep into written English. Doubling comparatives and superlatives is not acceptable, and is always avoided by careful speakers and writers.

Some adjectives have irregular comparative forms and superlative forms. These include the following:

Adjective	Comparative	Superlative
good	better	best
bad	worse	worst
little	less	least
many	more	most

A very few adjectives are ungradable, i.e. they have no comparative or superlative, for example:

lone
single
unique.

Pronoun

A pronoun is a word that takes the place of a noun. The seven types of pronoun are *personal, possessive, reflexive, relative, demonstrative, indefinite* and *reciprocal pronouns.*

- *personal pronouns*
  I, me, you, he, him, she, her, it, we, us, you, they, them

- *possessive pronouns*
  my, mine, your, yours, his, her, hers, its, our, ours, your, yours, their, theirs

- *reflexive pronouns*
  myself, yourself, himself, herself, itself, ourselves, yourselves, themselves

- *relative pronouns*
  who, whom, whose, which, that

- *demonstrative pronouns*
  this, that, these, those

- *indefinite pronouns*
  all, another, any, anybody, anyone, anything, both, each, either, neither, everybody, everyone, everything, few, many, nobody, no one, none, nothing, one, several, some, somebody, someone, something

- *reciprocal pronouns*
  each other, one another

Personal and possessive pronouns take a different form according to whether they are the subject or object of a verb.

The *subjective* forms are:

I, my, you, your, he, his, she, her, it, its, we, our, they, their.

The *objective* forms are:

me, mine, yours, his, hers, its, ours, yours, theirs.

> Note that there is no apostrophe before the *s* in the possessive pronouns *hers*, *yours*, *ours* and *theirs*. Do not confuse *its* meaning 'belonging to it' with *it's*, the short form of *it is*.

It is a very common error to use the subjective form of a personal pronoun when the objective form should be used, and vice versa. It is *not* correct to write:

You and him are the only likely candidates.
Most of the work was left to Gregor and I.

It is correct to write:

You and he are the only likely candidates.
Most of the work was left to Gregor and me.

When a pronoun is used after a preposition it is always in the objective case, for example:

There isn't much love lost between them and us.

Article

The *definite* article is the word *the*. The *indefinite* article is the word *a* and its alternative form *an*.

The *a* form of the indefinite article is used before words that begin with a consonant sound, for example:

a box   a road
a gardenia   a walrus.

The *an* form is used before words that begin with a vowel sound, for example:

an appetite   an ostrich
an enormous effort an unbelievable coincidence.

Note that it is the sound of the initial letter that matters and not the spelling, thus *a* is used before words beginning with *a u* or *eu* when they are pronounced with the *y* sound /ewe/, for example:

a unit
a euro.

Similarly *an* is used before words beginning with the letter *h* when this is not pronounced, for example:

an heir
an hour
an honest man.

It was quite common to use *an* before words that begin with an *h* sound and an unstressed syllable, for example:

an hotel
an historic occasion

but nowadays most people use *a* in such cases.

Adverb

An adverb is a word that modifies, qualifies or adds information about a verb, an adjective, another adverb, or a whole sentence. It usually answers one of the following questions: 'When?' 'Where?' 'Why?' 'How?' 'How far?' 'How long?' 'How often?' 'To what degree or extent?' 'Under what conditions?'

Many adverbs end in -*ly*, but note that not all words ending in -*ly* are adverbs. Some are adjectives, for example:

costly   lonely
elderly   manly
friendly   timely.

Some adverbs do not end in -*ly*, for example:

fast, as in We ran fast.
long, as in We didn't have to wait long.
hard, as in They're working hard.

Adverbs like *only* and *even* should be placed as close as possible to the word they are modifying. Notice the difference in meaning created by placing *only* in different locations, as in:

She drinks **only** wine at the weekend.
She drinks wine **only** at the weekend.
Only she drinks wine at the weekend.

Similarly, and in order to avoid ambiguity, *even* should be placed immediately before the word it is intended to modify. Compare the meanings of the following sentences:

He **even** finds it difficult to relax on holiday.
He finds it difficult to relax **even** on holiday.
Even on holiday he finds it difficult to relax.

Preposition

A preposition shows how two elements in a sentence or clause relate to each other in time or space. In the sentence

> The cat sat on the mat.

on is a preposition; in the sentence

> She is at home.

at is a preposition; in the sentence

> They left after lunch.

after is a preposition; and in the sentence

> He sat between us.

between is a preposition.

The element, usually a noun or pronoun, that follows a preposition is said to be governed by the preposition.

It is sometimes difficult to decide which preposition should follow certain words. If you are in doubt you should consult a reliable dictionary or usage book.

This is the kind of usage that sometimes changes according to modern preference. For example *different from* used to be the only form that was considered correct but now *different to* is considered acceptable, especially in informal English.

In American English, *different than* is quite acceptable.

Conjunction

Conjunctions join word, phrases and clauses and indicate the relationship between the joined elements (or conjoins).

Finding the Word: Grammar

- A *co-ordinating* conjunction links elements of equal importance. The most familiar co-ordinating conjunctions are:

and
or
but.

Thus, *and* links the words in

bread and butter

or links the phrases in

a kilo of cheese or half a kilo of potatoes

and *but* links the clauses in

We asked for more money but we didn't get it.

- A *subordinating* conjunction, such as those shown below, links a subordinate clause to a main clause:

because
since
though
that
in case
when

In the sentence

We left at three o'clock because that's when the bus left.

the subordinating conjunction *because* links the subordinate clause *that's when the bus left* with the main clause *We left at three o'clock.*

Interjection

An interjection is an exclamation which, like a clause, is grammatically complete, for example:

Oh dear!
Aargh!

Phrases, sentences and clauses

Phrase

A phrase is two or more words, usually not containing a finite verb, that form a complete expression or constitute a part of a sentence.

There are various types of phrase including *noun* phrase, *prepositional* phrase, and *participial* phrase.

- A *noun phrase* is a group of words containing a noun as its main word and functioning like a noun in a sentence, i.e. it can function as the subject, object or complement of a sentence. In the sentence

The large black dog bit him.

the noun phrase is *the large black dog.*

- A *prepositional phrase* is a group of words made up of a preposition followed by its object. Prepositional phrases are very common in English.

In the sentence

We sheltered under the oak tree.

the prepositional phrase is *under the oak tree*; and in the sentence

We escaped by the skin of our teeth.

the prepositional phrase is *by the skin of our teeth*.

- A *participial phrase* includes a present participle or a past participle.

In the sentence

Gathering up his papers, he hastily left the room.

the participial phrase is *gathering up his papers*; and in the sentence

All things considered, it was a satisfactory result.

the participial phrase is *all things considered*.

Sentence

A sentence has certain defining characteristics.

It begins with a capital letter, and ends with a full stop, or an exclamation mark or question mark.

It is a group of words – or even a single word – that makes sense without additional information, for example:

The boy broke the window.
Help!

- A sentence with only one main clause is called a *simple* sentence, for example:

  The boy broke the window.

- A sentence made of two main clauses linked by a conjunction is called a *compound* sentence, for example:

  We went out early and we came back late.

- A sentence made up of a main clause and one or more subordinate clauses is called a *complex* sentence, for example:

  Since he is not in the office he cannot give you a reply.
  When he sees her he will be surprised.
  The party is going ahead although it is raining.

The basic elements making up sentences and clauses are: the *subject* and *predicate*, the *object*, the *verb*, the *complement* and the *adverbial*.

- The *subject* of a sentence is that which is spoken of (a noun, pronoun, or noun phrase) and which determines the number of the verb. If the subject is singular, the verb is singular and if the subject is plural, the verb is plural. In the sentence

  Birds fly.

  the subject is the noun *birds*.

  In the sentence

Finding the Word: Grammar

She hit the child.

the subject is the pronoun *she*, and in the sentence

The people in the town dislike him.

the subject is the noun phrase *the people in the town*.

- The *predicate* is all the parts of a clause or sentence that are not contained in the subject. The predicate typically includes the verb and the object. In the sentence

The little girl was exhausted and hungry.

the predicate is *was exhausted and hungry*. In the sentence.

The tired old man slept like a top.

the predicate is *slept like a top*.

- The *object* of a sentence is the person or thing that is receiving or affected by the action of the verb. The object is part of the predicate. There may be a *direct* object and an *indirect* object. Effectively, the indirect object is the object of the direct object.

The *direct* object can be a noun, a noun phrase, a noun or nominal clause or a pronoun. In the sentence

She bought milk.

the subject is *she, bought* is a transitive verb which takes an object, and *milk* is the direct object.

In the sentence

She bought loads of clothes.

the subject is *she*, *bought* is a transitive verb, and *loads of clothes* is the direct object.

The *indirect* object usually refers to someone or something benefiting from the action. In the sentence

Her father gave the boy food.

the noun *food* is the direct object and the noun *boy* is the indirect object. Notice that the sentence could be rephrased as

Her father gave food to the boy.

- The *complement* is the equivalent of the object in a clause that contains a linking verb such as the verb *to be*. In the sentence

Jack was a professional footballer.

the linking verb *was* is followed by the complement a *professional footballer*.

- The *adverbial* element may be a single word adverb or an adverbial phrase. It may qualify the verb in the sentence or clause, or the whole sentence. See, for example, *exactly* and *frankly* in the sentences below:

That will fit exactly.
Frankly, I think her hair is a mess.

Clause

A clause is a string of words containing a subject and predicate.

- A *main* clause is like a sentence in that it can stand alone. A main clause can be joined to another clause using a conjunction, thus the following sentence is a sentence made up of two main clauses:

He went to the city and he stayed there for a few days.

- A *subordinate* clause occurs in a sentence with a main clause and is dependent on the main clause or on another subordinate clause. Subordinate clauses often begin with a subordinating conjunction, for example:

because   that
since   when.

In the sentence

They will leave when the others arrive.

the main clause is *They will leave* and the subordinate clause is *when the others arrive*. A subordinate clause can come before a main clause, for example:

Since he is too young to go to school, he goes to a playgroup.

- An *adverbial clause* is a subordinate clause that modifies the main clause by adding information about time, place, condition, manner, purpose and result, for example:

He left after the meal was over.

They left it where they found it.
We cannot go unless we get permission.
He looked at her as if he hated her.
They will have to work long hours in order to get the job done on time.
He fell awkwardly so that his leg was bent under him.

Adverbial clauses usually follow the main clause but very often the order can be changed, so that the adverbial clause precedes the main clause, as in:.

Wherever I went, I saw signs of poverty.

- A *relative* clause is a subordinate clause that functions like an adjective. It is introduced by a relative pronoun. Examples of relative clauses introduced by relative pronouns are:

There's the man who I saw robbing the bank.
She is the person to whom you must apply.
This is the chap whose partner won the prize.
They all approved of the stand which he had taken.
I'll show you the car that I would like to buy.

Relative pronouns refer back to a noun or noun phrase in the main clause. These nouns and noun phrases are known as antecedents. The antecedents in the example sentences are respectively *man*, *person*, *chap*, *stand* and *car*. Sometimes the relative clause divides the parts of the main clause, for example:

The woman whose daughter is missing is too upset to talk to the press.
The people who we met on holiday were French.
The house that we liked best was too expensive.

- A *conditional* clause is a type of adverbial clause which expresses a condition and is introduced by the conjunction *if*, for example:

If he is talking about leaving, he must be unhappy.
If you tease the dog, it will bite you.
I would have sacked him, if I had been in charge.

Agreement

In English the most common form of grammatical agreement is that between subject and verb.

- *Singular* verbs are used with *singular* nouns, as in:

She looks well.
He is working late.
Elvis has left the building.

- *Plural* verbs are used with *plural* nouns, as in:

They look well.
They are working late.
All the Elvis impersonators have left the building.

- There can be some uncertainty about which verb to use with the *collective* nouns that represent a single unit but where that unit is made up of a number of individuals, for example:

audience	crew	jury
board	crowd	orchestra
cast	family	party
choir	gang	public
class	government	staff

committee   group   team
company   herd   tribe.

Can these nouns be used with a plural verb, as well as with a singular verb?

The answer is that they are quite routinely treated as *plural* in British English but rarely so in American English.

- *Compound* subjects, that is two or more nouns acting as the subject and joined with *and*, are used with a *plural* noun, for example:

My friend and I are going to the cinema tonight.
Cups, plates and cutlery came clattering down.

However, when the two nouns together represent something that is considered an *indivisible whole*, use a *singular* verb, as in:

Snakes and ladders is the children's favourite board game.
Brandy and soda is an excellent restorative.

- *Indefinite pronouns*, such as the pronouns shown below, are *singular*:

anyone
everyone
no one
someone
either
neither.

They should be followed by a singular verb, as in:

Each of the flats is self-contained.
Everyone is welcome.
No one is allowed in without a ticket.
Neither is quite what I am looking for.

Agreement in both number and gender is equally applicable to *personal pronouns*, for example:

She blames herself.
He could have kicked himself.
They asked themselves why they had got involved.

Apposition

When a noun or noun phrase is followed by another noun or noun phrase which describes it, the second noun or noun phrase is said to be in apposition to the first. For example, in the sentence

Peter Jones, the managing director, has resigned.

Peter Jones and *the managing director* are in apposition.

Double passive

A double passive is a clause that contains two verbs in the passive, the second being an infinitive, for example:

The goods are expected to be despatched some time this week.

Some examples of double passives are clumsy or ungrammatical and should be avoided, for example:

Redundancy notices are planned to be sent out next week.

Gender

When there is an indefinite pronoun and the sex of the person is unspecified, it used to be considered acceptable to use *his* to represent both sexes, for example:

Each of the pupils was asked to hand in his work.

As women achieved greater equality, the use of masculine terms to refer to both sexes was challenged, and alternatives were brought forward, for example:

Each of the pupils was asked to hand in his/her (or his or her) work.

However, this is now considered to be clumsy and artificial. Use of the plural pronoun, *their*, was then promoted as an acceptable alternative, though it is strictly speaking ungrammatical, for example:

Each of the pupils was asked to hand in their work.

Another, often better, solution is simply to recast the sentence entirely, for example:

All the pupils were asked to hand in their work.

Punctuation

Punctuation's role is to make meaning clearer, and to improve readability. It is essentially a means of representing on the printed page the natural pauses and tone heard in speech. It divides text into sentences, and parts of a sentence; it separates quotations and comments from surrounding text; and it indicates where there is emphasis and omission.

> A badly punctuated letter is almost as off-putting as a badly spelled letter.

The function of all those little marks – semi-colons, commas, inverted commas and apostrophes – seems to be a bit of a mystery to some people. The same errors and omissions appear again and again and cause so much irritation and concern amongst careful writers that endless columns in newspapers and magazines – and even best-selling books – have been written offering guidance to offenders. Changes to the school curriculum and modern teaching methods are routinely blamed for a decline in standards, but while there certainly has been a move away from formal instruction in grammar and punctuation, it is perhaps a little unjust to lay the entire blame on the education system. Several other explanations can be given for the scant attention so often paid to punctuation.

The modern style in the UK – including amongst careful writers – is for 'open punctuation': that is, the minimum punctuation required to structure a text so that it is readily understood. Open punctuation, it is argued, makes for a less cluttered appearance and allows the reader to maintain an even flow, unhindered by too many little stops and starts. In the United States too, where there is a much more rigid attitude to what constitutes 'correct' punctuation, texts nowadays have less punctuation than they might have had a hundred years ago.

It is often recommended that short 'punchy' sentences are used to make business letters and reports readable and effective. Clearly, how to punctuate correctly is rather less of a consideration where sentences are kept short and simple in structure.

Nowadays, much written work is produced at speed on word

processors. Anyone with a PC can turn out a wide range of written material very quickly and easily. While the word processor is a boon in many respects, the user has not only to compose the text, but must also be the typist, the page designer, and the subeditor. More or less anyone can sit down at a keyboard and in a shortish time learn how to be a passably good typist. On the other hand, punctuation is learned, not by leaping in without any knowledge or practice, but as part of the broader and more complex process of acquiring a solid understanding of how written language works.

People often don't allow enough time to check over their word processed documents.

In newer and more informal media, very little – sometimes no – punctuation is used. People who make frequent use of email and messaging may make the mistake of assuming that the informal style they use there will be acceptable in other contexts.

If each generation pays less attention to correct punctuation, it will become more and more difficult to recover the situation, with teachers as ignorant of the subject as their students. But, there is nothing very complicated or mysterious about punctuation, and only a short time is needed to learn the basic rules.

The punctuation marks and how to use them

Capitals *or* upper-case letters

- The first word of a sentence begins with a capital letter, for example:

  The room had two beds.

- The first letter of a name or proper noun is always a capital letter, for example:

Mary Ann
South America
Singapore
Zimbabwe
October
Lent
Monday
Microsoft.

- Registered trademarks used like common nouns are often written with an initial capital letter, for example:

Hoover
Jacuzzi
Xerox.

However, when a verb has been formed from a trademark noun, the verb can be written with a lower-case letter. Thus, although the noun *Hoover* may be written with a capital letter, the verb is more commonly written *hoover, hoovers, hoovering, hoovered*.

Full stop, point *or* period

- Full stops (.) are used to mark the ends of sentences. Full stops are also used in abbreviations, and in mathematical and scientific notation to indicate a decimal point.

- A sentence – i.e. a statement that is complete in itself – should start with a capital letter and end with a full stop, for example:

The fat cat sat on the mat.
Thanks.

The only exceptions to this rule are when the sentence is a question or an exclamation in which case it will end in a question mark or an exclamation mark.

- In a continuous block of text, each sentence is ended with a full stop and the first letter of the next sentence starts with a capital letter.

- There should be no space between the last letter in the sentence and the full stop.

- When punctuating direct speech (which is written within quotation marks) and when the direct speech is part of, and placed at the end of, a longer sentence, the full stop should come before the closing quotation marks, not after them, for example:

He shouted, 'Hey! That's my jacket.'

It is not necessary to add a second full stop outside the closing quotation mark.

- When the sentence is re-ordered so that the direct speech comes before the verb, the full stop at the end of the direct speech is replaced by a comma, for example:

'Hey! That's my jacket,' he shouted.

- When words in quotation marks come at the end of a sentence, but are not part of direct speech, the full stop comes outside the closing quotation marks, for example:

The front of each official document was stamped 'Top Secret'.

Capital letters *and* full stops in abbreviations

- Abbreviations made up of the first part of the full word should be followed by a full stop, for example:

Prof. = Professor
approx. = approximately
fig. = figurative.

You may see such abbreviations printed without full stops, and while this may be acceptable in addresses, it should be avoided elsewhere.

- Where the abbreviation is made up of an initial letter followed by one or more letters from within the full form of the word, the abbreviated form never has full stops, for example:

TV = television
cm = centimetre
kg = kilogram.

- Abbreviations that include the first and last letter of a word are called *contractions*, for example:

Mr or Mr. = Mister
Rd or Rd. = Road
do or do. = ditto.

A full stop is optional at the end of a contraction, though nowadays they tend to be written without (unless leaving out the full stop could result in a misreading). Contractions usually follow the form of the whole word; if the whole word starts with a capital letter, the contraction should also start with a capital letter. However, it is also quite common to write all the letters of the contraction in capital letters (upper case), especially in addresses.

- *Acronyms* are abbreviations formed from the first letters of several words in a phrase, with the letters making, and being pronounced, as a new 'word'. Many acronyms are written with all upper-case letters, for example:

UNIDO = United Nations Industrial Development Organization.

Others have only the first letter in upper case, for example:

Benelux = Belgium, Netherlands and Luxembourg.

And others are treated like ordinary words and written entirely in lower case letters, for example:

scuba = self-contained underwater breathing apparatus.

There should be no full stops in acronyms.

- *Initialisms*, like acronyms, are made up of the first letters of several words in a phrase, but they are distinct from acronyms in that each letter is said separately. In the past, initialisms were written with full stops after each letter, but now they are nearly always written without full stops, for example:

EU = European Union
US = United States
WHO = World Health Organization
FoE = Friends of the Earth
plc = public limited company.

Finding the Word: Punctuation

Many initialisms that have been created for, and are used in, email and messaging are now typed entirely in capitals, though they come from lower-case fully formed words, for example:

BTW = by the way
WRT = with regard to
AFAIK = as far as I know.

Initialisms that come from Latin phrases are written in lower-case letters with full stops. These include:

a.m. = ante meridiem
p.m. = post meridiem
e.g. = exempli gratia
i.e. = id est.

Full stops can be omitted if italic is used, but to avoid criticism from traditionalists it is advisable to put in the full stops when using any of these abbreviations in a formal letter.

- When an abbreviation with a full stop after its last letter comes at the end of a sentence, there is no need to write another full stop, for example:

The train is due to arrive at 7 p.m.

Question *or* query mark
- When a sentence is a question rather than a statement it should end with a question mark (?) rather than a full stop, for example:

Where did he go?

Questions can consist of a single word, for example:

Why?

- If the question is a quotation using the actual words of the speaker, a question mark comes at the end of the question, inside the closing quotation mark or marks, for example:

'Can I help you?' she asked suspiciously.

- A full stop rather than a question mark should be used at the end of a sentence that contains an indirect question, for example:

He asked me when I would be ready to go.

- A question mark is also sometimes used to show that something – especially a birth or death date – is uncertain or approximate.

Exclamation mark

- When the sentence is a statement expressing strong feeling of some kind then an exclamation mark (!) can be used instead of a full stop, for example:

What a nerve he has!

- Exclamations can be one word, for example:

Help!

An occasional exclamation mark can be effective but do not pepper your letters with them. Be especially careful about using exclamation marks in formal letters.

Finding the Word: Punctuation

Comma

The comma (,) is probably the most commonly used punctuation mark after the full stop.

- The individual items in a series of three or more items should be separated by commas, for example:

  At the sports club we can play tennis, squash, badminton and table tennis.
  We need to buy bread, milk, fruit and sugar.
  They are studying French, German and Spanish.

  Whether or not a comma is inserted before the final *and* in the sentence is a matter of choice, though it is more common to omit it in Britain and include it in America.

- The individual items in a list can be quite long, as in:

  I opened the door, let myself in, threw my bags on the bed and flung myself down on the couch.
  They consulted the map, planned the trip, got some foreign currency and were gone before we realized it.

  Be aware that if the last item in the list contains *and* in its own right, omitting the comma before the last item may cause your reader to misinterpret what is written, as in:

  In the pub they served ham salad, shepherd's pie, pie and chips and spicy sausages.

  For clarity, put a comma before the final *and*:

  In the pub they served ham salad, shepherd's pie, pie and chips, and spicy sausages.

- Where there is a list of adjectives before a noun, commas between the adjectives are now optional.

Thus it is correct to write:

She wore a long, red, sequinned dress.

And it is equally correct to write:

She wore a long red sequinned dress.

- Commas are always used to separate terms of address or question tags from the rest of the sentence, as in the following sentences:

Ladies, please make yourselves at home in the lounge.
It's the fifth today, isn't it?
Ladies and gentlemen, please take your seats.

- Put a comma between main clauses when the two main clauses are long, and especially when the subjects of the two clauses are different, for example:

Jake wanted to stay for the weekend, but we had arranged to visit our daughter.
Great minds think alike, and fools seldom differ.

- If main clauses have the same subject or object it is usually not necessary to separate them with a comma, as in:

She swept the floor and dusted the table.

Finding the Word: Punctuation

- Put a comma in between a main clause and a following conditional clause, for example:

  Do come for tea, if you think you'll have time.

- Put a comma in after an adverb linking the sentence in which the adverb appears to the previous sentence, for example:

  We lost. However, we are not downhearted.

- When a subordinate clause comes before the main clause and where the subordinate clause starts with words like *when*, *how*, *since* and *although*, put a comma in after the last word of the subordinate clause, as in the following sentence:

  Although many people registered objections, the scheme was approved by the council.

  Some people argue that it is quite acceptable to leave out the comma in such constructions, but the comma makes the sentence much easier to read, and – just for this reason – it should be put in.

- Where a subordinate clause describes a result or consequence of the action in the main clause, the main clause and subordinate clause should be separated by a comma, for example:

  He left the house an hour early, so arrived long before the appointed time.

- A comma is sometimes used to show that words used earlier in the sentence have been left out, for example:

  Some people will be terribly offended; others, amused.

- A comma is sometimes used to create a visual break, at which the reader is expected to pause appropriately. It can also prevent the reader from misinterpreting what is written. In some sentence structures, a comma can alter the meaning completely, as in these slightly improbable examples:

  For one week only, pine furniture prices will be reduced by 50%.
  For one week, only pine furniture prices will be reduced by 50%.

- Commas can be left out between main clauses and ordinary relative clauses, for example:

  The thing that really made people sit up and take notice was his beautiful speaking voice.

- A *pair* of commas is used around the type of relative clause that inserts parenthetical information into the sentence:

  The largest dinosaurs, which weighed many tons, were gentle herbivores.

  In such a sentence the clause within the commas can be removed without altering the basic meaning.

- A pair of commas is used to enclose supplementary or subordinate information within a sentence, for example:

Mr Bush, the US President, cut short his holiday in Texas.

- A pair of commas is also used to enclose a commenting word or phrase in the middle of a sentence, for example:

Then he took a running jump, mad fool, and landed on the other bank.

> Where pairs of commas are needed, take care to include the second comma. To check whether a pair of commas is needed, and also to check where they should be placed, leave the word, phrase or clause out of the sentence. If the sentence makes sense without the word, phrase or clause, this shows that it must be enclosed by a pair of commas.

Apostrophe

The apostrophe (') is the punctuation mark that probably causes the most difficulty to inexperienced writers. Errors in placing, and the omission of, apostrophes are some of the most commonly seen punctuation errors.

- The main use of the apostrophe is to indicate possession, for example:

the cat's tail = the tail of the cat
John's front door = the front door belonging to John
the children's lunches = the lunches of the children
the horses' hooves = the hooves of the horses.

Possessive nouns are usually formed by adding *'s* to the singular noun, for example:

the girl's mother
Peter's car;

or by adding an apostrophe to plural nouns that end in *s*, for example:

the teachers' cars;

or by adding *'s* to irregular plural nouns that do not end in *s*, for example:

women's shoes.

For a name or singular noun that ends in *s*, *x* or *z*, the apostrophe may or may not be followed by *s*. In words of one syllable the final *s* is usually added, for example:

James's house
the fox's lair
Roz's dress.

The final *s* is most often omitted in names, particularly those of three or more syllables, for example:

Euripides' plays.

Often the presence or absence of final *s* is a matter of convention rather than rule.

- The apostrophe is also used to indicate omitted letters in contracted forms of words, as in:

can't
you've.

It is also sometimes used in dates to indicate missing century numbers, as in:

the '60s and '70s.

More generally apostrophes are no longer used to indicate omitted letters in shortened words that have become more common than the longer forms, for example:

phone
flu.

- Sometimes an apostrophe is added to a plural when it shouldn't be, for example:

apple's 50 pence.

This adding of an apostrophe where none is needed is called a *grocer's apostrophe* because it is so often seen on the handwritten notices advertising food and household goods.

- There is now an increasing tendency to omit the apostrophe in possessive forms, so that *the soldier's tale* is written *the soldiers tale*.

Like the grocer's apostrophe, this is never acceptable, because of the ambiguity created by its omission. In the unpunctuated example above, the reader is quite likely to be left wondering if the tale is about one soldier or several soldiers.

- Never put an apostrophe in the possessive pronouns its, hers, yours or theirs.

A GUIDE TO LETTER-WRITING

> The possessive form of the pronoun *it* should be written *its*, without an apostrophe, for example:
>
> The dog howled **its** long mournful howl.
>
> The short form of *it is* is written *it's*, for example:
>
> **It's** a sunny day.
>
> Similarly, the possessive form of the pronoun *who* is spelled *whose*, for example:
>
> **Whose** turn is it next?
>
> The short form of *who is* is written *who's*, for example:
>
> **Who's** going to read next?

Colon

The colon (:) is very much like the dash but is used in more formal contexts.

- A colon is used before a part of a sentence which explains, clarifies, interprets or amplifies what has appeared before in the same sentence, for example:

  The standard of schoolwork here is very high: it is almost university standard.

  What follows the colon may be a complete sentence, a list or even a single word.

- A colon can be used to introduce lists or long quotations, for example:

  The school has sent a list of things each pupil needs for the new term: blazer, two pairs of trousers, three shirts, sweater, black shoes, sports clothes and leisure wear.

- It is *not* correct to use a colon after the verb to be, as illustrated by the following example:

  The best and most useful thing to do is: keep calm.

  This sentence should be reworded, as in:

  The best and most useful thing to do is to keep calm.

- Do *not* use a colon instead of a comma to introduce direct speech. For example, this is wrong:

  He said: 'I'm ready. Let's go.'

  And the following is correct:

  He said, 'I'm ready. Let's go.'

- Colons are used to indicate ratios, as in:

  2:1.

- In certain types of business correspondence, such as memos, a colon is used between standard headings and the text that follows those headings on the same line, for example:

A GUIDE TO LETTER-WRITING

> To: Andrew Madley
> cc: Patricia Ogilvie, Brian Tweedsdale
> From: Anita Forthing
> Date: 1 March 2005
> Subject: Sales Meeting

- In much the same way, a colon can be used in book titles where there is a main title followed by a subtitle or a subsidiary title, for example:

Nineteenth Century Emigration: a statistical survey

Semi-colon
- A semi-colon (;) can be used to join two clauses and so make a longer more complex sentence. The semi-colon takes the place of a comma followed by a conjunction such as *and* or *but*, for example:

There is nothing more to discuss; the matter is closed. We had hoped for a big win; sadly, we won only £10 between us.

A semi-colon is only used where two clauses may otherwise stand as two complete sentences. Wherever a semicolon is used, a full stop can, theoretically, be used instead.

- The semi-colon is used to form subsets in a long list or series of names, for example:

The young woman wants to be a journalist and she has contacted *The Times* in London; *The Washington Post* in Washington; *The Globe and Mail* in Toronto; *The Age* in Melbourne; *The Tribune* in Chicago.

Brackets

Brackets, in common with commas and dashes, interrupt the flow of the main statement, but brackets indicate a more definite or clear-cut interruption. Brackets are used to enclose information that is in some way additional to the main statement. The information so enclosed is called *parenthesis* and the pair of brackets enclosing are called *parentheses*. The information enclosed in the brackets is supplementary or explanatory and could be removed without changing the overall meaning or grammatical completeness of the main statement.

- There are various shapes of brackets. Round brackets () are the most common type. Square brackets [] are sometimes used to enclose information that is contained inside other information already in brackets, for example:

  (Christopher Marlowe [1564–93] was a contemporary of William Shakespeare.)

- Material within brackets can be one word, for example:

  In one local wine bar we had some delicious crêpes (pancakes).
  They didn't have the chutzpah (nerve) to challenge her.

- Brackets are also used to enclose date ranges, for example:

  Robert Louis Stevenson (1850–94) is considered to be the master of the romantic adventure novel.

- Brackets can enclose a phrase, for example:

  They served lasagne (a kind of pasta) and some delicious veal.

- Brackets can enclose a clause, for example:

  We were to have supper (or so they called it) later in the evening.
  They went for a walk round the loch (as a lake is called in Scotland) before leaving.

- Brackets can enclose a complete sentence, for example:

  He was determined (we don't know why) to tackle the problem alone.
  She made it clear (nothing could be more clear) that she was not interested in the offer.

- Sentences that appear in brackets in the middle of another sentence are not usually given an initial capital letter or a full stop, for example:

  They were extremely keen (she had no idea why) to buy her house.

- If material within brackets comes at the end of a sentence the full stop comes outside the second bracket, for example:

  For some reason we agreed to visit her at home (we had no idea where she lived).

- If the material in the brackets is a sentence and this is placed between two other whole sentences the bracketed sentence is treated like a normal sentence and given an initial capital letter and a closing full stop, for example:

  He never seems to do any studying. (He is always watching television.) Yet he does brilliantly in his exams.

Finding the Word: Punctuation

- Punctuation of the main statement is unaffected by the presence of the brackets and their enclosed material, except that any punctuation that would – in the absence of the bracketed material – come after the word where the brackets now break the sentence, now comes after the closing bracket, for example:

  He lives in a place (I am not sure exactly where), miles from anywhere, that is very difficult to reach.

Dash

The dash (–) often serves much the same purpose as brackets, but is considered by some to be informal. It should be used sparingly, especially in writing formal pieces of prose, such as business letters.

Depending on it too much may lead to careless writing, with ideas set down at random rather than in a clear and logical order.

- The dash indicates a short break in the continuity of a sentence, for example:

  I was amazed when he turned up at the meeting – I thought he was still abroad.

- The dash is sometimes used in pairs to indicate a break in a sentence, for example:

  We could only hope – hope and pray – that they would reach the children in time.

If two dashes are needed and the inserted material is long, take care to include the second dash.

- The dash can also be used in place of a colon in two-part sentences consisting of an itemized or detailed list followed by a general or summing-up statement, for example:

Silver, jewellery, paintings, hi-fi system, television – the burglars removed everything of value from the house.

Quotation marks or inverted commas

Inverted commas or quotation marks are always used in pairs. There are two types of quotation marks: single quotes ('...') and double quotes ("..."). British style tends to favour single quotes, while American style favours double quotes.

- Quotation marks are used to indicate that the words that appear between them are the actual words that someone has said (otherwise known as direct speech). It is fairly rare to use direct speech in letters.

> It is a very common error to put quotes around indirect or reported speech.

- Quotation marks or inverted commas are also sometimes used around the titles of books, plays, or films, for example 'Bleak House', 'The Merchant of Venice', 'Death and the Maiden'. This is now a rather old-fashioned use of inverted commas. Titles are now more commonly printed in italic, for example:

Bleak House by Charles Dickens.
She has a starring role in the *Merchant of Venice*.

- Inverted commas are used to emphasize or draw attention to a particular word, sentence or phrase within a piece of writing, for example:

She wants to know how to spell 'picnicked'.

- Punctuation marks that belong to, or are part of, quoted speech should be kept within the quotation marks. Any punctuation that belongs to the surrounding sentence goes outside the quotation marks. Usually a sentence containing a quotation is punctuated like any other sentence and the only additional punctuation required is the quotation marks themselves.

> For guidance on punctuating addresses and the other elements of a letter *see* Chapter 4.

Word Formation and Spelling

English is peppered with difficult, often illogical, spellings. This has come about because the language has changed and evolved over hundreds of years while at the same time it has absorbed vocabulary – sometimes at an astonishing rate – from other languages. Add to these factors the propensity in the English-speaking world to create new words by tacking together two or more words or parts of words, and the fact that there has never been a concerted attempt to iron out spelling anomalies – in British English, at least – and you have the current, often perplexing, situation.

> Always check over the spelling in your letters. Use a computer spell checker and/or a good dictionary. Never just guess at a spelling you do not know. You'll almost certainly be caught out.

This section provides a few pointers on how words are formed, and gives guidance on some particularly tricky words and word endings. As with other sections in this chapter, the information given here is not comprehensive and you should also refer to a good dictionary or usage book.

More spelling guidance is given in the section on British English and American English spelling on page 199 and a list of words that are difficult to spell is provided on pages 212–230.

Word formation

How the plurals of nouns are formed

- For most nouns -*s* is added to the singular noun to form the plural, for example:

cat/cats
machine/machines
boot/boots.

This includes singular nouns that end in a vowel followed by -*y*, for example:

monkey/monkeys
day/days
boy/boys.

- For singular nouns ending in a consonant followed by -*y*, the *y* is dropped and -*ies* is added for the plural, as in:

baby/babies
berry/berries
fairy/fairies
spy/spies.

However, note that proper nouns ending in a consonant followed by -*y* simply have -*s* added for the plural, as in:

the four Marys.

- For singular nouns ending in -*s*, -*x*, -*z*, -*ch* and -*sh* the plural is formed by adding -*es*, for example:

bus/buses
mass/masses
fox/foxes
chintz/chintzes
church/churches
dash/dashes.

- For most singular nouns ending in -*f*, the *f* is replaced by -*ves* in the plural, for example:

loaf/loaves
wife/wives
calf/calves
half/halves.

For other words ending in -*f*, -*s* is simply added to the singular form in the usual way, for example:

belief/beliefs
chief/chiefs
gulf/gulfs
proof/proofs.

Some words ending in -*f* can have either the -*s* or the -*ves* ending in the plural, for example:

hoof/hoofs or hooves
dwarf/dwarfs or dwarves.

- Nouns that end in -o often just add -s to make the plural form, for example:

  photo/photos
  piano/pianos
  radio/radios
  soprano/sopranos
  video/videos.

  For others -es is added:

  domino/dominoes
  echo/echoes
  go/goes
  hero/heroes
  potato/potatoes
  tomato/tomatoes
  torpedo/torpedoes
  veto/vetoes.

  Quite a number can be spelled either way, for example:

  buffalo/buffaloes or buffalos
  grotto/grottoes or grottos
  halos/haloes or halos
  mango/mangoes or mangos
  mosquito/mosquitoes or mosquitos
  tornado/tornadoes or tornados
  volcano/volcanoes or volcanos.

- Some nouns in English have irregular plural forms, for example:

  man/men
  woman/women

child/children
mouse/mice
foot/feet
ox/oxen
goose/geese.

- Some nouns adopted into English from other languages retain the foreign plural form in English, for example:

larva/larvae
stimulus/stimuli
phenomenon/phenomena
criterion/criteria
crisis/crises.

Nowadays, however, there is often an anglicized plural that is an equally acceptable alternative to the foreign plural, for example:

appendix/appendices *or* appendixes
formula/formulae *or* formulas
gateau/gateaux *or* gateaus
soprano/soprani *or* sopranos
stadium/stadia *or* stadiums.

- For some irregular nouns the singular form is unchanged in the plural, for example:

sheep/sheep
grouse/grouse (*the game bird*)
salmon/salmon.

- Sometimes there is an alternative regular plural ending in *s*, for example:

A GUIDE TO LETTER-WRITING

fish/fish or fishes.

- A very few nouns have a regular plural and an irregular plural form, for example:

brother/brothers or brethren.

- With compounds that have a noun as their first element the plural is usually formed by adding *s* to the first element rather than at the end of the compound, for example:

passer-by/passers-by
court-martial/courts-martial
brother-in-law/brothers-in-law.

How the inflections of verbs are formed

As has been seen in the Grammar section of this chapter (page 121), verbs can change their endings in the first person singular, the present participle, the past tense and the past participle.

- For most verbs the *third person present singular* is formed by adding -*s* to the end of the base form of the verb, for example:

laugh/laughs
jump/jumps
recommend/recommends
walk/walks.

However, for verbs ending in -*o*, -*ch*, -*sh*, -*ss*, -*x*, -*z* and -*zz*, the ending is -*es*, for example:

veto/vetoes
thatch/thatches

lash/lashes
miss/misses
fix/fixes
buzz/buzzes.

For a verb that ends in a consonant followed by -*y*, the *y* is changed to -*ies*, for example:

copy/copies
marry/marries.

But, for verbs that end in a vowel followed by -*y*, the *y* is kept, for example:

buy/buys
say/says.

- When forming the *present participle*, if the base form of a verb ends in a consonant followed by -*e*, the *e* is dropped before adding -*ing*, for example:

love/loving
drive/driving
fake/faking
create/creating.

Where the base form ends in -*ie*, the *i* is changed to *y* and the *e* is dropped before adding -*ing*, for example:

die/dying
tie/tying.

Where the base form ends in -*ee*, -*oe*, or -*ye*, the final *e* is kept and -*ing* is added, for example:

see/seeing
toe/toeing
dye/dyeing.

Note also that the *e* is kept in the following verbs:

age/ageing
singe/singeing.

For verbs ending in a short vowel followed by a consonant, the final consonant is doubled when adding *-ing*, for example:

sob/sobbing
grin/grinning
tap/tapping
pet/petting.

Where the base form ends in *-c*, this is changed to *ck* when adding *-ing*, for example:

panic/panicking
mimic/mimicking
frolic/frolicking.

- The *simple past tense* is the base form followed by *-ed*, for example:

laugh/laughed
jump/jumped
walk/walked
blink/blinked
rain/rained.

Finding the Word: Word Formation and Spelling

However, when the base form ends in *-e*, only *-d* is added for the simple past tense, for example:

agree/agreed
love/loved
fake/faked
create/created.

Regular verbs with a doubled final consonant in the present participle also have a doubled final consonant in the simple past tense, for example:

sob/sobbing/sobbed
grin/grinning/grinned
tap/tapping/tapped
pet/petting/petted.

Where the base form ends in *-c*, the *c* is changed to *ck* when adding *-ed*, for example:

panic/panicked
mimic/mimicked
frolic/frolicked.

- For regular verbs the *past participle* is formed in the same way as the simple past tense.

- For irregular verbs see Appendix 4.

How comparatives *and* superlatives of adjectives are formed

- The usual way to form comparatives and superlatives of adjectives is to add *-er* and *-est* to the absolute form of the adjective, for example:

tall/taller/tallest.

- However, for words consisting of a single syllable that also have a long vowel and end in -e, the e is dropped before adding -er or -est, for example:

safe/safer/safest.

- For words consisting of a single syllable that also have a long vowel and end in a single consonant, the final consonant is doubled, for example:

sad/sadder/saddest.

- Where an adjective ends in a consonant followed by -y, the y is changed to i before adding -er or -est, for example:

happy/happier/happiest.

- Words ending in -l usually just add the usual -er or -est ending, for example:

cool/cooler/coolest.

The one exception is *cruel* spelled with a double *ll*, thus:

cruel/crueller/cruellest.

How adverbs are formed

- The usual way to form an adverb is simply to add -ly to the absolute form of the adjective, for example:

hopeless/hopelessly
beautiful/beautifully.

Finding the Word: Word Formation and Spelling

- If an adjective ends in *-ll*, then only *-y* is added to form the adverb, for example:

full/fully.

- For adjectives of more than one syllable that end in *-y*, the adverb is formed by changing the *y* to *-ily*, for example:

happy/happily.

How some other derivatives are formed

Derivatives are words formed from a root word of a different part of speech, for example a noun may be formed from a verb, an adverb from an adjective, and so on. Sometimes the spelling of the derivative is not immediately obvious, and errors can result. Here are some guidelines:

- For nouns deriving from a verb ending in *-er* or *-ear*, the *r* at the end is not doubled when *-ence* or *-ance* is added to create a noun, for example:

refer/reference
appear/appearance.

- For nouns deriving from a verb ending in *-ur*, the *r* at the end of the verb is doubled when *-ence* is added to create a noun, for example:

concur/concurrence
recur/recurrence
occur/occurence.

- In British English, for adjectives formed from nouns that end in *-our* the *u* is kept, for example:

honour/honourable
favour/favourable
colour/colourful.

The *u* is also kept for nouns formed from verbs ending in -*our*, for example:

labour/labourer
pour/pourer
harbour/harbourer
scour/scourer.

However, British English is inconsistent in that the *u* is dropped in certain adjective derivatives, for example:

glamour/glamorous
honour/honorary
humour/humorous
rigour/rigorous
vigour/vigorous.

- The *o* is dropped from a verb ending in -*ounce* when forming a noun ending in -*iation*, for example:

denounce/denunciation
pronounce/pronunciation.

Spelling pitfalls

Days *and* months

Generally, spellings for days of the week and months of the year give little difficulty. However, those highlighted in bold at the top of the next page are frequently misspelled:

Finding the Word: Word Formation and Spelling

Monday	January	July
Tuesday	**February**	August
Wednesday	March	September
Thursday	April	October
Friday	May	November
Saturday	June	December.
Sunday		

Silent, unpronounced *and* mispronounced letters

Words are often misspelled when they contain a letter that is silent, or if they contain a letter that is not pronounced.

For example, there is a silent *b* in *debt* and *subtle*; a silent *e* in *subtlety* and *righteous*; a silent *p* in *psychology* and *psychiatry*; and a silent *t* in *mortgage*.

The *i* in *parliament* is rarely pronounced, as is the *c* in *Arctic* and *Antarctic*; and certain words, such as *itinerary* and *vehement*, often have whole syllables elided or not pronounced.

Here are some more examples of silent letters likely to be omitted or to otherwise cause spelling problems:

- Words spelled with a silent *c* following *s*, for example:

    abscess
    descent
    omniscient
    acquiesce
    convalescent.

- Words with a silent *c* before *k* or *q*, for example:

    acknowledge
    acquainted
    acquire.

- Words with silent *d* before *j*, for example:

  adjourn
  adjunct
  adjust.

- Words with silent *g* before *n*, for example:

  gnash
  gnarled
  align
  foreign
  reign.

- Words with silent *k* before *n*, for example:

  knapsack
  knead.

- Words in which silent *u* comes after *g*, for example:

  guarantee
  guard
  beleaguered.

- Words with silent *h* after *r*, for example:

  diarrhoea
  haemorrhage
  rhythm.

Vowel combinations ('i before e except after c')

The spelling mnemonic that most people remember from their

Finding the Word: Word Formation and Spelling

school days is '*i* before *e* except after *c*'. More often than not the rule works, as in:

achieve	ceiling
believe	conceive
niece	deceive
siege	receive.
yield	

But there are also exceptions, for example:

ancient	leisure
caffeine	protein
counterfeit	seize
foreign	sovereign
forfeit	weight
heifer	weir
height	weird.

Therefore the simple '*i* before *e* except after *c*' rule needs sometimes to be augmented, using pronunciation as a guide.

Where the vowel combination follows *c* or *t* pronounced like the *sh* in sheep, the order is always *i-e*, as in:

ancient	patient
conscience	quotient
deficient	species
efficient	sufficient.

Where the vowels are pronounced to rhyme with the *a* in *say*, the order is often *e-i*, as in:

beige	neigh
deign	reign

eight   rein
feign   sleigh
freight   their
heir   veil
inveigh   vein
inveigle   weigh.

Where the vowels are pronounced to rhyme with the *i* in *might*, the order is often *e-i*, as in:

either   neither
height   seismology.
kaleidoscope

But, when the *i* as in *might* sound is followed by the letter *r*, the word is spelled according to the '*i* before *e* except after *c*' rule and the order is *i-e*, as in:

fiery
hieroglyphics
hierarchy.

Some more tricky vowel combinations

Here are some quick tips for vowel combinations that also cause spelling difficulties:

- *a* comes before *e* in *aerial, aerobics, aeroplane, anaesthetic, haemoglobin, leukaemia*. See also the differences betweeen British and American spelling (page 199).

- *o* comes before *e* in *oestrogen, foetus, amoeba, diarrhoea, homoeopathic, manoeuvre*. See also page 200.

- *a* comes before *i* in *dairy* but *i* comes before *a* in *diary*.

Finding the Word: Word Formation and Spelling

- *a* comes before *u* in *gauge*, but *u* comes before *a* in *guard* and *language*.

- *u* comes before *o* in *buoy* and *buoyant*.

- *u* comes before the first *e* in *Portuguese*.

- *o* comes before *u* in *silhouette*.

Single *or* double consonant

There are a few rules that can help you decide whether or not to double a consonant. Some of these have been discussed already in the section on how to form verbs.

- In words of one syllable ending in a single consonant preceded by a single vowel, the consonant is doubled when an ending starting with a vowel is added, for example:

   drop/dropped
   pat/patted
   rub/rubbed.

- For words of more than one syllable that end in a single consonant preceded by a single vowel, the consonant is doubled if the stress is on the last syllable, for example:

   begin/beginning
   occur/occurring
   prefer/preferred
   commit/committed.

- In similar words where the stress is not on the last syllable, the consonant does not double, for example:

bigot/bigoted
develop/developed.

- Exceptions to this rule include words ending in *l*. The *l* doubles even in cases where the last syllable is unstressed, for example:

travel/traveller
appal/appalling.

- The final consonant is doubled in verb inflections if the verb has two syllables and the second is stressed, for example:

occur/occurring/occurred
enthral/enthralling/enthralled
fulfil/fulfilling/fulfilled.

- It is a common error to spell words that should have a double consonant with only one consonant, for example:

address
appoint
disappoint
suppress.

If in doubt, consult a dictionary.

- It is a common error to put a double consonant in certain words that should have only one consonant, for example:

anoint   biased
apartment   inoculate
canister   iridescent
banister   omit.

Finding the Word: Word Formation and Spelling

- It is a very common error to leave out one consonant from a pair in a word that has two or more pairs of consonants, for example:

  accommodation   embarrassing
  aggression   millennium
  committee   Mississippi.

- It is also a very common error to confuse which consonant should be single and which double in words that contain a single consonant and a pair of consonants, for example:

  appal   harass
  accumulate   Mediterranean
  Caribbean   necessary
  commemorate   parallel
  desiccate   Philippines.
  disappear

Consonant clusters

Words that contain a cluster of two, three, or more consonants are very easy to misspell. Here are a few tips for some of the commonest errors concerning consonant clusters:

- an *n* comes before the *m* in *enmity* and *environment*.

- an *m* comes before the first *n* in *mnemonic*.

- note the order of the letters (*p-h-t-h*) in the four-consonant cluster in *diphtheria* and *ophthalmic*.

- there is a *p* between the *m* and the *t* in *symptom*.

- there is a double *h* in *withhold*, but only one *h* in *threshold*.

Word endings

There are quite a number of word endings (suffixes) that are confused because they differ only in a single vowel and there is very little to distinguish them in spoken English.

-able or -ible?

These two endings can be confused because they are often pronounced in a similar way. The commoner ending is -*able*, and new words are always given the -*able* ending.

Note that if -*able* is removed from the word, often a complete word remains, but if the same is done with -*ible* what remains is an incomplete word. The -*ible* ending is not used after vowels.

Here are some words with the -*able* ending:

acceptable	conquerable	indomitable
adaptable	creditable	inestimable
admirable	culpable	inevitable
advisable	despicable	inexcusable
affable	detachable	inexorable
agreeable	detestable	inflammable
amenable	drinkable	insatiable
amiable	enviable	inscrutable
amicable	equitable	inseparable
applicable	excusable	intolerable
available	fashionable	invariable
bendable	formidable	irrevocable
breakable	foreseeable	knowledgeable
capable	hireable	lamentable
changeable	hospitable	malleable
communicable	implacable	memorable
comparable	indefinable	nameable
computable	indispensable	navigable

Finding the Word: Word Formation and Spelling

noticeable
palpable
payable
peaceable
permeable
persuadable
pliable
portable
predictable

preferable
probable
reliable
repeatable
replaceable
respectable
saleable
shockable
sociable

transferable
unconscionable
unforgettable
unmistakable
unstoppable
usable/useable
variable
viable
vulnerable.

Some words with the *-ible* ending:

accessible
admissible
audible
collapsible
combustible
compatible
comprehensible
contemptible
convertible
corruptible
credible
defensible
deducible
digestible
dirigible
discernible
divisible
edible
eligible

expressible
fallible
feasible
flexible
forcible
gullible
horrible
incorrigible
indelible
indestructible
inexhaustible
invincible
irascible
irrepressible
irresistible
legible
negligible
ostensible
perceptible

perfectible
permissible
persuasible
plausible
possible
reprehensible
repressible
reproducible
resistible
responsible
reversible
risible
sensible
susceptible
tangible
terrible
unintelligible
visible.

Some words can be spelled with either the *-able* or the *-ible* ending:

collectable/collectible
detectable/detectible
preventable/preventible.

-acy *or* -asy?

Again, these endings are often confused. There are more words with the *-acy* ending, but it is not safe to assume that it is always the one to use.

Some words with the *-acy* ending:

accuracy	democracy	pharmacy
adequacy	diplomacy	privacy
bureaucracy	fallacy	supremacy.
conspiracy	fantasy	
delicacy	intimacy	

Some words with the *-asy* ending:

apostasy
ecstasy
idiosyncrasy.

-ant *or* -ent?

Words with *-ant* or *-ent* endings are usually adjectives. The nouns derived from these words often end in *-ance* or *-ence*. Note that for some words the *-ant* or *-ent* ending indicates which part of speech the word is, as in *confidant/confident*. Some verbs have a noun ending in *-nce* or *-ncy* but no adjective ending in *-ant* or *-ent*. It is usually correct to spell the noun with *-ance*, as in *annoy/annoyance*, but there are exceptions such as *exist/existence* and *interfere/interference*.

Finding the Word: Word Formation and Spelling

Some words ending with -*ant*:

arrogant	confidant (*noun*)	malignant
assistant	defiant	vacant.
blatant	dependant (*noun*)	
brilliant	flippant	

Some words ending with -*ent*:

adolescent	decent	independent
absorbent	dependent	innocent
complacent	descent	reminiscent
confident	dissident	transparent.

-ary *or* -ery?

It is very easy to confuse these two, or to omit the vowel and use only -*ry*. The ending -*ary* is much more common and is used to form adjectives and nouns, for example:

complimentary
stationary (*adjective*)
secretary.

The much less common -*ery* ending is almost always used to form nouns, for example:

confectionery
jewellery
stationery (*noun*).

-ative *or* -itive?

It is easy to confuse these two endings because they are pronounced in a very similar way. Note that the -*ative* ending is much more common.

Words ending in -*ative* include:

- affirmative
- alternative
- demonstrative
- illustrative
- imaginative
- qualitative
- representative
- sedative
- vegetative.

Words ending in -*itive* include:

- acquisitive
- additive
- competitive
- fugitive
- inquisitive
- intuitive
- repetitive.

-ise *or* -ize?

Most words ending in -*ise* in British English can also be spelled -*ize*, and vice versa, for example:

colonise/colonize
organise/organize.

However, there are some words that must always be spelt with –*ize*:

capsize
prize (to value)
seize.

And some words that must always be spelt with -*ise*:

- advertise
- advise
- appraise
- apprise
- arise
- bruise
- chastise
- circumcise
- comprise
- compromise
- cruise
- despise
- devise
- disguise
- enterprise
- excise
- exercise
- franchise

Finding the Word: Word Formation and Spelling

improvise	promise	surmise
incise	raise	surprise
liaise	revise	televise.
practise	rise	
praise	supervise	

-or, -er *or* -ar?

It is a very common error to misspell words with these endings. The *-er* and *-or* endings are commonly used in 'doer' nouns, that is, names for people or things that perform the action of a verb. The *-er* ending is the one that is nearly always used when new nouns are formed from verbs. Both are also used in other types of noun and in adjectives. The *-ar* ending is the least common and is used for some nouns and adjectives.

Some words ending with *-or*:

accelerator	contributor	impostor
actor	councillor	incubator
ambassador	counsellor	indicator
ancestor	creator	inferior
auditor	creditor	inspector
author	debtor	interior
aviator	decorator	inventor
bachelor	dictator	investigator
calculator	director	investor
chancellor	distributor	jailor
collector	doctor	janitor
commentator	editor	legislator
competitor	educator	major
conductor	equator	mayor
conqueror	escalator	minor
conspirator	exterior	narrator
contractor	governor	objector

operator	refrigerator	survivor
orator	sailor	tailor
posterior	senator	tenor
predecessor	solicitor	tractor
professor	spectator	traitor
projector	sponsor	translator
proprietor	successor	ulterior
protector	superior	vendor
radiator	supervisor	ventilator
rector	surveyor	visitor.

Some words ending with -*er*:

announcer	knocker	singer
builder	lawyer	sorcerer
cooker	lecturer	talker
cruiser	mariner	teacher
dancer	opener	trailer
foreigner	plasterer	treasurer
jeweller	prisoner	worker.

Some words ending with -*ar*:

altar	grammar	
angular	guitar	registrar
beggar	hangar	regular
burglar	insular	scholar
calendar	muscular	similar
caterpillar	particular	singular
cellar	peculiar	spectacular
circular	perpendicular	vicar
collar	pillar	vinegar
dollar	polar	vulgar.
familiar	popular	

British English and American English

British English and American English are the principal varieties of English, in terms of numbers of speakers worldwide. There are many differences between them. Aside from the obvious pronunciation differences, which needn't concern us for the purposes of letter-writing, there are many differences between the two, in spelling, vocabulary and, to a lesser extent, grammar and usage.

The influence of the United States, its culture and its products, has meant that American spelling and usage is now more familiar to more people in more countries than British English. Historically, and especially at the height of the British Empire, the reverse would have been the case.

If you are communicating with people in the United States or one of the many countries that has adopted the conventions of American English, it is a good idea to know and recognize the differences, to avoid any confusion or misunderstanding.

Spelling

Certain spellings formerly used only in American English have now been adopted into British English, for example, the British English *-ise* ending of verbs is increasingly being dropped in favour of the American English *-ize* ending, thus finalise is spelled *finalize* and recognise is spelled *recognize*. You can correctly use either spelling in British English, as long as you are consistent within the same document. There are some exceptions: words that can be spelled only with the *-ise* ending and others that may be spelled only with the *-ize* ending (see page 196).

British and American spelling is, however, quite distinct in many other instances, some of which are dealt with overleaf.

- Words that end in -*our* in British English are spelled -*or* in American English, for example:

  colour/color.

  However, some derivatives of words that end in -*our* in British English are spelled -*or* in both British and American English, for example:

  vigorous.

- Most words that end in -*re* in British English are spelled -*er* in American English, for example:

  centre/center.

- Some words ending in -*ogue* in British English are spelled -*og* in American English, for example:

  prologue/prolog.

- For verbs that end in a *vowel + single consonant*, the past tense and present participle forms of the verb are spelled with a double consonant in British English, but with a single consonant in American English, for example:

  travelled/traveled   labelling/labeling
  kidnapped/kidnaped.

- The letter combinations -*ae* and -*oe* used in British English become -*e* alone in American English, for example:

  mediaeval/medieval
  amoeba/ameba.

Here are some more examples of spelling differences.

British English	**American English**
acknowledgement	acknowledgment
aeroplane	airplane
aluminium	aluminum
anaesthetic	anesthetic
appal	appall
artefact	artifact
axe	ax
behaviour	behavior
bevelled	beveled
calibre	caliber
cancelled	canceled
candour	candor
catalogue	catalog
centilitre	centiliter
centimetre	centimeter
centre	center
channelled	channeled
councillor	councilor
counselling	counseling
counsellor	counselor
cheque	check
colour	color
defence (*noun*)	defense
demeanour	demeanor
diarrhoea	diarrhea
disc	disk
dishevelled	disheveled
dishonourable	dishonorable
distil	distill
draught	draft
endeavour	endeavor

enrol	enroll
equalled	equaled
faeces	feces
favour	favor
fibre	fibre
flavour	flavor
foetus	fetus
fuelled	fueled
fulfil	fulfill
fulfilment	fulfillment
glamour, glamorous	glamor, glamorous
grey	gray
grovelled	groveled
gynaecology	gynecology
haemoglobin	hemoglobin
haemorrhage	hemorrhage
honour	honor
humour, humorous	humor, humorous
instil	instill
jeweller	jeweler
jewellery	jewelry
kilometre	kilometer
levelled	leveled
licence (*noun*)	license
litre	liter
manoeuvre	maneuver
marvellous	marvelous
maths	math
metre	meter
modelled	modeled
monologue	monolog
mould, mouldy	mold, moldy
moult	molt
moustache	mustache

neighbourhood	neighborhood
odour	odor
oesophagus	esophagus
offence	offense
omelette	omelet
paediatrician	pediatrician
paedophile	pedophile
parcelled	parceled
pencilled	penciled
plough	plow
practice (*noun*)	practice (*noun*)
practise (*verb*)	practice (*verb*)
pretence	pretense
programme (on radio/ TV)	program
prophecy (*noun*)	prophesy
pyjamas	pajamas
rigour	rigor
rumour	rumor
sceptic	skeptic
shovelled	shoveled
skilful	skillful
smoulder	smolder
snivelled	sniveled
spectre	specter
storey	story
sulphur	sulfur
theatre	theater
totalled	totaled
towelling	toweling
travelled	traveled
traveller	traveler
tranquillize, tranquillise	tranquilize
tumour	tumor
tunnelled	tunneled

tyre	tire
unequalled	unequaled
vigour	vigor
wilful	willful
woollen	woolen

Vocabulary

The famous quote about Britain and the United States being 'divided by a common language' is especially apt in relation to vocabulary. There are lots of examples of completely different words for the same thing. While there is still some two-way traffic, some American English words are now displacing their British English equivalents, for example *backpack* is now more commonly used than *rucksack* and *ATM* (*automated teller machine*) than *cashpoint*. It is probably inevitable that this process will continue in those spheres – especially popular culture and business and commerce – in which the United States is the dominant influence.

British English	**American English**
aubergine	eggplant
autumn	fall
bad tempered	mean
(bank)note	bill
bath	tub, bathtub
beach hut	cabana
biscuit	cookie
black pudding	blood sausage
blinds	shades
blinkers	blinders
bonnet (of car)	hood
boot (of car)	trunk
bottom drawer	hope chest
braces	suspenders

break (in school, etc)	recess
breve	double whole note
broad bean, butter bean	lima bean
bum	fanny
bumper	fender
burgle	burglarize
candy floss	cotton candy
canola oil	rapeseed oil
car park	parking lot
caretaker	janitor
catapult	slingshot
changing room	locker room
chemist, pharmacy	drugstore
chips	French fries
clingfilm	Saran wrap, plastic wrap
coffin	casket
condom	rubber
coriander	cilantro
cornflour	corn starch
courgette	zucchini
crisps	chips
crossroads	intersection
crotchet	quarter note
cupboard, fitted wardrobe	closet
current account	checking account
curtains	drapes
cutlery	flatware, silverware
CV (curriculum vitae)	resumé
docker	longshoreman
double cream	heavy cream
draughts (the game)	checkers
drawing pin	thumbtack
dressing gown	robe
dummy	pacifier

A Guide to Letter-Writing

dustbin	trash can
esate agent	realtor
estate car	station wagon
first floor	second floor
flat	apartment
flyover	overpass
fortnight	two weeks
foyer	lobby
fringe	bangs
full stop	period
garden	yard
gear lever	stick shift
glowworm	lightning bug
grill	broil
ground floor	first floor
hair grip, Kirby grip	bobby pin
handbag	purse
hessian	burlap
holiday	vacation
homely	ugly, unattractive
icing sugar	powdered sugar
indicators	blinkers
jelly	Jell-o
lawyer	attorney
lend	loan (*verb*)
level crossing	grade crossing
lollipop	popsicle
maize	corn
mange tout	snow pea
methylated spirits	denatured alcohol
minced beef	ground beef
minim	half note
motorway	freeway
nappy	diaper

Finding the Word: British and American English

normality	normalcy
noughts and crosses	tic-tac-toe
number plate	license plate
off licence	liquor store
offal	variety meats
pants	undershorts, panties
paraffin	kerosene
pavement	sidewalk
pedestrian crossing	crosswalk
pepper, red/green	bell pepper
Perspex	Plexiglas
petrol	gas
pig	hog
pinafore	jumper
plait	braid
plot (of land)	lot
porridge	oatmeal
pram	baby carriage
prawn	shrimp
press stud	snap
quaver	eighth note
queue	line
railway	railroad
receptionist	desk clerk
ring road, circular road	beltway, loop
rocket (the herb)	arugula
rosé	blush
roundabout	traffic circle
rubber	eraser
rubbish, refuse	trash
Sellotape	Scotch tape
semibreve	whole note
semi-detached house	duplex
semi-quaver	sixteenth-note

semolina	cream of wheat
silencer	muffler
skip	dumpster
skirting board	baseboard
socket	outlet
soft drink	soda
spanner	wrench
spring onion	scallion
stream	creek
sultana	golden raisin
surgical spirit	rubbing alcohol
suspenders	braces
swede	rutabaga
tap	faucet
tarmac	asphalt, blacktop
telegram	wire
tights	pantyhose
timber	lumber
tissue	Kleenex
torch	flashlight
tram	streetcar
tramp	bum
trolley	cart
trousers	pants
truncheon	nightstick
turn-ups	cuffs
undertaker	mortician
vest	undershirt
waistcoat	vest
windscreen	windshield
zip	zipper

Grammar and usage

Differences in grammar principally relate to the use of verbs and prepositions.

- In informal American English the *present perfect tense* is used much less than in British English, for example:

  American English:
  I can't find my shoe. Did you see it anywhere?
  British English:
  I can't find my shoe. Have you seen it anywhere?

  American English:
  I feel queasy. I think I ate too much.
  British English:
  I feel queasy. I think I've eaten too much.

- In informal American English it is accepted that the *simple past tense* may be used with *already, just* and *yet*, whereas in British English the *present perfect* tense is preferred, for example:

  American English:
  Did you go round the track already?
  British English:
  Have you been round the track already?

  American English:
  Is Harry here? No, he just left.
  British English:
  Is Harry here? No, he's just left.

American English:
Did you do it yet?
British English:
Have you done it yet?

- In certain contexts, the verb *have* used in British English is replaced with the verb *take* in American English, as in:

have a bath/take a bath
having a little holiday/taking a short vacation.

- Certain *simple past* and *past participle* forms of verbs are different, for example:

British English		American English	
past	past participle	past	past participle
dived	dived	**dove** or dived	dived
got	got	got	**gotten**
leaned or **leant**	leaned or **leant**	leaned	leaned
learned or **leant**	learned or **leant**	learned	learned
pleaded	pleaded	pleaded or pled	pleaded or **pled**
sawed	sawn	sawed	sawn or **sawed**
proved	proved	proved	proved or **proven**
spilled or spilt	spilled or **spilt**	spilled or spilt	spilled
spat	spat	spat or **spit**	spat or **spit**

Finding the Word: British and American English

- In American English, there has always been a much more pronounced tendency to create verbs from nouns. This was a habit much abhorred by British commentators in the past, but now is almost as likely to happen in Britain as the United States.

- In American English, the preposition *to* is often left out after *to write*:

  American English:
  I'll write you as soon as I get there.
  British English:
  I'll write to you as soon as I get there.

- British English prefers *different from* and *different to*, whereas American English prefers *different than*:

  British English:
  His recipe is different from mine.
  American English:
  His recipe is different than mine.

- British people do something *at the weekend*, Americans do it *on the weekend*.

Words That Are Difficult To Spell

A
abbreviation
abscess
absence
abundance
abysmal
abysmally
abyss
accelerate
accelerator
accept
acceptable
access
accessible
accessories
accident
accidental
accommodate
accommodation
accompaniment
accompany
accumulate
accurate
accustomed
ache
achieve
achievement
aching
acknowledge
acknowledgement
acquaint
acquaintance
acquiesce
acquiescence
acquire
acquisition
acquit
acquittal
acquitted
acreage
across
actual
additional
additive
address
adequate
adequately
adieu
adjacent
admissible
admittance
adolescence
adolescent
advantageous
advertisement
advice [noun]
advisable
advise [verb]
aerate
aerial
aesthetic
affect
affiliation
afforestation
aggravate
aggravation
aggregate
aggression
aggressive
aghast
agnosticism
agoraphobia
agreeable
agreeably
agreed
aisle
alcohol
alfresco
alibis
align
alignment
allegation
allege
allergic
alleys
alligator
allocate
allotment
allotted
almighty
almond
alms
alphabetically
already
although

Finding the Word: Words That Are Difficult to Spell

altogether	anxiety	ascent
aluminium	anxious	asphalt
amateur	apartheid	asphyxiate
ambiguous	apologize/	asphyxiation
amethyst	apologise	aspirin
ammunition	apology	assassin
amount	appal	assassinate
anachronism	appalling	assessment
anaesthetic	apparatus	assistance
analyse	apparently	associate
analysis	appearance	asthma
anarchist	appendicitis	asthmatic
ancestor	appendix	astrakhan
ancestry	appreciate	atheist
ancillary	approach	athlete
anecdote	appropriate	atmosphere
anemone	approval	atrocious
angrily	approximate	attach
anguish	approximately	attempt
ankle	aquarium	attendance
annihilate	aquiline	attendant
annihilation	arbiter	attitude
anniversary	arbitrary	aubergine
announcement	arbitration	auburn
annulled	archaeology	auctioneer
annulment	architectural	audible
anonymous	Arctic	aural
anorak	arguably	author
anorexia	argument	authority
answered	arrangement	automatic
Antarctic	arrival	autumn
antibiotic	arthritis	auxiliary
anticipate	artichoke	awful
antithesis	ascend	awkward

B

bachelor
bagatelle
baggage
bailiff
ballast
ballerina
ballet
balloon
balloted
banana
banister
banjo
banjoes/banjos
bankruptcy
banquet
barbecue
barometer
barrister
basically
basis
bassoon
battalion
bayonet
bazaar
beautiful
beauty
becoming
befriend
begin
beginning
beguile
behaviour
beleaguer

belief
believe
belligerent
benefit
benefited
bequeath
berserk
besiege
bettered
bevelled
bewitch
bias
bicycle
biennial
bigamous
bigoted
bilingual
biscuit
bivouacked
bizarre
blancmange
blasphemous
blasphemy
bleary
blitz
bodily
bonfire
bootee
borough
boundary
bouquet
bourgeois
boutique
bracketed

Braille
brassiere
breadth
breath (*noun*)
Breathalyzer/
 Breathalyser
breathe (*verb*)
brief
brilliant
Britain
broccoli
brochure
bronchitis
bruise
brusque
buccaneer
Buddhist
budding
budgerigar
budgeted
buffeted
bulimia
bulletin
bumptious
bungalow
buoyancy
buoyant
bureau
bureaucracy
bureaux
burglar
burglary
burial
bury

Finding the Word: Words That Are Difficult to Spell

business
buttoned

C
cabbage
cafeteria
caffeine
calendar
calibre
camouflage
campaign
campaigned
cancelled
cancerous
candour
cannabis
cannibal
canoe
canvassing
capability
capillary
capitalist
caravan
carbohydrate
carburettor
career
careful
caress
caricature
caries
carriage
cartoonist
cashier
cassette

castanets
casualty
catalogue
catarrh
catechism
category
catering
caterpillar
cauliflower
caustic
cautious
cavalier
cedar
ceiling
Cellophane
cemetery
centenary
centilitre
centimetre
centre
certainty
challenge
champagne
championed
chancellor
changeable
channelled
chaos
characteristic
chasm
chassis
chauffeur
cheetah
cherish

chief
chilblain
chintz
chiropody
chisel
chocolate
choir
cholesterol
choreographer
choreography
chorus
Christian
chronically
chrysanthemum
cigarette
cinnamon
circuitous
cistern
citation
cite
civilian
claustrophobia
clientele
clique
coalesce
cocoa
coconut
coffee
cognac
coincidence
colander
collaborate
collapsible
colleague

college
colonel
colonnade
coloration
colossal
colour
column
comically
commandeer
commemorate
commentator
commercial
commiserate
commission
commissionaire
commissioner
commitment
committal
committed
committee
communicate
commuter
companion
comparative
comparison
compatibility
compatible
compelled
competent
competitive
computer
computerization/
  computerisation
conceal

concealment
concede
conceit
conceivable
conceive
concession
concurrent
concussion
condemned
condescend
confectionery
conference
confetti
congeal
congratulations
conjunctivitis
conned
connoisseur
connotation
conscience
conscientious
conscious
consequently
consignment
consolation
conspicuous
constitute
consumer
contemptible
continent
continuous
contraception
contradictory
controlled

controller
controversial
convalesce
convenient
convertible
conveyed
convolvulus
coolly
co-operate
co-operative
co-ordinate
copying
coquette
corduroy
co-respondent
coronary
correspondence
corridor
corroborate
corrugated
cosmopolitan
cosseted
councillor
counselling
counsellor
counterfeit
coupon
courageous
courteous
crèche
credible
credited
crematorium
creosote

Finding the Word: Words That Are Difficult to Spell

crescent
crisis
criterion
crocheted
crocodile
croupier
crucial
crucifixion
cruel
cruelly
cruise
cryptic
cubicle
cupboard
cupful
curable
curiosity
curious
currency
curriculum vitae
customary
cynic
cynicism
cynosure

D
dachshund
daffodil
dahlia
dairy
dais
damage
dandruff
darkened

debatable
debauched
debility
debris
debt
debtor
deceased
deceit
deceive
deciduous
decipher
decoyed
decrease
decreed
defamatory
defeat
defence
defendant
defied
definite
definitely
degradation
dehydrate
deign
deliberate
delicatessen
delicious
delinquent
delirious
demeanour
democracy
demonstrate
denouement
denunciation

dependence
dependent
depot
depth
derailment
dermatitis
derogatory
descend
descendant
describe
description
desiccate
desperate
detach
detachable
detergent
deterred
deterrent
deuce
develop
developed
development
device [noun]
devise [verb]
diabetes
diagnosis
dialogue
dialysis
diametrically
diaphragm
diarrhoea
diary
difference
different

difficult
digestible
dilapidated
dilemma
dilettante
diminish
diminution
dining
dinosaur
diphtheria
diphthong
disadvantageous
disagreeable
disagreed
disagreement
disappearance
disappeared
disappoint
disapproval
disastrous
disbelief
disbelieve
discern
discipline
discotheque
discouraging
discourteous
discrepancy
discrimination
discussion
disease
disguise
dishevelled
dishonourable

disillusion
disinfectant
disinherited
dismissal
disobeyed
disparage
dispelled
disposal
dispossess
dissatisfaction
dissatisfy
dissect
disseminate
dissent
dissident
dissimilar
dissipated
dissipation
dissociate
dissolute
dissolve
dissuade
distil
distilled
distillery
distinguish
distraught
disuse
divisible
documentary
doggerel
dominant
domineering
donate

donor
doubt
dough
dragooned
drastically
draughty
drooled
drooped
drunkenness
dubious
duly
dumbfounded
dungarees
duress
dutiful
dynamite
dysentery
dyslexia
dyspepsia

E

eccentric
ecclesiastic
ecologically
economically
ecstasy
eczema
effective
effervescence
efficacious
efficient
effrontery
eighth
eightieth

elaborate
electrician
elevenses
eligible
emancipate
embarrass
embarrassment
emergence
emergent
emolument
emotional
emphasize/
 emphasise
employee
emptied
enable
encourage
encyclopedia
endeavour
endurance
energetically
enervate
engineer
enough
ensuing
entailed
enthusiasm
enumerate
epilepsy
equalize/equalise
equalled
equipped
erroneous
erudite

escalator
escapism
espionage
essence
essential
estranged
etiquette
euthanasia
eventually
evidently
exaggerate
exaggeration
exasperate
exceed
exceedingly
excellent
excessive
exchequer
excommunicate
exercise
exhaust
exhibit
exhilarated
exorcize/exorcise
explanation
exquisite
extinguish
extraneous
extravagant

F
fabulous
facetious
facsimile

faeces
Fahrenheit
fallacious
fanatic
farcical
fascinate
fascist
fatigue
fatuous
fax
February
feeler
feign
ferocious
festooned
feud
feudal
fevered
fiasco
fibre
fictitious
fiend
fierce
fiery
filial
finesse
flabbergasted
flaccid
flammable
flannelette
flotation
fluent
fluoridate
fluoride

A Guide to Letter-Writing

fluoridize/
  fluoridise
focal
foliage
forcible
foreigner
forfeit
formative
forthwith
fortieth
fortuitous
fortunately
frailty
frankincense
fraudulent
freedom
freight
frequency
friend
frolicked
fuchsia
fuel
fuelled
fugitive
fulfil
fulfilled
fulfilment
fullness
fulsome
furious
furniture

G
gaiety

galloped
garrison
garrotted
gases
gateau
gauge
gazetteer
generator
genuine
gesticulate
ghastly
ghetto
gigantic
gingham
giraffe
glamorous
glamour
glimpse
global
gluttonous
glycerine
gnarled
gnash
goitre
gossiped
government
graffiti
grammar
grandeur
gratefully
gratitude
gratuitous
greetings
gregarious

grief
grieve
grovelled
gruesome
guarantee
guarantor
guard
guardian
guest
guillotine
guinea
guise
guitar
gymkhana
gynaecology
gypsy/gipsy

H
haemoglobin
haemorrhage
halcyon
hallucination
hammered
handfuls
handicapped
handkerchief
happened
harangue
harass
harlequin
haughty
hazard
hearse
height

Finding the Word: Words That Are Difficult to Spell

heightened	hypocrisy	incandescent
heinous	hypothesis	incessant
heir	hypothetical	incipient
herbaceous	hysterectomy	incognito
hereditary	hysterical	incommunicado
heroism		inconceivable
hesitate	**I**	incongruous
hiccup, hiccough	icicle	incontrovertible
hideous	ideological	incorrigible
hierarchy	idiosyncrasy	incredulous
hieroglyphics	ignorance	incriminate
hijack	illegible	incubator
hilarious	illegitimate	incurred
hindrance	illiterate	indefatigable
hippopotamus	imaginative	indefinable
holiday	imitation	indefinite
holocaust	immaculate	independence
honorary	immediate	independent
honour	immemorial	indescribable
hooligan	immoral	indict
hormonal	immovable	indictment
hormone	impasse	indigenous
horoscope	impeccable	indigestible
horrible	imperative	indomitable
horticulture	imperceptible	indubitable
hullabaloo	imperious	ineligible
humorous	impetuous	inescapable
humour	impresario	inexcusable
hurricane	imprisoned	inexhaustible
hurried	imprisonment	infallible
hygiene	inaccessible	infatuated
hyphen	inadmissible	inferred
hypnosis	inappropriate	infinitive
hypochondria	inaugural	inflamed

inflammable
inflationary
ingratiate
ingredient
inhabitant
inheritance
inhibition
iniquitous
initiate
initiative
innate
innocuous
innumerable
innumerate
inoculate
insecticide
inseparable
insincere
insistence
instalment
instantaneous
intercept
interference
interior
intermediate
intermittent
interpret
interpretation
interrogate
interrupt
interview
intrigue
intrinsically
intuition

intuitive
invariably
inveigle
inveterate
involuntary
involvement
irascible
irrelevant
irreparable
irreplaceable
irresistible
irresponsible
irrevocable
irritable
italicize/italicise
itinerant
itinerary

J

jackal
jeopardize/
   jeopardise
jettisoned
jeweller
jewellery
jodhpurs
juggernaut
jugular

K

kaleidoscope
karate
keenness
khaki

kidnapped
kilometre
kiosk
kitchenette
kleptomania
knick-knack
knowledgeable

L

labelled
laboratory
labyrinth
lackadaisical
laddered
lager
language
laryngitis
larynx
lassitude
latitude
laundered
launderette
layette
league
leanness
ledger
legendary
legible
legitimate
length
lengthened
leukaemia
levelled
liaise

Finding the Word: Words That Are Difficult to Spell

liaison
lieu
lieutenant
lilac
limousine
lineage
linen
lingerie
linguist
liqueur
literature
litre
livelihood
loneliness
loosened
loquacious
lucrative
lucre
luggage
lugubrious
luminous
luscious
lustre
luxurious
lyric

M

macabre
maelstrom
magician
magnanimous
mahogany
maintenance
malaise

malaria
malignant
manageable
management
mannequin
manoeuvre
mantelpiece
manually
margarine
marijuana
marquee
martyr
marvellous
marzipan
masochist
massacre
matinee
matriarch
mayonnaise
meagre
measurement
medallion
medieval
mediocre
melancholy
meningitis
meringue
messenger
meteorological
metropolitan
microphone
microwave
midday
migraine

mileage
milieu
millionaire/
   millionnaire
mimicked
mimicry
miniature
miraculous
mirrored
miscellaneous
mischief
mischievous
misogynist
misshapen
misspell
misspent
modelled
modelling
morgue
mortgage
mosquito
mountaineer
moustache
multitudinous
muscle
museum
mysterious
mythical

N

naive
narrative
naughty
nausea

nautical
necessary
necessity
negligence
negligible
negotiate
neighbourhood
neither
neurotic
neutral
niche
niece
nineteenth
ninetieth
ninth
nocturnal
nonentity
notably
noticeably
notoriety
nuance
numbered
numerate
numerous
nutrient
nutritious

O
obedient
obese
obituary
oblige
oblique
oblivious

obnoxious
obscene
obscenity
obsessive
obstetrician
occasion
occupancy
occupier
occupying
occurred
occurrence
octogenarian
odour
offence
offered
official
officious
ominous
omission
omitted
oncology
oneself
opaque
ophthalmic
opinion
opponent
opportunity
opposite
orchestra
ordinary
original
orthodox
orthopaedic
oscillate

ostracize/
 ostracise
outlying
outrageous
overdraft
overrate
overreach
overwrought
oxygen

P
pacifist
paediatrician
paedophile
pageant
pamphlet
panacea
panegyric
panicked
papered
parachute
paradigm
paraffin
paragraph
paralyse
paralysis
paraphernalia
parcelled
parliament
paroxysm
parquet
partially
participant
particle

Finding the Word: Words That Are Difficult to Spell

partner	physiotherapist	preferred
passenger	picketed	prejudice
passers-by	picnic	preliminary
pastime	picnicked	prepossessing
patterned	picturesque	prerequisite
pavilion	pioneered	prerogative
peaceable	pious	prescription
peculiar	piteous	presence
pejorative	pitiful	preservative
pencilled	plaintiff	prestige
penicillin	plausible	prestigious
peppered	pleurisy	pretentious
perceive	pneumonia	prevalent
perennial	poignant	priest
perilous	politician	primitive
permissible	pollution	privatization / privatisation
permitted	polythene	privatize/privatise
pernicious	porridge	procedure
perpetrate	portrait	proceed
persistence	portray	procession
personnel	positive	professional
persuasion	possession	profiteering
perusal	possibility	prohibit
pessimism	posthumous	promiscuous
pessimistically	potato	pronunciation
pesticide	potatoes	propeller
phantom	practice (*noun*)	proposal
pharmacy	practise (*verb*)	proprietor
pharyngitis	precede	prosecute
pharynx	precedent	protagonist
phenomenon	precinct	protein
phial	precipice	provocation
phlegm	precocious	prowess
physician	preference	

psalm
psalmist
pseudonym
psyche
psychiatric
psychic
psychoanalyse
psychology
publicly
pursuit
putative
pyjamas

Q
quarrelsome
questionnaire
queue
quintet

R
rabies
radioed
radios
railing
ransack
rapist
rapturous
reassurance
rebelled
rebellious
recalcitrant
receipt
receive
recommend

reconnaissance
reconnoitre
recruitment
recurrence
redundant
referee
reference
referred
regatta
regrettable
regretted
rehabilitation
reign
relevant
relief
relieve
reminisce
reminiscence
remuneration
rendezvous
repertoire
repetitive
reprieve
reprisal
requisite
rescind
resemblance
reservoir
resistance
resourceful
responsibility
restaurant
restaurateur
resurrection

resuscitate
retrieve
reunion
reveille
revelry
revenue
reversible
rhapsody
rheumatism
rhododendron
rhyme
rhythm
ricochet
righteous
rigorous
rigour
risotto
riveted
rogue
roughage
royalty
rucksack
ruinous
rummage
rumour

S
sabotage
sacrilege
saddened
salmon
salvage
sanctuary
sandwich

Finding the Word: Words That Are Difficult to Spell

sanitary	shield	sphinx
sapphire	shovelled	sponsor
satellite	shuddered	spontaneity
scaffolding	siege	spontaneous
scandalous	significant	squabble
scenic	silhouette	squandered
sceptic	simply	squawk
sceptre	simultaneous	staccato
schedule	sincerely	staggered
scheme	sixth	stammered
schizophrenic	sixteenth	statistics
schooner	sixtieth	statutory
sciatica	skeleton	stealth
science	skilful	stereophonic
scissors	slanderous	stirrup
scruple	slaughter	storage
scrupulous	sleigh	straitjacket
scurrilous	sleight of hand	strait-laced
scythe	sluice	strategic
secretarial	smattering	strength
secretary	smithereens	strenuous
sedative	snivelled	stupor
sedentary	soccer	suave
sensitive	solemn	subpoena
separate	solicitor	subtle
sergeant	soliloquy	succeed
serrated	soloist	successful
serviceable	sombre	successor
serviette	somersault	succinct
settee	sophisticated	succulent
shampooed	sovereign	succumb
shattered	spaghetti	suddenness
sheikh	spectre	suede
sheriff	spherical	sufficient

suffocate
suicide
sullenness
summoned
supercilious
superfluous
supersede
supervise
supervisor
supplementary
surgeon
surveillance
surveyor
susceptible
suspicious
sycamore
symmetry
sympathize/
 sympathise
symphony
synagogue
syndicate
synonym
syringe

T
tableau
tableaux
taboo
taciturn
taffeta
tangerine
tangible
targeted

tattoo
technique
teenager
televise
temperature
tenuous
terrifically
terrifying
territory
terrorist
therapeutic
therefore
thief
thinness
thirteenth
thirtieth
thirty
thorough
thoroughfare
threshold
thrombosis
throughout
thwart
thyme
tightened
titillate
titivate
tobacconist
toboggan
toffee
tomato
tomatoes
tomorrow
tonsillitis

topsy-turvy
tornadoes
torpedoes
torpor
tortoiseshell
tortuous
totalled
tourniquet
towelling
traffic
trafficked
tragedy
traitorous
tranquillity
tranquillizer/
 tranquilliser
transcend
transferable
transferred
transparent
travelled
traveller
tremor
triggered
trilogy
troublesome
trousseau
truism
trustee
tsetse
tuberculosis
tumour
tunnelled
tureen

Finding the Word: Words That Are Difficult to Spell

turquoise
twelfth
tyranny

U
unanimous
unconscious
undoubted
unduly
unequalled
unique
unnecessary
unprecedented
unremitting
unrequited
unrivalled
upheaval
uproarious

V
vaccinate
vacuum
vague
variegate
vegan
vehement
vendetta
veneer
ventilator
veranda
verandah/
  veranda
vermilion
veterinary

vetoes
vice versa
vicissitude
videoed
vigorous
vigour
viscount
visibility
vivacious
vociferous
voluminous
volunteered
vulnerable

W
walloped
weakened
wearisome
Wednesday
weight
weird
whereabouts
wherewithal
whinge
widened
width
wield
wintry
witticism
wizened
woebegone
wooden
woollen
worsened

worship
worshipped
wrapper
wrath
wreak
writhe

X
xylophone

Y
yield
yoghurt

Z
zealous
zigzagged

Words That Can Be Confused

There are many pairs of words in English that have the same spelling but different meanings, or sound the same but are spelled differently. To avoid errors in writing, these words – sometimes called confusables – need special attention. In general, if you are in any doubt about the spelling or meaning of a word look it up in a dictionary, checking both the spelling and the meaning. It is often helpful to use a dictionary that has definitions and example phrases or sentences with the defined word used in context.

Remember it isn't a good idea to depend on a computer spell-checker to alert you when you've confused one word with another. Many spellcheckers will accept words that are correctly spelled, even where they have been used in the wrong context. For example, many spellcheckers will accept as correct the sentence

> The *affect* of the cuts was felt throughout local *counsel* offices.

when the correct spellings should be:

> The *effect* of the cuts was felt throughout local *council* offices.

Here is a list of these confusable words, together with some examples of usage to help you to differentiate them.

abrogate	The king abrogated all responsibilities for government.
arrogate	He arrogated to himself various rights and privilege.

Finding the Word: Words That Can Be Confused

aboard	to get aboard a ferry
abroad	to travel abroad
abuse	to abuse the children; to shout abuse
misuse	to misuse the word
accede	to accede to all their requests
exceed	to exceed the baggage allowance
accept	to accept a gift
except	There was one for everyone except Mary.
access	The ramps provided access to the building.
excess	an excess of fat in the diet
acetic	acetic acid
ascetic	ascetics and holy men
acme	the acme of perfection
acne	spots, pimples and acne
activate	He activated the safety cut-out.
actuate	actuated by sheer malice
ad	a short TV ad
add	add two and two
adapter	the adapter of the novel for TV
adaptor	an electrical adaptor
addition	an addition to the family
edition	a new edition of the book

adherence	adherence to Marxism
adhesion	adhesion is rapid so work quickly
adjacent	the house adjacent to the school
adjoining	a bedroom with adjoining bathroom
contiguous	here the boundaries of the two estates are contiguous
admission	reduced admission charges to the theatre
admittance	The sign said 'No admittance'.
adopted	an adopted child
adoptive	his adoptive parents
adverse	He had an adverse reaction to the drug.
averse	She was not averse to the idea.
advice	to seek legal advice
advise	We advise you to go.
aesthetic	an aesthetic feast of paintings, sculpture and rich textiles
ascetic	ascetic monklike habits
affect [verb]	He was badly affected by the news.
effect [noun]	the effects of the drug
afflict	afflicted with neuralgia
inflict	inflicting pain on others
affluent	an affluent suburb
effluent	The effluent from the factory was poisoning the river.

Finding the Word: Words That Can Be Confused

ail	What ails you?
ale	local ales and beers
aisle	The bride walked down the aisle followed by three bridesmaids.
isle	the isle of Skye
air	She puts on airs. He went flying through the air.
heir	the heir to the throne
alias	His alias was Solomon Shifty.
alibi	He had an alibi for the night of the murder.
all	all the children
awl	with a sharp end like a cobbler's awl
allegory	an allegory for faithfulness
allergy	an allergy to pollen
alley	a dark alley
allay	He tried to allay our fears.
allude	He alluded to the affair.
elude	The robbers eluded the police.
allusion	He made no allusion to recent events.
delusion	under the delusion that he is immortal
illusion	an optical illusion

allusive	an allusive reference
elusive	a rare and elusive bird
altar	praying at the altar
alter	to alter a dress
alteration	making an alteration to his will
altercation	There was an altercation between two obviously very angry drivers.
alternately	striped alternately red and green
alternatively	we could drive there – alternatively we could walk
amateur	an amateur dramatic group
amateurish	an amateurish attempt at blackmail
ambiguous	an ambiguous expression
ambivalent	ambivalent about the result
amend	to amend the law
emend	He was asked to emend the text before publication.
amiable	an amiable old gent
amicable	an amicable agreement
among	among the hay stacks
between	between the house and the barn
amoral	He was amoral – he had no moral standards.
immoral	immoral earnings from vice
immortal	immortal gods

Finding the Word: Words That Can Be Confused

angel	heavenly angels
angle	a right angle
annals	the annals of European history
annuals	planting annuals and perennials
annex [verb]	to annex a neighbouring country
annexe [noun]	to build an annexe to the house
antagonist	a fearsome antagonist
protagonist	a leading protagonist of women's rights
antiquated	antiquated rules
antique	an antique clock
arc	the arc of a rainbow in the sky
ark	Noah's ark
arisen	A problem had arisen.
arose	There arose a murmur of discontent.
artist	Van Gogh and other famous artists
artiste	a circus artiste
ascent [noun]	the first ascent of Everest
assent [verb]	He readily gave his assent to the proposal.
assay	to assay gold and silver
essay	He wrote an essay on the Romatic poets.
assistance	to need immediate medical assistance
assistants	the magician and his two lovely assistants

assure	I assure you it's genuine.
ensure	Please ensure the door is securely locked.
insure	He insured the horse for 250,000.
astrology	Believers in astrology read horoscopes.
astronomy	Astronomy is the scientific study of the stars and the planets.
ate	We ate bread and cheese.
eaten	He'd eaten too much.
aural	an aural impairment requiring a hearing aid
oral	both oral and written language exams; oral and dental hygiene
averse	not averse to a little luxury
adverse	adverse weather conditions
awl	shaped like a cobbler's awl
all	all the children
axes	He had two axes for chopping wood.
axis (*pl* axes)	the Earth spinning on its axis; one axis, two axes
bad	bad weather
bade	he bade me sit
bade	he bade me sit
bid	He bid $100.

Finding the Word: Words That Can Be Confused

bail	The accused was granted bail.
bale	a bale of cotton
bale out	to bale out water; to bale out of an aircraft
baited	The hook was baited with a worm. He baited the trap with meat.
bated	with bated breath
ball	a tennis ball
bawl	'Stop!' he bawled, at the top of his voice.
ballet	dancing in the ballet
ballot	There was a strike ballot of the union members.
banns	to read the marriage banns
bans	bans imposed on imports
bare	bare skin
bear	a polar bear
barn	hay in the barn
baron	mediaeval barons
barren	a barren wilderness
base	the base of the mountain
bass	a deep bass voice
bath	She had a bath every day.
bathe	to bathe in the sea

A GUIDE TO LETTER-WRITING

baton   He passed the baton to the next runner.
batten   The felt was held down with a wooden batten.

bazaar   a church bazaar
bizarre   a bizarre situation

beach   a sandy beach
beech   a beech tree

bean   beans and pulses
been   Where have you been?
being   You're being silly, like a being from another planet.

beat   to beat a drum
beet   sugar beet

beau   Miss Lisa went walking out with her new beau.
bow   She was wearing a pink bow in her hair.

became   What became of them?
become   What will become of us?

beer   I'd love a cold beer.
bier   Snowwhite's bier was decked with flowers.

befallen   What has befallen him?
befell   Disaster befell them.

began   The child began to cry.
begun   It had begun to rain.

Finding the Word: Words That Can Be Confused

belief	He had belief in his own abilities.
believe	He believes that he can succeed.
bell	church bells
belle	the belle of the ball
bellow	bellow like a bull
below	The river flowed below the bridge.
bereaved	the bereaved widow
bereft	bereft of sympathy
beret	a jaunty French beret
berry	shiny red holly berries
bury	to bury their dead
berth	There was a berth at the marina for their yacht.
birth	the birth of their fourth son
beside	The bride stood beside the groom.
besides	Besides, he has no money.
	Who, besides you, was there?
biannual	Twice a year they all met together at a biannual conference.
biennial	Biennial plants flower in their second year.
bight	the Great Australian Bight
bite	Don't bite the hand that feeds you.
bit	The dog bit the postman.
bitten	She was bitten by a rat.

blew	The wind blew softly.
blown	He was blown across the street by the fierce wind.
blew	The hat blew away.
blue	He chased after the blue hat.
bloc	The African bloc of countries left the talks.
block	a block of flats
blond	a blond boy
blonde	a blonde girl
boar	a wild boar
boor	He's an ill-mannered boor.
bore	I thought the film was a bore.
board	oak boards
bored	I am bored with sums.
boast	He liked to boast about how much money he had.
boost	to boost profits
bonny	bonny Scotland
bony	long bony fingers
bookie	to place a bet at the bookie
bouquet	a bouquet of roses
bootee	a baby's bootee
booty	The pirate's booty consisted of gold and silver coins.

Finding the Word: Words That Can Be Confused

born	born in the twentieth century
borne	I could not have borne the pain.
borough	the borough of Queens, New York
burgh	Lanark is a Scottish royal burgh.
bough	She sat in the tree on a low-hanging bough.
bow	Please bow to the queen.
bound	They were bound by ties of blood.
bounded	The farm was bounded on the west by dense forest.
boy	a cheeky little boy
buoy	a buoy marking the shipping channel
brae	a steep brae
bray	to bray like a donkey
brake	to apply the brake
break	to break an egg
brassiere	'Bra' is short for brassiere.
brazier	They held their hands out to the glowing brazier.
breach	to breach the rules; a breach in the sea wall
breech	a breech birth
bread	bread and cheese
bred	The fisherman was born and bred in Iceland.

breath	to take a deep breath
breathe	to breathe deeply
bridal	a bridal bouquet
bridle	the horse's bridle
broach	to broach a subject
brooch	an emerald brooch
broke	They were broke; they had no money left.
	She broke down and cried.
broken	His leg is broken.
	The vase is broken.
buffet [*buffit*]	He heard the wind buffet the shutters.
buffet [*boofay*]	The hotel served a buffet rather than a formal dinner.
business	a business meeting
busyness	the busyness of the bees
but	small but perfectly formed
butt	the butt of jokes; a water butt
buy	to buy a new car
by	to pass by on the other side
bye	bye for now
cache	a cache of arms
cash	to pay cash
caddie	a golf caddie
caddy	a tea caddy

Finding the Word: Words That Can Be Confused

calf	a newborn calf
calve	The cow is due to calve.
callous	a callous murder
callus	a callus on my heel
came	She came home yesterday.
come	I hope he will come home soon.
canned	The tomatoes are chopped and canned for export.
could	He could probably do it just as well as you can.
cannon	the roar of the cannon
canon	He's a canon of the cathedral.
	the canon of English literature
can't	I can't help it.
cant	mere cant, and utterly lacking in sincerity; thieves' cant
canvas	under canvas at the camp site
canvass	to canvass local opinion
carat	a ten-carat diamond
caret	The caret symbol looks like an upside down 'Y' and shows where to insert a word.
carrot	a carrot cake
cartilage	The footballer damaged the cartilage in his knee.
cartridge	a shotgun cartridge

carton	a carton of milk
cartoon	a Disney cartoon
cast	He was cast adrift in a small boat.
caste	the Indian caste system
cavalier	cavaliers and roundheads; a cavalier attitude
cavalry	A cavalry charge won the battle.
cede	England had to cede territory to France.
seed	bird seed
ceiling	a low ceiling
sealing	sealing wax; sealing the two edges of the envelope
cell	a prison cell
sell	to sell shoes or other merchandise
cellular	a cellular structure; a cellular phone
cellulose	cellulose and other plant material
censor	to censor a film
censer	The priest was swinging a brass censer.
censure	a vote of censure
cent	It won't cost you a cent.
scent	the scent of violets
sent	She sent him away.
centenarian	Someone aged 100 is a centenarian.
centenary	on the centenary of Dickens' birth

Finding the Word: Words That Can Be Confused

cereal	He enjoyed eating breakfast cereal.
serial	She enjoyed listening to a serial on the radio.
ceremonious	He gave a ceremonious bow.
ceremonial	The duke wore his ceremonial robes to the coronation.
chafe	These rubber boots chafe my legs.
chaff	to separate the wheat from the chaff
charted	They charted his progress.
chartered	a chartered accountant
chased	The huntsman was chased by a wild boar.
chaste	the chaste smile of a young virgin
cheap	to sell cheap goods
cheep	the cheep of baby birds
check	to check your luggage; [American] to pay by credit card or check
cheque	[British] to pay by credit card or cheque
checked	a checked jacket
chequered	a chequered career
chilli	hot chilli powder
chilly	a chilly wind from the north
choir	a choir of angels
quire	a quire of paper

choose	Choose the one you like best.
chose	I chose the one I liked best.
chosen	She had chosen to wear pink.
chord	to play a chord on the guitar
cord	the spinal cord
chute	There was a rubbish chute to the basement.
shoot	to shoot an arrow in the air
cite	Please cite some examples.
sight	It was a sight that astonished everyone.
site	a building site
clothes	She was not wearing any clothes.
cloths	one cloth, two cloths
coarse	a coarse fabric
course	a race course; in the course of the week
collage	a collage of scraps of paper, fabric and dried flowers
college	He planned to attend college and further his education.
coma	She fell into a coma.
comma	Put a comma after this word.
commissionaire	The commissionaire held the door open for us.
commissioner	the police commissioner

Finding the Word: Words That Can Be Confused

complement	The fruit complements the rich ice cream perfectly.
compliment	to pay someone a compliment
complementary	complementary oufits; a complementary angle
complimentary	He was very complimentary about my drawings.
	a complimentary ticket
concert	She wanted to sing at the school concert.
consort	the king's consort, Princess Adelaide
confidant	He is a man who will be both friend and confidant.
confidante	a female friend and confidante
confident	I am confident of success.
conscience	to have a conscience about lying
conscientious	a conscientious, hardworking boy
conscious	She was conscious of her failings.
console [*kon-sol*]	He tried to console the grieving relatives.
consul	If you lose your passport, contact the British consul.
contemptible	contemptible behaviour
contemptuous	a contemptuous sneer
content	The content of the book was mainly humorous.
content	She was relaxed and content with life.

A Guide to Letter-Writing

continual	continual interruptions
continuous	a continuous stream of oaths
coop	a hen coop; to coop someone up somewhere
coup	a military coup
coral	a coral reef
corral	to drive mustangs into a corral
co-respondent	the co-respondent in a divorce case
correspondent	the political correspondent for *The Times*
cornet	play the cornet; an ice-cream cornet
coronet	the duke's coronet
cornflour	She thickened the sauce with cornflower.
cornflower	a blue cornflower and a blood-red poppy
corps	the army service corps
corpse	Detectives examined the corpse of the murder victim.
cost	The dress cost £50.
costed	He costed the project in minute detail.
council	a city council
counsel	Counsel him to wait a while.
councillor	a town councillor
counsellor	a marriage counsellor
courtesy	They informed him merely as a courtesy.
curtsy	to curtsy to a queen

Finding the Word: Words That Can Be Confused

creak	In my old age, my knee joints creak when I move.
creek	Beavers were building a dam across the creek.
credible	not a very credible story
credulous	He is a foolish credulous person who believes all he is told.
crevasse	The climber suddenly fell down a deep ice crevasse.
crevice	a crevice between the two stones
criterion	the single criterion
criteria	all the criteria
crochet	to crochet a shawl
crotchet	In music, a crotchet is called a quarter note in the US.
cue	The actor missed his cue and had to be prompted. a billiards cue
queue	a queue all the way round the building
curb	to curb your enthusiasm; [American] to step off the curb
kerb	[British] to step off the kerb into the road
currant	sultanas, raisins and currants
current	current affairs
cygnet	swans with their cygnets
signet	a signet ring

cymbal	One cymbal is struck against the other.
symbol	a symbol of freedom
dairy	milk from the local dairy
diary	I pencilled the date into my diary.
dam	the Hoover dam
damn	Damn your eyes!
dammed	The river was dammed.
damned	He's damned to a life of misery.
dear	dear old Mrs Hobbs
deer	They were hunting deer.
decry	to decry the government's record on health care
descry	to descry a ship on the horizon
decent	a decent man; a decent burial
descent	The descent from the summit of Everest was full of danger.
deduce	to deduce something from the available evidence
deduct	to deduct tax from wages
defective	a defective window lock
deficient	a diet deficient in vital minerals and vitamins
definite	a definite smell of gas
definitive	the definitive book on Polish literature

Finding the Word: Words That Can Be Confused

defuse	to defuse a bomb
diffuse	There was a subtle, diffuse scent of flowers in the summer air.
dependant	a married man with dependants
dependent	to be dependent on drugs
deprecate	The rest of the family deprecated his foolish vanity.
depreciate	A new car will depreciate in value from the day it is bought.
desert	the Gobi desert
dessert	I would like to have raspberry sorbet for dessert.
detract	Nothing could detract from his achievement.
distract	The nurse distracted the little girl while she was getting an injection.
device [noun]	a cunning device
devise [verb]	He tried to devise a means of cooking without pots and pans.
devolution	Devolution for Scotland and Wales was an important issue in the election.
evolution	the evolution of the species
dew	Morning dew is good for your skin.
due	The bill is now due.
did	Did you do it?
done	It was done by someone else.

A Guide to Letter-Writing

die	He will die a slow death.
dye	Please dye the curtains green.
died	died in combat
dyed	dyed a vivid pink
dinghy	a sailing dinghy
dingy	a dingy little bedsit
disbelief	He looked at me in disbelief.
disbelieve	I don't disbelieve him.
discreet	a discreet distance; a discreet woman
discrete	There is a a discrete possibility that all will not go well.
discus	to throw the discus
discuss	He wanted to discuss the plan with other department heads.
disinterested	The disinterested party was to arbitrate.
uninterested	The young boy was completely uninterested in school work.
doe	A female deer, hare or rabbit is a doe.
dough	He kneaded the bread dough for ten minutes.
doily	The cake was placed on a paper doily.
dolly	The little girl was holding a dolly.
draft	the first draft of a letter; [American] to draft men into the army
draught	a chilly draught; a long draught of beer

Finding the Word: Words That Can Be Confused

dragon	tales of monsters and dragons
dragoon	to dragoon someone into doing something
drawn	a drawn and haggard appearance; a portrait drawn with a pencil
drew	He drew a small sketch. The knife drew blood. He drew on his past experience.
drank	I drank my coffee before it got cold.
drunk	The drunk man had drunk more than ten pints of beer.
driven	The stake was driven into the ground.
drove	The dog drove the sheep into the pen.
dual	The car had dual controls.
duel	to fight a duel
ducks	ducks and swans
dux	the dux of the school
dudgeon	to leave in high dudgeon
dungeon	The prisoner was thrown into a dark dungeon.
dully	The day began dully, with great grey clouds in the sky.
duly	We were duly reminded to have our passports ready.
dyeing	Dyeing cloth can be messy.
dying	He was dying of cancer.

earthly	He had no earthly chance of winning.
earthy	an earthy sense of humour
easterly	an easterly wind
eastern	an eastern custom
eclipse	a total eclipse of the moon
ellipse	An ellipse is flatter than a circle.
economic	economic policies
economical	an economical way to travel
eerie	an eerie screech
eyrie	the eagle's eyrie
elder	my elder brother
eldest	He's the eldest of three sons.
elicit	It was his task to elicit information.
illicit	The strikers held an illicit meeting.
eligible	He was eligible to join the club.
legible	Do you have legible handwriting?
emigrant	an emigrant from Scotland
immigrant	an immigrant to the United States
emigrate	to emigrate from their homeland
migrate	Many birds migrate south for the summer.
emigration	Irish emigration peaked in the nineteenth century.
immigration	Immigration to the United Kingdom is on the rise.

Finding the Word: Words That Can Be Confused

eminent	an eminent scientist
imminent	his imminent arrival
emission	an emission of gases
omission	An apostrophe can mark the omission of letters.
emphasis	Give the line more emphasis.
emphasize	Try to emphasize your good points.
employee	a loyal employee
employer	a fair employer
entomologist	an entomologist's guide to butterflies
etymologist	an etymologist studying the history of words
envelop	Clouds and mist envelop the mountains.
envelope	Put the letter in a brown envelope.
equable	an equable temperament
equitable	an equitable settlement
ere	ere long
err	to err on the side of caution
erotic	an erotic dance
erratic	an erratic radio signal
escapement	the clock's escapement mechanism
escarpment	He climbed the escarpment.
ewe	a ewe and her lambs
yew	a dark yew tree
you	you and me

executioner	The executioner raised his axe.
executor	He was appointed as executor of the will.
exercise	If you want to get fit, try to exercise every day.
exorcize/ exorcise	The priest was able to exorcize the demons.
expand	to expand and contract
expend	Do not expend energy unnecessarily.
expansive	an expansive manner
expensive	an expensive car
expatiate	to expatiate on the topic of the free market
expiate	trying to expiate his sins
extant	an extant manuscript
extinct	an extinct animal like the mammoth
fain	I would fain be his wife.
feign	Some animals feign death to escape predators.
faint	to fall down in a faint; a faint glimmer
feint	The fencer distracted his opponent with a feint.
fair	We took the children to the fair. a fair fight
fare	I have paid my train fare. He fared well in the fight.

Finding the Word: Words That Can Be Confused

fallen	The leaves have fallen.
fell	He fell dead at her feet.
felled	He felled trees to build a cabin.
fatal	a fatal blow
fateful	on that fateful day
fate	His fate is sealed.
fête	at the village fête
farther	farther than the eye can see
father	My father is a banker.
faun	A faun is a rural deity in Roman legend.
fawn	Don't fawn all over me.
	a young deer fawn
	Fawn is a light greyish-brown colour.
feat	a great feat of strength
feet	The clown had big feet.
fearful	Being in the thunderstorm was a fearful experience.
fearsome	a fearsome growl
ferment	A brewer has to ferment barley and hops to make beer.
foment	to foment civil unrest
fiancé	her fiancé
fiancée	his fiancée
filed	The dentist filed the tooth down.
filled	She filled the hall with admirers.

final	his final performance
finale	the act just before the big finale
fir	a fir tree
fur	a fur coat
fission	nuclear fission
fissure	a fissure in the rock
flair	He shows flair and imagination in his work.
flare	The captain of the drifting ship sent up a warning flare.
flammable	flammable materials
inflammable	an inflammable gas
flaunt	to flaunt new clothes
flout	to flout the rules
flea	a flea bite
flee	to flee the country
flew	We flew business class.
flu	Flu can be a dangerous thing for elderly people.
flue	He cleaned out the chimney flue.
flew	We flew first class.
flown	Have you flown first class?
flocks	flocks of starlings
phlox	tall sugar-pink phlox plants

Finding the Word: Words That Can Be Confused

floe	an ice floe
flow	the flow of lava
flounder	He continued to flounder about out of his depth.
founder	Ships often founder on the reefs.
flour	Dough is made with flour and water.
flower	a flower of the rose family
floury	floury rolls
flowery	a flowery speech
font	The minister baptized the baby at the font.
fount	the fount of all wisdom
forage	The dog was forced to forage for scraps of food.
foray	a foray into enemy territory
forbade	I forbade him to leave.
forbidden	He was forbidden to go out.
forceful	He has a strong and forceful personality.
forcible	a forcible entry; a forcible argument
fore	to the fore
four	four and four is eight
forebear	a forebear of mine
forbear	His father forbear from punishing him.

foregone	a foregone conclusion
forgone	I have forgone many pleasures.
forwent	He forwent his usual Sunday walk.
foresaw	He foresaw his own death.
foreseen	She could not have foreseen what happened next.
foreword	The author wrote the foreword to his book.
forward	to move forward not back
forgave	The priest forgave him his sins.
forgiven	His sins were forgiven.
forgot	She forgot her coat.
forgotten	Have you forgotten my name?
formally	The young man bowed formally to the king.
formerly	Mrs Woods, formerly Miss Green
forsaken	He's forsaken all hope.
forsook	She forsook her family.
fort	a hill-fort
forte	His forte is making speeches.
forty	I'll be forty at my next birthday.
forth	to ride forth
fourth	the fourth in line to the throne
foul	a foul smell
fowl	geese and other fowl

Finding the Word: Words That Can Be Confused

found	lost and found
founded	They founded the city of Rome.
franc	a French franc
frank	a frank discussion
freeze	The lakes freeze over in winter.
frieze	A decorative frieze ran along the walls.
froze	the river froze
frozen	the water was frozen
funeral	a funeral march
funereal	a slow funereal pace
gabble	to gabble incoherently
gable	the gable end of the house
gaff	He used a gaff to land the salmon.
gaffe	It was a major gaffe on the part of the minister.
gait	the pony's gait
gate	He shut the gate.
galleon	The Spanish galleon sailed the seas.
gallon	a gallon of water
gambit	his opening gambit
gamut	the whole gamut from A to Z
gamble	The man refused to gamble all his money away.
gambol	Lambs gambol round their mothers.

gaol	Pay the fine or end up in gaol.
goal	to score a goal
gave	My boss gave me two days' notice.
given	I'd rather have been given more time to sort things out.
genie	He let the genie out of the bottle.
genius	Einstein was a genius.
genus	a genus of sparrow
genteel	some genteel company
gentile	Is he a Jew or a gentile?
gentle	a gentle breeze
gild	to gild the lily
guild	a guild of tradesmen
gilt	a gilt necklace
guilt	I felt no guilt.
glacier	A glacier was moving very slowly down the mountain.
glazier	The glazier mended the broken window.
gone	Has he gone away?
went	He went away yesterday.
gorilla	The gorilla is an endangered species.
guerrilla	He joined the guerilla army.
gourmand	A gourmand will eat anything.
gourmet	A gourmet is an expert on the subject of good food.

Finding the Word: Words That Can Be Confused

gradation	There were gradations of colour among the trees on the hillside.
graduation	She wore a gown at her graduation.
grate	a fire in the grate
great	one of the great writers of the nineteenth century
grew	He grew tall.
grown	Hasn't he grown tall?
grief	His grief was great when his father died.
grieve	She was allowed to grieve for her lost youth.
grill	She was told to grill the chicken pieces.
grille	The impact damaged the car's radiator grille.
griped	He complained and griped about almost everything.
gripped	He gripped the axe with both hands.
grisly	a grisly tale of blood and guts
gristly	The gristly meat was very tough.
grizzly	a grizzly bear
grope	to grope about in the dark
group	a group of monkeys
ground	The coffee mill ground the coffee beans. The parachutist hit the ground with a thud.
grounded	The bad weather grounded all the aircraft.

hail	to hail a taxi
	Snow was forecast for the next day.
hale	to be hale and hearty
hair	long brown hair
hare	a mountain hare
half [noun]	half a grapefuit
halve [verb]	Please halve the grapefruit.
hallo	Hallo, how are you?
halo	She saw an angel with a halo.
hangar	an aircraft hangar
hanger	a coat hanger
hanged	The duke was hanged for treason.
hung	She hung the pictures on the wall.
hart	The white hart was small for a male deer.
heart	heart and soul
heal	A doctor's job is to heal the sick.
heel	He had a hole in the heel of his sock.
hear	to hear noises
here	Here he is!
heard	We heard loud noises.
herd	A herd of buffalo thundered by.
hereditary	a hereditary disease
heredity	His behaviour showed traits governed by heredity.

Finding the Word: Words That Can Be Confused

heron	a tall grey heron
herring	shoals of silver herring
hew	to hew a tree
hue	the purple hue of the heather
hewed	They hewed wood.
hewn	The statue was hewn from the solid rock.
hid	She hid in the cupboard.
hidden	She stayed hidden for an hour.
higher	higher up the mountain
hire	He was told to hire a room for the meeting.
him	Do you know him?
hymn	to sing a hymn in church
hoar	hoar frost
whore	She behaved like a whore.
hoard	to hoard money
horde	a horde of football fans
hoarse	His voice became hoarse.
horse	Bucephalus, Napoleon's horse
hole	a hole in the ozone layer
whole	He ate the whole cake.
holy	the holy book of Islam
holey	a holey jumper
wholly	The artist was wholly absorbed in his work.

honorary	an honorary title
honourable	an honourable man
hoop	to jump through a hoop
whoop	a whoop of delight
hoped	She hoped they were safe.
hopped	He hopped around on one leg.
human	a human being
humane	the humane treatment of animals
humiliation	His army had to suffer the humiliation of defeat.
humility	He began to behave with a proper humility.
idle	an idle threat
idol	to worship an idol
illegible	an illegible signature
ineligible	With only a year's service, he's ineligible for promotion.
immorality	vice and immorality
immortality	the immortality of the soul
impetuous	an impetuous young man
impetus	The roar of the crowd was the impetus for action.
imply	Did he imply that I was incompetent?
infer	I infer from what you say that you were angry.

Finding the Word: Words That Can Be Confused

impracticable	An impracticable task is one that cannot be done.
impractical	an impractical solution
	She was an impractical person.
inapt	His comments were particularly inapt.
inept	an inept idiot
incredible	an incredible achievement
incredulous	He wore an incredulous expression.
indigenous	the indigenous people of the Kalahari
indigent	an indigent beggar
industrial	an industrial plant
industrious	the industrious ant
ingenious	an ingenious scheme
ingenuous	a trusting, ingenuous young girl
inhuman	an inhuman absence of emotion
inhumane	inhumane treatment
inimical	Conditions on Mars were found to be inimical to life.
inimitable	His inimitable style of humour was always popular.
intelligent	an intelligent ape
intelligible	a faint, barely intelligible voice
interment	The funeral service was followed by the interment of the body.
internment	a disused internment camp

inveigh	Who was there to inveigh against the blatant injustice of the judgement?
inveigle	He managed to inveigle his way into the meeting.
invertebrate	An invertebrate has no backbone.
inveterate	an inveterate smoker
its [= *belonging to it*]	The pony tossed its head.
it's [= *it is*]	It's a long way from home.
jam	butter and jam to jam on the brakes There was a huge traffic jam in the busy street.
jamb	to lean against the door jamb
jib	The pony might jib at that high fence. A jib sail is set forward of the foremast.
jibe	It was a spiteful jibe.
judicial	a judicial review
judicious	a judicious move
junction	a railway junction
juncture	at this juncture
key	the key to a door
quay	They began to unload the cargo onto the quay.
knave	You rogue, you knave!
nave	the nave of the cathedral

Finding the Word: Words That Can Be Confused

knead	The baker slowly began to knead the dough.
kneed	His attacker kneed him in the groin.
need	I need hospital treatment.
knew	She knew my name.
known	She hadn't known it yesterday.
knew	I knew the answer.
new	a new car
knight	a knight in shining armour
night	a long dark night
knightly	knightly chivalry
nightly	It happens nightly.
knit	He knit his brow.
	Knit me a warm scarf.
knitted	She knitted me a warm scarf.
nit	I can see a nit in her hair.
knot	to tie a knot
not	It's not fair!
knotty	a knotty problem
naughty	You naughty child!
know	I know who he is.
no	He's no friend of mine.
known	Have you known him long?
knew	I knew him in school.

A Guide to Letter-Writing

laid	The hen laid an egg.
lay	The kittens lay in a manger.
laid	laid end to end
lied	He lied about his age.
lain	It had lain undisturbed for centuries.
lane	a three-lane motorway
lair	the wolf's lair
layer	a layer of blubber under the skin
lama	a Tibetan lama or priest
llama	The llama's wool is used to make clothing
laterally	The crab moved laterally.
latterly	Latterly, they'd lived in Italy.
lath	a lath and plaster wall
lathe	to turn wood on a lathe
lea	the grassy lea
lee	in the lee of the mountain; on a lee shore
lead	to lead the way
led	The path led through a thicket.
leak	The bath sprung a leak.
leek	Chop a leek or a large onion for the soup.
lessen	to lessen the impact
lesson	a history lesson

Finding the Word: Words That Can Be Confused

liable	to be liable for costs
libel	to sue for libel
liar	a liar and a cheat
lyre	plucking a golden lyre
licence [*noun*]	a driving licence
license [*verb*]	It was their job to license the sale of alcohol.
lightening	She bought peroxide for lightening her hair.
lightning	thunder and lightning
lineament	facial lineaments
liniment	a soothing liniment
liqueur	a coffee liqueur
liquor	strong liquor
literal	the literal meaning
literary	a literary prize
literate	Most peasants were not literate.
load	a heavy load
lode	The mother lode lay close to the entrance of the mine.
loan	a bank loan
lone	a lone wolf
loath/loth	They were loath to challenge his authority. We were loth to get up.
loathe	I loathe getting up early.

local	the local shops
locale	an ideal locale for a new shopping centre
looped	She looped the wool over the needle.
loped	The wolf loped along keeping pace with the deer.
lopped	He lopped the top off the bush.
loose	a loose shirt
lose	to lose money
loot	the robbers' loot
lute	Not many people know how to play the lute.
lumbar	She had pain in the lower lumbar region.
lumber	The useless bits and pieces were stored in the lumber room.
	Don't lumber me with that stuff.
luxuriant	luxuriant vegetation
luxurious	The young girl lived in a luxurious apartment
macaroni	macaroni and cheese
macaroon	a macaroon bar
made	made in Sweden
maid	The maid turned down the bed.
magnate	a shipping magnate
magnet	Iron filings are drawn to a magnet.

Finding the Word: Words That Can Be Confused

mail	to mail a letter
male	A male elephant is called a bull elephant.
main	the main road
mane	a horse's mane
maize	maize flour
maze	the maze at Hampton Court
maniac	a maniac is loose
manic	His behaviour is rather manic today.
manner	Her manner was aloof.
manor	the lord of the manor
mare	a mare and her foal
mayor	the mayor of New York
marina	There were lots of yachts in the marina.
merino	merino wool
marshal	The general began to marshal his troops.
martial	judo and other martial arts
marten	a pine marten
martin	a sand martin
mask	a Halloween mask
masque	Balls and masques were popular at court.
mat	A letter lay on the mat.
matt	matt brown

mean	a mean old man
mien	He had a solemn mien.
meat	meat and potatoes
meet	Meet me at seven tonight.
	The huntsmen attended the meet before the hunt began.
mete out	to mete out punishment
medal	a silver medal
meddle	Do not meddle with things you know nothing about.
mediate	He tried to mediate between the feuding clans.
meditate	There was no time to meditate on life's mysteries.
metal	a metal spoon
mettle	to show one's mettle
mews	Horses were once stabled in the mews.
muse	his creative muse
might	the might of Rome
mite	a tiny crawling mite
militate	His poor health was to militate against his success as an athlete.
mitigate	Some environmental laws are created to mitigate the effects of pollution.
miner	a coal miner
minor	a minor problem

Finding the Word: Words That Can Be Confused

minister	minister of this parish
minster	York Minster
mistaken	I think you may be mistaken.
mistook	I mistook him for his twin brother.
moat	The castle was surrounded by a moat.
mote	Motes of dust were caught in the sunlight.
modal	a modal verb
model	a model citizen
module	the command module of a spacecraft
momentary	a momentary lapse
momentous	on this momentous occasion
momentum	to gather momentum
moose	Moose wander the streets of Anchorage.
mouse	a house mouse
mousse	Chocolate mousse is delicious.
moral	the moral of the story
morale	Morale on the ship was very low.
morality	Many people question the morality of capital punishment.
mortality	There was a high mortality rate amongst the elderly residents.
motif	the central motif in a design
motive	What was his motive for killing her?
mucous [*adj*]	mucous membrane
mucus [*noun*]	mucus from the nose

multiple	multiples of six
multiply	He was asked to multiply six by six.
muscle	He's strained a muscle.
mussel	cockles and mussels
mystic	a renowned mystic and holy man
mystique	part of her mystique
naturalist	a famous naturalist
naturist	Naked naturists were walking on the beach.
naught	His plans came to naught.
nought	A one and a nought together is the number ten.
naval	naval uniform
navel	She wore a jewel in her navel.
navvy	He was a navvy working on the railways.
navy	a navy ship
nay	All those who don't agree say 'nay'.
nèe	Mrs Gibbons nèe Foster
neigh	The horse gave a loud neigh.
negligent	She was found to be negligent in her duty.
negligible	There was a negligible amount of radio-activity.
net	a fishing net
nett	to pay wages nett; his nett income

Finding the Word: Words That Can Be Confused

northerly	a northerly wind
northern	the northern states
nougat	Nougat with hazelnuts is a popular sweet.
nugget	a nugget of gold
oar	A gondola is a boat propelled by a single oar.
ore	iron ore
obsolete	Recent advances have rendered the process obsolete.
obsolescent	obsolescent technology
of	a cup of tea; a glass of wine
off	We are off on holiday.
	to fall off something
official	an official letter
officious	He was approached by an officious little man with a clipboard.
ordinance	by royal ordinance
ordnance	military ordnance or supplies
organism	An organism can be any living plant or animal including any bacterium or virus.
orgasm	to reach orgasm
outdid	She outdid all others.
outdone	They were outdone.
overcame	She overcame many difficulties.
overcome	There were many difficulties to overcome.

A GUIDE TO LETTER-WRITING

overran   Hordes of rampaging tribesmen overran the village.
overrun   The city was overrun.

overtaken   He was overtaken by a truck.
overtook   The truck overtook him on a bend.

overthrew   They overthrew the dictator.
overthrown   The dictator was overthrown.

packed   They packed the hall.
pact   a suicide pact

pail   a pail of water
pale   She went pale as a sheet.

pain   a pain in my side
pane   The ball broke a pane of glass.

pair   a pair of shoes
pare   to pare the skin off an apple
pear   Would you prefer a pear or a banana?

palate   the soft palate on the roof of your mouth
palette   an artist's palette
pallet   a pallet of bricks

par   Par for the golf course was 72.
parr   A salmon parr is a salmon of up to two years of age.

passed   She passed her driving test.
past   She enjoyed driving past the school.

Finding the Word: Words That Can Be Confused

pastel	pastel shades
pastille	a throat pastille
pâté	chicken liver pâté
patty	a meat patty or burger
peace	peace in our time
piece	a piece of cheese
peak	the distinctive peak of the Matterhorn
peek	Please take a peek at the baby.
pique	He left the room in a fit of pique.
peal	the peal of church bells
peel	orange peel
pearl	a freshwater pearl
purl	a purl stitch in knitting
peasant	a red-faced peasant
pheasant	a brace of pheasant
pedal	to pedal faster
peddle	to peddle wares around a town
peer	a peer of the realm
pier	The pier was damaged by the storm.
pendant	She wore a heavy silver pendant.
pendent	a shrub with pendent blooms
perquisite	tips and other perquisites such as the use of a company car
prerequisite	A pass in maths is a prerequisite for entry

perpetrate	to perpetrate a crime
perpetuate	Please do not perpetuate these myths.
personal	my personal opinion
personnel	army personnel
petrel	The petrel, a tiny bird, stays at sea for most of its life.
petrol	a petrol engine
phenomena	to study natural phenomena
phenomenon	a rare phenomenon
pidgin	Pidgin English is a language made up of two or more languages including English.
pigeon	a racing pigeon
pined	She pined for her lover.
pinned	The general pinned the medal on his lapel.
piped	They piped the oil across Asia.
pipped	to be pipped at the post
place	a place of my own
plaice	plaice and other flat fish
plain	plain cooking
plane	a fighter plane
plaintiff	the plaintiff and the defendant in a court case
plaintive	The young wolf let out a plaintive cry.

Finding the Word: Words That Can Be Confused

plait	She asked her friend to plait her hair.
plate	a dinner plate
plum	plum jam; a plum job
plumb	to plumb the depths
politic	It would not be politic to disagree with him.
political	a political meeting
pool	a pool of blood
pull	to pull the plug
poplar	a poplar tree
popular	a popular song
pore	to pore over the documents A pore is a small opening in the skin.
pour	to pour tea
pored	He pored over the documents.
poured	She poured some tea.
poser	He set us a bit of a poser.
poseur	He's such a poseur!
practicable	It's not practicable to do it that way.
practical	a practical solution
practice [*noun*]	Practice makes perfect.
practise [*verb*]	She had to practise every day.
pray	to pray to God
prey	The wolf's usual prey was in short supply.

precede	Will the speeches precede or follow dinner?
proceed	They will proceed on a signal from the commander.
premier	The Russian premier was greeted by the US president.
premiere	The premiere of the film was attended by many famous stars.
price	The salesman decided not to cut the price.
prise	to prise open a jar
prize	to win first prize
principal	the principal reason; a school principal
principle	a first principle; a man of principle
private	The wedding was a private function.
privet	A privet hedge enclosed the garden.
prodigy	a child prodigy
protégé	a protégé of the famous director
profit	to profit by others' mistakes
prophet	a prophet of doom
program	a computer program
programme	a TV programme
proof	The police need more proof.
prove	They can't prove he did it.
property	You're trespassing on private property.
propriety	The duchess always behaved with the utmost propriety.

Finding the Word: Words That Can Be Confused

prophecy [*noun*] Cassandra had the gift of prophecy.
prophesy [*verb*] The cult leader continued to prophesy the end of the world.

prostate	the prostate gland in men
prostrate	The people lay prostrate before their king.
put	to put on a coat
putt	The golfer left himself with a short putt to the hole.
quash	to quash the rumours
squash	to squash a fly
quiet	quiet as a mouse
quite	It was quite a long journey.
racket	Stop that racket!
racquet	a tennis racquet
radar	The planes flew so low they were undetectable by radar.
raider	The pine marten is a raider of birds' nests.
raged	He raged and beat his fists on the table.
ragged	a ragged beggar
rain	Heavy rain was forecast for the day of the wedding.
reign	in the reign of Elizabeth I
rein	She was told to keep the horse on a short rein.

raise	to raise a flag
raze	The demolition expert was told to raze the building to the ground.
rampant	a rampant infection
rampart	Guards could be seen pacing the castle rampart.
ran	I ran all the way home.
run	Earlier, I'd run all the way to school.
rang	Who rang a moment ago?
ringed	They ringed all the eagle chicks.
rung	He had rung several times that day.
rap	a rap on the door
wrap	Wrap yourself in this towel.
raped	The woman was raped by her attacker.
rapped	He rapped on the door.
rapt	The children sat in front of him, rapt with attention.
wrapped	The parcel was wrapped in brown paper.
rated	The film is rated PG.
ratted	Who ratted on him to the police?
read	Have you read Little Women?
red	a red poppy
read	When did you read *Little Women*?
reed	a tall species of reed

Finding the Word: Words That Can Be Confused

real	in real life
reel	a reel of cotton
refuge	to take refuge from a storm
refugee	a refugee from the war
regal	a regal lion
regale	He often used to regale us with stories of his adventures.
relief	Analgesics provide relief from the symptoms of flu.
relieve	The doctor gave her patient some morphine to relieve her pain.
respectful	a respectful silence
respective	The two women went off to meet their respective husbands.
rest	to take a short rest
wrest	The thief tried to wrest the handbag from the old lady's grip.
retch	to retch at a disgusting smell
wretch	a pathetic wretch
review	The theatre critic wrote a scathing review.
revue	Many comedians have their first success in a student revue.
rhyme	Is there a word to rhyme with 'orange'?
rime	The frosty rime on the trees and shrubs glinted in the sun.

ridden	She'd never ridden before.
rode	He rode a magnificent black horse.
right	Is this right or wrong? Is this left or right?
rite	an ancient Druid rite
wright	The shipwright had helped to build many ships.
write	He loved to write poems.
ring	to ring a bell
wring	to wring out a cloth; to wring someone's neck
risen	He'd risen at six.
rose	He rose and made himself a cup of tea.
road	The road was icy.
rode	He rode at full tilt.
rowed	They rowed out to the ship.
rode	He rode a magnificent white stallion.
roe	Some people like to eat fried cods' roe.
row	a row of chairs
role	He played a leading role in local politics.
roll	a roll of wallpaper
rose	He rose at five in the morning.
risen	The sun had just risen.
rote	The children were learning the rules off by heart, that is by rote.
wrote	He wrote many plays.

Finding the Word: Words That Can Be Confused

rough	a rough surface
ruff	The little bird had a ruff of feathers around its neck.
rout	The soldiers were determined to rout enemy.
route	a more direct route to work
run	I'd run a mile.
ran	He ran the marathon.
rung	We'd rung the doorbell several times.
wrung	She wrung her hands in despair.
rye	Do you like rye bread?
wry	a wry smile
sail	to sail a yacht
sale	There were some good bargains in the spring sale.
salon	a hairdressing salon
saloon	Some saloon cars have four doors, some have two.
sang	We sang all the songs we knew.
sung	Have you ever sung in public?
sank	The snake sank its fangs into my leg.
sunk	The cake had sunk in the middle.
sunken	The sick child had sunken cheeks.
saviour	The new coach was the saviour of the failing football team.
savour	He wanted time to savour the moment.

saw	I saw him fall.
seen	Have you seen this film?
sawed	They sawed the trees into planks.
sawn	Sawn wood was sent to the factory.
scared	scared of mice
scarred	scarred for life
scene	a scene of destruction
seen	Owls are rarely seen during the day.
sceptic	a religious sceptic
septic	The wound became septic and she had to take antibiotics.
scraped	He scraped together enough money to buy a new car.
scrapped	He scrapped his old car.
sculptor	a famous sculptor
sculpture	Her sculptures were large and abstract.
seam	I burst the back seam of my trousers.
seem	Didn't it seem strange to you?
sear	to sear meat in a dry frying-pan
seer	a seer's prophesy
secret	Tell me a secret.
secrete	The pores secrete sweat.
sensual	a sensual experience
sensuous	slow sensuous movements

Finding the Word: Words That Can Be Confused

series	a radio series
serious	Crime is a serious subject.
sew	to sew a button on
so	So, this is your sister.
sow	to sow corn
sewed	She sewed all evening.
sewn	She'd sewn on the buttons first.
sewer	An open sewer carried away the surface water and sewage.
	She was a skilful sewer.
sower	a sower of seeds
sewn	The label was sewn into the jacket's lining.
sown	These seeds were sown last autumn.
sextant	He was told to plot their position using a sextant.
sexton	the sexton of the local church
shaken	shaken not stirred
shook	He shook his fist at the other motorist.
shear	to shear a sheep
sheer	a sheer drop
sheared	He sheared the sheep.
sheered	The pipe was sheered off.
shorn	The young boy had his hair shorn.
shelf	on the top shelf
shelve	to shelve a cupboard; to shelve a project

shoe	a ballet shoe
shoo	She tried to shoo the hens away.
showed	He showed us into a side room.
shown	We were shown into a side room.
shrank	My jumper shrank in the wash.
shrunk	It had shrunk by two sizes.
singeing	The cat lay singeing its tail at the fire.
singing	Singing a happy song always made him feel better.
sinuous	a sinuous snake
sinus	a blocked sinus
skies	the skies above and the earth beneath
skis	He skis in Switzerland every winter.
slain	The dragon was slain after a great and lengthy fight.
slew	The knight slew the dragon.
slated	a slated roof or floor
	The theatre critic slated the actor's performance.
slatted	a slatted blind
slay	He tried to slay the dragon.
sleigh	They rode in a horse-drawn sleigh through the snow.
sloe	She made sloe gin every autumn.
slow	a slow pace

Finding the Word: Words That Can Be Confused

sloped	The hill sloped gently towards the sea.
slopped	Water slopped out of the bucket.
smelled/smelt	She smelled/smelt the roses in the garden below.
smelt	They smelt iron in the foundry's furnace.
sniped	He sniped at us with sarcastic comments.
snipped	She snipped the heads off the flowers.
soar	to soar above the clouds
sore	She had a very sore head.
sociable	a sociable person
social	a social event
solder	He was able to solder the two pieces of metal together.
soldier	The soldier came home on leave.
sole	the sole survivor
soul	He loved her body and soul.
some	some people
sum	a large sum of money
son	He was the son of a miner.
sun	The earth moves round the sun.
soot	The chimneysweep was covered in soot.
suit	a suit of clothes
southerly	a southerly wind
southern	a southern county

A Guide to Letter-Writing

sowed	The farmer sowed seed.
sown	The seed was sown in the late autumn.
spared	She was spared further distress.
sparred	The boxers sparred with each other.
speciality	a speciality of the restaurant
specialty	Diseases of the intestine are his specialty.
species	a species of marsupial
specious	a false and specious argument
sped	They sped along at over 100 miles per hour.
speeded	We speeded up and overtook him.
spoke	He spoke first.
spoken	He had spoken to me yesterday.
sprang	The kitten sprang out of the box.
sprung	The boiler had sprung a leak.
staid	He's becoming very staid in his old age.
stayed	They stayed in touch by letter.
stair	Every second stair in the staircase creaked.
stare	It's rude to stare at people.
stake	He knew he had to drive a stake through the vampire's heart.
steak	He loved to eat steak and chips every night for his supper.

Finding the Word: Words That Can Be Confused

stalk	The lion was able to stalk its prey in the long grass.
	a flower stalk
stock	They had a good stock of dry goods.
stank	His boots stank of manure.
stunk	His clothes had stunk of cigarette smoke for days.
stared	She stared at me in amazement.
starred	The young actress starred in a West End play.
stationary	a stationary vehicle
stationery	the stationery cupboard
statue	a statue of Nelson
statute	written in statute; on the statute book
staunch	He was a staunch supporter of his local football team.
stanch	to stanch the blood from a wound.
steal	The boy tried to steal someone's bike.
steel	a steel door
step	to take one step forwards
steppe	the Russian steppes
stile	to climb over a stile
style	a painting in the Dutch style
stimulant	Caffeine is a stimulant.
stimulus	The plant reacts to the stimulus of light.

stocked	Is your larder stocked for the winter?
stoked	He stoked the engine's boiler.
storey	a single storey building
story	Please tell us a story.
straight	She decided to go straight home to her mother.
strait	The ship had to sail through a narrow strait.
straightened	He straightened his tie.
straitened	The old couple were now in straitened circumstances.
strewed	They strewed flowers at his feet.
strewn	The path was strewn with flowers.
strife	The depression caused strife and political unrest.
strive	to strive to succeed
striped	A tiger has a striped coat.
stripped	First he stripped the paint off the walls.
striven	They had striven to make amends.
strove	She strove to succeed.
sty	a pig's sty
stye	a stye on the eyelid
style	The author had a distinctive writing style.
stile	He climbed over the stile.

Finding the Word: Words That Can Be Confused

suede	suede shoes
swede	He did not enjoy eating boiled swede.
suite	a suite of rooms
sweet	Sweet foods are usually not good for you.
summary	The police inspector provided a summary of progress so far.
summery	summery clothes
sundae	an ice cream sundae
Sunday	Saturday and Sunday
sung	The national anthem is sung at morning assembly.
sang	They sang songs all the way.
super	a super day
supper	Supper is at eight o'clock.
surplice	the bishop's surplice
surplus	surplus goods
swam	He swam in the lake.
swum	Have you ever swum underwater?
swelled	The sail swelled in the wind.
swollen	Many rivers are swollen with the recent heavy rain.
swingeing	There were swingeing cuts in the budget.
swinging	The monkeys were swinging through the trees.

swore	He swore revenge.
sworn	He had sworn revenge.
tacks	The carpet tacks were all in place.
tax	Do you pay income tax?
tail	The pig has a curly tail.
tale	The old sailor knew many tales of the sea.
taken	He's taken a bus into town.
took	He took the train yesterday.
taped	They taped around the windows to stop draughts.
tapped	He tapped on the window to catch their attention.
taught	He taught maths and science for many years.
taut	Her skin was taut after the facial.
tea	tea and cakes
tee	A golf tee can be made of wood or plastic.
team	a football team
teem	to teem with fish
tear	to tear along the dotted line
tare	The lorry had a tare weight of 6 tons.
tear	A tear rolled down her cheek.
tier	a three-tier wedding cake

Finding the Word: Words That Can Be Confused

teeth	lovely white teeth
teethe	When do babies usually start to teethe?
temporal	the spiritual and temporal life of a community
temporary	He had to find temporary lodgings while his house was being built.
tendon	The athlete strained a tendon.
tenon	a mortise and tenon joint
tenor	a tenor voice
tenure	His tenure in office was short.
testimonial	She had glowing testimonials from several important people.
testimony	The witness gave his testimony to the court.
their	Their house is next to mine.
there	Are you there?
they're	They're coming tomorrow.
theirs	Is this land yours or theirs?
there's	There's my mother.
thorough	a thorough investigation
through	to look through binoculars
thrash	to thrash an opposing team
thresh	to thresh corn
threw	He threw the ball.
through	The ball went through the window.

A GUIDE TO LETTER-WRITING

threw	She threw the ball up into the air.
thrown	The ball was thrown up into the air.
throes	in the throes of war
throws	two throws of the dice
throne	One day he will ascend the throne as king.
thrown	They were thrown sideways by the blast.
through	through thick and thin
thorough	a thorough cleaning
thyme	parsley and thyme
time	a long time ago
tic	a nervous tic
tick	There was a tick after every correct answer.
tiled	He tiled the bathroom.
tilled	The farmer tilled the soil.
timber	a timber frame
timbre	the timbre of a voice
toe	She stubbed her toe on a rock.
tow	Their car could tow a caravan.
tomb	the tomb of the Unknown Warrior
tome	Dusty tomes lined the shelves of his library.
too	He loves me and I love him too.
to	Go to the end of the road.
two	Two and two is four.

Finding the Word: Words That Can Be Confused

took	He took his pills an hour ago.
taken	Have you taken your medicine?
topi	He was wearing a topi to protect his head from the sun.
toupee	We saw a bald man trying on a toupee.
tore	He tore it in half.
torn	The ticket had been torn in half.
tortuous	There was a tortuous route up the mountain.
torturous	I had to spend a torturous hour listening to him go on and on.
trait	a character trait
tray	a tray for the tea things
treaties	International treaties are common among the countries of the world.
treatise	He had prepared a treatise on ethics.
trod	The horse trod on my foot.
trodden	You've trodden on something smelly.
troop	The soldier was well enough to join his troop training in the desert.
troupe	a troupe of monkeys
turban	Sikh men wear turbans.
turbine	a gas turbine
tycoon	a media tycoon
typhoon	a typhoon in the China Sea

A Guide to Letter-Writing

unaware	We were unaware of his presence.
unawares	He tried to catch her unawares.
unconscionable	an unconscionable rogue
unconscious	an unconscious patient
undid	By one foolish act, he undid all his good work.
undone	He often left his work undone.
uninterested	to be uninterested in politics
disinterested	to take a disinterested view
unwanted	She gave all her unwanted items of furniture and clothing to charity.
unwonted	It was an unwonted piece of good fortune.
urban	the urban landscape
urbane	a cultured and urbane man
vacation	a summer vacation
vocation	Teaching is his vocation.
vain	a vain attempt; a vain man
vane	A weather vane shows which way the wind is blowing.
vein	The drug was injected into the vein.
vale	the vale of Evesham
veil	The bride wore a veil over her face.
venal	Venal and dishonest officials are open to bribery.
venial	A venial sin is a sin easily forgiven.

Finding the Word: Words That Can Be Confused

veracity	The prosecution tried to question the veracity of his statement.
voracity	The voracity of his appetite was making him overweight.
vertex	Can you see the keystone at the vertex of the arch?
vortex	The car was swept up into the vortex of the tornado.
vicious	a vicious dog
viscous	A viscous fluid is thick and sticky.
vigilant	The security firm kept a vigilant guard on the factory.
vigilante	They formed a vigilante group bent on revenge.
wafer	an ice cream wafer
waver	He didn't waver from his purpose.
waged	The two countries waged war for five years.
wagged	The puppy wagged its tail.
waif	a waif and stray
waive	to waive a fee
wave	to wave goodbye
waist	a slim waist
waste	to waste money
wander	He likes to wander in the hills.
wonder	I wonder who she is?

A GUIDE TO LETTER-WRITING

want	You always want more.
wont	He went alone, as is his wont.
warden	She was warden of the sheltered housing.
warder	a prison warder
ware	tinware; silverware
wear	to wear clothes
way	He found a quicker way home.
weigh	She had forgotten to weigh the flour.
weak	a weak smile
week	seven days a week
weather	The weather forecast is good for the rest of the week.
whether	
weekly	Many magazines are published weekly.
weakly	The puppy whimpered weakly.
were	We were lost.
where	We asked where to go next.
westerly	a westerly breeeze
western	the western boundary
wet	Wet your hair and apply shampoo.
whet	He had an appetizer to whet his appetite.
which	Which is which?
witch	She was an evil witch.

Finding the Word: Words That Can Be Confused

whit	I don't care a whit.
wit	He was a man of wit and wisdom.
whoa	Whoa, not so fast!
woe	Oh, woe is me!
whose	Whose chair is this?
who's	Who's at the door?
willed	The marathon runner willed himself to go on.
would	He would have finished the race if he had not got cramp.
winded	The rider fell off his horse and winded himself.
wound	The path wound round and round the mountain.
withdrawn	His wife had withdrawn all their savings.
withdrew	The young man withdrew £10 from the bank.
woe	Woe betide you if you arrive late.
woo	The handsome prince came to woo the princess.
woke	She woke with a start.
woken	She asked to be woken in time for breakfast.
wonder	I wonder where they are.
wander	They tend to wander from place to place.

wood	The boat was made of wood.
wooed	He wooed her with flowers.
would	I would if I could.
wore	She wore green.
worn	I haven't worn these shoes before.
wove	They wove threads of gold and silver through the white.
woven	This material is woven on a loom.
wreak	It was their intention to wreak havoc on the enemy.
wreck	to wreck someone's plans; to cause the wreck of a ship
wreath	a funeral wreath
wreathe	We like to wreathe the Christmas tree with tinsel.
written	Have you written to your grandmother?
wrote	He wrote to the bank.
yoke	The farmer put the heavy wooden yoke on the two oxen.
yolk	The yolk of an egg is yellow.
yore	in days of yore
your	Please can I have your attention.

Part 2

Sample letters

This section of the book contains sample letters, with more precise guidance on specific categories of letter.

> These samples are intended as illustrations of how letters may be worded and should not be copied exactly.

Before you start writing, here are a few useful questions, which may help you to get your letter into shape:

- What is the purpose of this letter?
- Is it a personal or a business letter?
- Is it a formal or informal letter?
- Who is going to read the letter and in what circumstances will they be reading it?
- Do I have a clear ideas of my aims? What do I hope to get out of writing this letter or what do I hope the recipient will get out of it? (It is sometimes a good idea to jot down your most important aims beforehand.)
- What specific information do I need to provide in this letter? Facts should be mustered and presented in a clear and accessible way.

Employment

Many of the formal letters we write relate to employment. Here, as with most kinds of business letter, you should, in general, aim for brevity.

Letters of application generally take two forms – letters applying for advertised posts and speculative letters written to investigate possible job opportunities.

Speculative letters are mostly written by younger people who are just leaving school or further education and looking for their first job. Young job-seekers should be prepared to bombard the firms operating in the areas in which they are most interested. They should also be prepared for disappointment: there may be no job available and they may get a letter of rejection; or, more discouragingly, they may not receive any acknowledgement at all of their letters. It can be extremely depressing for job-seekers to send off multiple letters and be met with complete silence. The most likely reason is that the employer receives so many speculative job applications they cannot reply to all of them and so getting no reply is not usually a reflection of the employer's opinion of the applicant.

If you are writing a letter that is not in reply to an advertisement and you don't know to whom to address the letter, a quick phone call to the firm should provide you with the relevant name, or at the very least, the department. Reasonably large firms will have a personnel or human resources' manager.

If your letter is a reply to an advertisement you should obviously answer any questions or comply with any requirements made in the advertisement. Sometimes a CV is asked for, in which case the cover letter should be a brief one stating why you are right for the job. Usually, you will need to send a CV and a brief typed letter which sells you and your skills to the firm.

The CV (called 'the résumé' in the United States) is a central part of most job applications. Because presentation is so important, many people choose to have their CVs compiled by a professional agency. Even if you don't do this, your CV must be neatly set out and give a general air of professionalism.

CVs often look remarkably similar so it can be a good idea to personalize either the CV or the covering letter, or both, to bring attention to your application. However, don't make the design or layout too idiosyncratic just in order to attract attention.

Both the CV and the covering letter should be typed unless otherwise stated, although it is quite common for firms to ask for covering letters to be handwritten.

Many firms and organizations send out application forms. These can be quite challenging, especially if they include such questions as 'Why do you want this post?' or 'What qualities do you feel you could bring to this post?' There are many specialist courses and publications on how to tackle job applications and interviews to best effect, and it may be worthwhile considering some of those.

Until quite recently it was the preferred practice to put just about everything the applicant had ever done, or was ever interested in, on the CV. For people in the middle of their career, this could make for a very long and crowded document which took a long time for prospective employers to digest. The preference nowadays is to keep the CV fairly brief, paring it down to a record of personal details, qualifications and employment.

Many employers now rely more on the letter accompanying the CV to spark their interest. These covering letters are a good opportunity for applicants to sell themselves to prospective employers. The covering letter's main purpose is to accompany your CV, to introduce you and your credentials to the employer, to generate interest in you and to encourage the employer to grant you an interview.

CV (curriculum vitae) and résumé

It is important that CVs are set out neatly and attractively. Many people nowadays choose to take advantage of the design features and templates offered in modern computer programs.

Employers are invariably dealing with many applications per vacancy and they are often also working to tight deadlines. They will make their first decision on your application by scanning your covering letter and your CV/résumé, and, while scanning, they will often be searching for a few keywords which

A GUIDE TO LETTER-WRITING

will alert them to the fact that you fit the profile of the person they are looking for. The processing of job applications is very tedious task for most employers, so if you make their life easier they are more likely to take a positive attitude to you.

And, make no mistake: any letter or CV/résumé that is difficult to read or navigate through will be discarded.

What a well-presented CV and covering letter should do

Attract the employer to read the CV immediately and before those of other applicants.
Get across the sense that you have wider skills than the brief descriptions in your CV.
Guide the employer to the key areas of your history.
Give the employer a positive picture of you and your abilities.
Get you an interview for the job.

The following two samples give some guidance on the kind of content that might appear in a simple one-page CV and in a one-page résumé.

Sample Letters

Curriculum vitae of an experienced candidate

CURRICULUM VITAE
John Smith

65 Queen's Road
Blackford
Whiteshire
BD14 7 RT
Telephone: 01341 666888
Email: j.smith290@rapiddigi.co.uk

Date of birth: 24 February 1981

Employment 2003–2005
Chief Translator, Chemec plc, Birchingham

Employment 2002–2003
Head of Translation, Publications Department, Chemec plc, Birchingham

Employment 2001–2002
Translator, Publications Department, Unitech Ltd, Newridge

Further education 1998–2001
Glasburgh University
Dean Square
Glasburgh
Blackshire
GB3 9RF
Degree: BA (Honours) French and German
Upper Second class

Secondary education 1992–1998
Raxworth Grammar School
25 Beach Road
High Raxworth
Braxshire
RX4 8DG
GCSEs: English, French, Maths, Spanish, History, German, Geography, Art
A levels: English Grade A, French Grade B, Spanish Grade B

Leisure activities
Hill-walking, photography, cinema, theatre

Referees

Robert Adams
Editorial Director
Chemec plc
37 Sea Way
Birchingham
BL5 9K6

Peter Schwartz
Head of Publications
Unitech Ltd
154 Plain Street
Newridge
NR4 8RT

US résumé of an experienced candidate

In the US, it is usual practice to restrict a résumé to a single sheet of paper, headed with the applicant's name, and with his or her career objectives somewhere near the top of the page.

HENRY APPLEGARD	
Date of Birth	March 10 1966
Objective	Vice-president Sales
Employment 2002–2006 MechHit Inc. Evendale NY	**National Sales Manager** Increased sales from $175 million to $285 million. Suggested new product lines that increased earnings by 28%.
Employment 1996–2002 Carter & Fotheringham Northlea NY	**Regional Sales Manager** Increased regional sales from $150 million to $200 million. Managed 150 sales representatives in 10 states.
Employment 1991–1996 McCord & Pickle Caronville NY	**Senior Sales Representative** Expanded sales team from 30 to 60. Developed and implemented incentive scheme for sales force. Developed training scheme for new recruits.
Employment 1989–1991 Hammerheads Inc. Chicago MI	**Sales Representative** Increased sales by 150%. Received company's highest sales award 1990, 1991.
Education 1985–1989 University of Michigan	**B.A., Business Administration and Computer Science.** Graduated summa cum laude.
Interests	Computers, sailing, theatre

Covering letter accompanying a CV

The covering letter that accompanies the CV can be just as, or more, important than the CV.

Dos

Your covering letter should contain a brief account of all the features, qualifications and experience that make you ideal for the advertised post:

- do generate the reader's interest in the first paragraph, and state your interest in the job;
- do promote your potential value by focussing on the employer's needs and highlighting your strengths and abilities;
- do provide a background summary of education and/or experience;
- do try to include a statement that encourages a positive response;
- do include a final statement of appreciation, such as:

Thank you.
Thank you for your consideration.

Don'ts

Any or all of the following can contribute to lack of impact and efficacy and should be avoided in your covering letter:

- don't ramble;
- don't be pushy;
- avoid self-deprecation – it can be irritating and professional interviewers are not usually convinced by an 'ever so humble' approach;
- don't exaggerate or brag;

- don't focus too much on your own needs, ignoring the needs of the employer;
- avoid a characterless or uninteresting writing style, laced with overused expressions;
- avoid bad grammar, spelling and punctuation;
- avoid a messy, muddled or cluttered appearance.

Some useful phrases for job application letters

I wish to apply for the post of [*job title*] advertised in the [*publication*] on [*date*].

I am writing to enquire whether you have a suitable vacancy in your organization.

I am sending this letter and CV to apply for the position of [*job title*] with your company.

The advertised post calls for qualifications and experience that correspond to my professional background.

As an experienced [*job description*], I believe I am the candidate you are looking for.

I am confident my experience qualifies me for the position of [*job title*].

It is my aim to work for a company where my qualifications and working experience would make a positive contribution.

I look forward to hearing from you and to being granted the opportunity of an interview.

I hope you will consider my application favourably and grant me an interview.

Employment issues

The fourteen sample letters that follow relate to employment issues.

Sample Letters

Job application in response to advertisement

Sender's Address
Sender's Contact Information

6 August 2005

Ms Diane Brand
Human Resources Manager
Moneywise Insurance Ltd
47 Castle Road
Laddington
Redshire
LD3 9 RT

Dear Ms Brand

I am writing in response to your advertisement in *The Chronicle* of 5 August 2005 for a temporary nursery assistant in your firm's crèche for the children of employees. I am very interested in the advertised post and think that I have the right experience and personality for the job.

I am used to dealing with young children and intend to make teaching my long-term career. I have just left school and am taking a year out before taking up a place at Neath Teachers' Training College next autumn. My aim on graduation is to teach younger children in primary school, and during my year out I want to build on my experience working with young children. I appreciate that the role of nursery assistant requires great energy, enthusiasm, initiative and patience and I know I can bring all these qualities to the post. In the past few years I have gained a great deal of experience caring for my younger siblings and am a trusted baby-sitter for several family friends and neighbours.

As to leisure activities, I play the piano and the guitar and like singing, dancing and painting.

References can be obtained from the head teacher of my school, Mr Peter Sharp, and from Ms Jean Peden, a neighbour for whom I baby-sit frequently. Their addresses and telephone numbers are given in my CV, which accompanies this letter.

I hope you will give my application favourable consideration and I look forward to hearing from you.

Yours sincerely

Eleanor Smart

Eleanor Smart

A GUIDE TO LETTER-WRITING

Speculative job application

>
> Sender's Address
> Sender's Contact Information
>
> 7 February 2003
>
> Ms Esther Martin
> Editorial Director
> Paragon Publishing Ltd
> 30 Blandford Lane,
> Kingsferry
> Whiteshire
> KF15 7KL
>
> Dear Ms Martin
>
> I am actively seeking a post in the publishing industry. Although I would welcome the opportunity to work in any aspect of publishing, my preference is the editorial area. I am about to graduate from Glasburgh University with an Honours Degree in English Language.
>
> Most of my family work in the publishing industry and it has been my ambition, since before I left school, to make it my career too. With that aim in mind I have had various temporary jobs and periods of work experience involving books, as you will see from my CV, which I enclose. This work has included editorial assistant on an encyclopedia, work in the design department of a publishing house, production assistant on a magazine, and a regular Saturday job at my local bookseller's. I have also been the assistant editor of our student newspaper for two years. I feel that with this accumulated experience I have the right background to fit in well in an editorial department.
>
> My pastimes include photography and writing. I have had several articles, mostly theatre reviews, published in The Forth Review, our local weekly newspaper.
>
> I am a good communicator and work well under pressure. I am well acquainted with computers, including desktop publishing and computer-aided design programs.
>
> Thank you for your consideration. I look forward to hearing from you.
>
> Yours sincerely
>
> *Sarah Brown*
>
> Sarah Brown

Request for a reference

> Sender's Address
>
> 1 June 2004
>
> Ms Jane White
> Head Teacher
> Newtown High School
> 21 High Street
> Newtown
> Blackshire
> SB12 7TY
>
> Dear Ms White
>
> I am writing to ask if I may use you as one of my referees for a job for which I am applying. The job is clerical assistant with Global Insurance.
>
> I left school at the end of the summer term and passed 6 GCSEs. Since then I have been working as an au pair in France.
>
> I was a pupil at Newtown High School from 1997–2003. In my last year I was in Ms Peter's form class.
>
> I hope that you will be able to help.
>
> Yours sincerely
>
> Joanna Thames
>
> JOANNA THAMES

Reply to employer requesting a reference

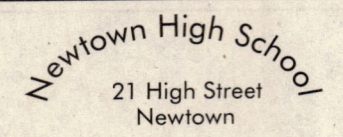

Newtown High School
21 High Street
Newtown

15 June 2004

Ms Penny Main
Personnel Manager
Global Insurance
3 High Street
Stonyburn
Blackshire
SB13 9TZ

Dear Ms Main

Thank you for your letter of 5 June asking for my views on the suitability of Joanna Thames for a post as clerical officer with your firm.

I got to know Joanna quite well as I took her form for a weekly discussion group when she was in her final year at Newtown.

Joanna is a very honest, hard-working girl and always tries to do her best. She is very pleasant and polite and gets on very well with people.

I am sure that if you decide to employ her she will be an asset to the firm.

Yours sincerely,

Jane White

Jane White

Thank you to someone who has provided a reference

Sender's Address

26 June 2004

Ms Jane White
Head Teacher
Newtown High School
21 High Street
Newtown
Blackshire
SB12 7TY

Dear Ms White

I am writing to thank you very much for agreeing to act as one of my referees for the post that I applied for with Global Insurance.

I am delighted to say that I got the job and I start at the beginning of July.

With many thanks for your help.

Yours sincerely

Joanna Thames

JOANNA THAMES

A GUIDE TO LETTER-WRITING

Invitation to attend an interview

B&P
B& P Industries
Hard Grind House
43 Banks Street
Workton

9 August 2003

Dear Miss Huddle

PERSONAL ASSISTANT TO CHIEF EXECUTIVE OFFICER

Thank you for your application for this post.

You are invited to attend an interview with me and Mr Jacques Fontainbleau, Chief Executive, on Thursday 14 August at 2.30 p.m.

Please let me know, by letter, telephone or email, whether this appointment will be convenient.

Yours sincerely

Avril Montagu

Avril Montagu
Personnel Director

Rejection of application for a job

B&P
B& P Industries
Hard Grind House
43 Banks Street
Workton

10 August 2003

Dear Miss King

PERSONAL ASSISTANT TO CHIEF EXECUTIVE OFFICER

Thank you for your application for the post of personal assistant to the Chief Executive Officer.

We have received many applications for this post and I am sorry to inform you that your qualifications do not match all our requirements closely enough to include you on the shortlist.

I realize you will be disappointed but I am sure you will find a suitable post elsewhere.

Yours sincerely

Avril Montagu

Avril Montagu
Personnel Director

A Guide to Letter-Writing

Job offer

Letters of appointment should detail the salary and other employment conditions. If a job description is being sent there will be no need to repeat the details from the job description in the letter offering the post.

B&P
B& P Industries
Hard Grind House
43 Banks Street
Workton

15 August 2003

Dear Miss Huddle

Thank you for attending the interview yesterday, and I am pleased to offer you the post of personal assistant to the Chief Executive Officer at a salary of £24,500 per annum. The starting date of your employment with us will be Monday, 1 September 2003.

You will be entitled to 5 weeks' annual paid holiday. Holiday dates will coincide with Mr Fontainbleau's wherever practicable.

Please confirm in writing that you accept this appointment on these terms and that you will be available to begin work on 1 September.

Yours sincerely

Avril Montagu

Avril Montagu
Personnel Director

Request for early retirement

> Sender's Address
>
> 1 July 2005
>
> Mark Howe
> Redford Engineering Ltd
> 37 Hanover Street
> Brunstane
> Brownshire
> BT14 7WB
>
> Dear Mr Howe
>
> I understand that the firm is offering early retirement to some older employees as part of a staff reorganization scheme. It is likely that I shall take advantage of this offer and I would like to receive details of the retirement settlement.
>
> The reason for my decision to retire early is that my wife is in poor health.
>
> I would like to leave at the earliest opportunity and therefore I hope we can reach agreement on a settlement as soon as possible.
>
> I look forward to hearing from you.
>
> Yours sincerely
>
> *Peter Smythe*
>
> Peter Smythe

A Guide to Letter-Writing

Written warning

Under employment or contract conditions, it is usually the case that an employee is entitled to receive a written warning before they can be dismissed. The warning letter will in most cases have been preceded by a verbal warning or discussion with the employee about their conduct. When writing warning letters it is usual to include details of the unsatisfactory conduct with dates, and to state the further steps that will be taken if the conduct is repeated.

Big & Co

10-12 Main St
Ourtown

5 October 2005

Dear Greta

As I discussed with you at our meeting this morning, I am sorry to say that your conduct has been unsatisfactory recently.

There have been three occasions during the past month when you were in breach of the company's rules. On 15 and 27 September, you failed to remove the cash from the bar till and place it in the office safe for safekeeping overnight; and, on 3 October, you left a junior member of staff in charge for two hours while you left the building on personal business.

I have accepted your explanations meantime, but I must emphasize that should there be a repeat of any of these incidents or any other breach of company rules, that the company will regard this with the utmost seriousness.

I will review the situation in one month's time.

Yours sincerely

Alan Harrington

Alan Harrington
Personnel Manager

Written second warning

Big & Co
10-12 Main St
Ourtown

27 October 2005

Dear Greta

At our meeting this morning, I had to give you a second warning for unsatisfactory conduct. I was informed that you neglected to remove the day's takings from the bar till to the office safe yesterday evening. This follows the two similar incidents detailed in my letter of 5 October.

I must inform you that any further unsatisfactory conduct will result in dismissal.

Yours sincerely

Alan Harrington

Alan Harrington
Personnel Manager

Dismissal with one month's notice

Big & Co
10-12 Main St
Ourtown

1 November 2005

Dear Greta

I confirm that you have agreed to leave the company at the end of the month, on 30 November. This follows my warning letters to you of 5 and 27 October, and two further incidents of breaking company rules. All these incidents have been discussed with you and reported under the company's general rules of employment.

If you find another position before the end of the month we will be happy to release you.

Yours sincerely

Alan Harrrington

Alan Harrington
Personnel Manager

Summary dismissal

BIG TIME INC
Hard Slog Towers
Big Cash Park
Overton

15 November 2005

Dear Jerry

I confirm that you are dismissed from the company with immediate effect, following the discovery that you have again been stealing small sums from the till. This action follows my warning letters of 14 and 28 October.

A cheque for one month's salary in lieu of notice is enclosed and I must ask you to return the key of your staff locker to the office before you leave the premises.

Yours sincerely

Robert Smith

Robert Smith
Personnel Manager

Resignation

No matter how much you may have hated the job you are resigning from, or however badly you think you have been treated, you should resist the temptation to rant and rave or be abusive in a resignation letter.

Try to write a letter which will not sour your relations permanently with your ex-employer. You may find that your paths cross again later and, in any event, anger will almost certainly be tempered by time. If possible, you should always exercise restraint, be courteous, and try to include something positive about your period of employment with them.

Sender's address

14 August 2006

Mr Frank Brown
Personnel Manager
Lomond Financial Services
35 Milton Street
Neathing
Whiteshire
NT12 8DR

Dear Frank

I am writing to inform you of my decision to resign from the company. As is required by the conditions of my contract, I am giving you four weeks' notice, beginning today.

As I discussed with you yesterday, I have accepted a post with Carlton Investment Services, which will provide me with improved opportunities for advancement.

Thank you for all your support and encouragement during my three years with Lomond Financial. I have very much enjoyed working with you and have gained much valuable experience.

Yours sincerely

Richard Todd

Richard Todd

Sample Letters

Business and Financial

There are many areas of personal business and finance that might conceivably require that you write a letter. If you think you may need to have written evidence of an offer, transaction or exchange, it is a good idea to conduct the business in writing and keep copies of all letters.

Estimates

Request for an estimate (1)

The Gables
Wellington Road
Norwood
NW8 5XX
Telephone: 1896 757600
Mobile: 09888 888 000

24 June 2005

Abbeyhill Roofing Ltd
46 Abbeyhill
Norwood
Whiteshire
NW2 4XY

Dear Sirs

ESTIMATE TO REPAIR STORM DAMAGE

The roof of my house was damaged in the recent gales and the ceiling of one of the bedrooms is now leaking. I have contacted my insurance company and they have asked me to get three written estimates before selecting a contractor to carry out the work.

I would be glad if you were able to inspect the property as soon as possible. If you are interested in submitting an estimate, please telephone to arrange a suitable time to carry out your inspection. It is important that the repair work is carried out urgently.

Yours sincerely

Tom Henderson

Tom Henderson

Request for an estimate (2)

> Sender's Address
> Sender's Contact Information
>
> 14 April 2004
>
> Mr Peter Glass
> Blackford Kitchen Design Ltd
> 16 Forth Rd
> Newhill
> Whiteshire
> NH15 3KT
>
> Dear Mr Glass
>
> I am considering installing a new kitchen in my house. The rest of the house is quite modern but the kitchen is very old-fashioned. It is rather an odd shape and I shall need professional help to plan it.
>
> If you are interested in discussing this perhaps you could telephone to make an appointment.
>
> I realize that it there is a considerable amount of work to be done but the job has to be completed before the end of July.
>
> Yours sincerely
>
> *John Peters*
>
> John Peters

Accepting an estimate

> Sender's Address
> Sender's Contact Information
>
> 7 March 2005
>
> Mr Mark Garden
> Central Construction Ltd
> Craigpark
> Whiteshire
> CP12 8TY
>
> Dear Mr Garden
>
> I am writing to confirm in writing my telephone acceptance of your
> estimate dated 5 March for work to the stonework of my garage.
>
> I understand that work will begin on 19 March and will take about two days.
>
> I look forward to seeing you on 19 March.
>
> Yours sincerely
>
> *Ann Blackridge*
>
> Ann Blackridge

Rejecting an estimate

> Sender's Address
> 18 March 2004
>
> Michael Little
> Greenfingers Landscape Gardeners
> 46 Station Road
> Craigpark
> Whiteshire
> CP12 P34
>
> Dear Mr Little
>
> Thank you for submitting an estimate for landscaping the garden at the above address and for doing so promptly.
>
> Unfortunately I am not accepting your estimate. It was a good deal higher than those submitted by other firms.
>
> Yours sincerely
>
> *Philip Smith*
>
> Philip Smith

Complaints

We often write to complain or to ask for damaged things to be fixed. In order to be most effective, these letters should be brief and to the point, without going into too much detail. Letters of complaint should be factual rather than emotional, and calm and restrained rather than abusive.

Legislation relating to the supply of goods and services

The following acts and regulations deal with the supply of goods and services in the UK: the Sale of Goods Act 1979; Supply of Goods and Services Act 1982; Sale and Supply of Goods Act 1994; and the Sale and Supply of Goods to Consumers Regulations 2002.

It is the seller, not the manufacturer, who is responsible if goods do not conform to contract. This means they must be as described, fit for purpose and of satisfactory quality. Goods are deemed to be of satisfactory quality if they reach the standard that a 'reasonable' person would regard as satisfactory, taking into account the price and any description. Aspects of quality include fitness for purpose, freedom from minor defects, appearance and finish, durability and safety. If goods do not conform to contract at the time of sale, purchasers can request their money back within a 'reasonable' time.

Under the Supply of Goods and Services Act 1982 traders are required to provide services to a proper standard of workmanship. Any material used or goods supplied in providing the service must be of satisfactory quality. In addition, if a definite completion date or a price has not been fixed then the work must be completed within a 'reasonable' time and for a 'reasonable' charge. The law treats failure to meet these obligations as breach of contract and consumers would be entitled to seek redress, if necessary through the civil courts.

A GUIDE TO LETTER-WRITING

> ## Writing letters of complaint
>
> Be firm.
> Set a reasonable timetable for things to be put right and stick to it.
> Quote the relevant legislation where necessary.

Sample Letters

Complaint about poor workmanship

Sender's Address
Sender's Contact Information

4 June 2005

Mr Frank Smith
Manager
Slating and Roofing Contractors
16 Scott Street
Craigpark
Whiteshire
CP19 6KM

Dear Mr Smith

REPAIRS TO ROOF AT 56 WOOD ROAD, CRAIGPARK

Your firm recently completed repairs to the roof of my house. I am writing to tell you that I am not at all satisfied with the work. The first time it rained, the ceiling in one of the upstairs bedrooms leaked.

I have tried without success to contact you by telephone and left several messages with your secretary, but my calls have not been returned.

The faulty work must be put right as soon as possible. Please get in touch either by telephone or by letter to make an appointment to come and inspect the roof and to arrange a date for it to be put right.

I chose your firm on the personal recommendation of a friend and I am extremely disappointed to have been let down.

I look forward to hearing from you by the end of the week at the latest.

Yours sincerely

Sarah Jones

Sarah Jones

Complaint about faulty or damaged goods

Sender's Address
10 May 2005

Dimble's Fashion Catalogue
65 Kingsway
Brownpool
Longshire
BP5 5TY

Dear Sirs

ORDER NUMBER: 272753/00

I have just received the dress I ordered for my granddaughter from your catalogue on 4 May 2005. It does not reach the standard that I have come to expect from your company.

I was annoyed and disappointed to find that the sewing on both the hem and the seam on the left-hand side was undone.

My granddaughter was very upset, particularly since she had planned to wear the dress to her birthday party. There is really nothing that can compensate her for this disappointment.

I will be glad to receive either a full refund or an undamaged dress together with your advice about how the damaged one is to be returned at your expense.

I would hope that any further orders that I place with your company will be dealt with in a more satisfactory way. Meanwhile I look forward to an early and satisfactory response to my complaint.

Yours sincerely

Roberta Atkinson

ROBERTA ATKINSON

Complaint about standards and service

> Sender's Address
> Sender's Contact Information
>
> 28 September 2005
>
> Mr Pierre Bouleau
> Bon Appetit
> 60 Princes Street
> Brownwich
> Broadshire
> BR13 8FY
>
> Dear Pierre
>
> My family and I have been regular clients of your restaurant since it opened two years ago. Until our visit last Saturday we had always been extremely satisfied and had recommended it to several of our friends.
>
> Unfortunately we will not be recommending it again unless things improve greatly. We were extremely disappointed by both the food and the service at our last visit. The food was not up to the standard we have come to expect from your restaurant, it was served cold, and your staff were slow, sullen and quite obviously couldn't have cared less.
>
> We gather from friends that you have opened another restaurant in the area and are spending your time concentrating on that. However, the clients of your original restaurant deserve your attention too – otherwise we will go elsewhere.
>
> I look forward to hearing your views on the subject.
>
> Yours sincerely
>
> *John Burns*
>
> John Burns

Complaint to a holiday tour company

Sender's Address
Sender's Contact Information

20 August 2004

Sunshine Holiday Tours Ltd
30 Dean Street
Brownwich
Broadshire
BR 15 7JX

Dear Sirs

My husband and I booked a coach holiday through your company in August of this year. We were on a tour of the Italian lakes that started from Brownwich on 6th August.

Everything about the holiday fell short of the claims made in your company's brochure. The coach was not air-conditioned and the accommodation throughout the trip was in badly equipped rooms with poor food and disgraceful service.

We complained to your courier several times during the trip but she declared that there was nothing she could do.

Since this holiday was not at all up to the expected standard or to the standard advertised by you, we are seeking compensation. We gather that several other people on the tour have also complained.

We look forward to hearing from you and receiving your suggestions for compensation.

Yours sincerely

Joan Rogers

Joan Rogers

Sample Letters

Financial matters

If you are unfortunate enough to experience difficulties in paying bills or loans, the golden rule is to contact the lender or creditor as soon as possible, preferably in writing. Remember also that any arrangement you come to should be a realistic one which you are confident you will be able to maintain.

More wide-ranging advice on money matters is available through local advice centres, such as CAB (the Citizen's Advice Bureau).

To a lender/creditor advising of difficulty paying

Sender's Address
Sender's Contact Information

10 May 2003

The Fairdeal Mortgage Company
Fairdeal House
Fardington
BT22 4TL

Dear Sirs

MORTGAGE ACCOUNT NUMBER 2007869

Due to recent redundacy, I am finding it difficult to meet all my financial commitments.

I am writing to ask if you will consider reducing my monthly mortgage payments meantime.

I can provide details of my current income and outgoings on request if you need this information to enable you to make a more detailed assessment.

I hope that you will give sympathetic consideration to my situation.

Yours sincerely

Harold Hoplance

Harold Hoplance

A GUIDE TO LETTER-WRITING

Personal and Social

Love letters

No guidance should really be needed in this case. Nonetheless, it is interesting to compare the styles of a couple of love letters written by famous people in the past.

From John Constable (English landscape artist) to Maria Bicknell before their marriage

> East Bergholt
> February 27, 1816
>
> I received your letter, my ever dearest Maria, this morning. You know my anxious disposition too well not to be aware how much I feel at this time. At the distance we are from each other every fear will obtrude itself on my mind. Let me hope that you are not really worse than your kindness, your affection, for me make you say – I think – that no more molestation will arise to the recovery of your health, which I pray for beyond every other blessing under heaven.
>
> —Let us think only of the blessings that providence may yet have in store for us and that we may yet possess. I am happy in love – an affection exceeding a thousand times my deserts, which has continued so many years, and is yet undiminished. Never will I marry in this world if I marry not you. Truly can I say that for the seven years since I avowed my love for you, I have foregone all company, and the society of all females (except my own relations) for your sake.
>
> —I am still ready to make my sacrifice for you – I will submit to any thing you may command me – but cease to respect, to love and adore you I never can or will. I must still think that we should have married long ago – we should have had many troubles – but we have yet had no joys, and we could not have starved. Your FRIENDS have never been without a hope of parting us and see what that has cost us both – but no more.
> Believe me, my beloved & ever dearest Maria,
> most faithfully yours

From Napoleon to Josephine

Spring 1797

To Josephine,

—I love you no longer; on the contrary, I detest you. You are a wretch, truly perverse, truly stupid, a real Cinderella. You never write to me at all, you do not love your husband; you know the pleasure that your letters give him yet you cannot even manage to write him half a dozen lines, dashed off in a moment!

—What then do you do all day, Madame? What business is so vital that it robs you of the time to write to your faithful lover? What attachment can be stifling and pushing aside the love, the tender and constant love which you promised him? Who can this wonderful new lover be who takes up your every moment, rules your days and prevents you from devoting your attention to your husband? Beware, Josephine; one fine night the doors will be broken down and there I shall be.

—In truth, I am worried, my love, to have no news from you; write me a four page letter instantly made up from those delightful words which fill my heart with emotion and joy.

—I hope to hold you in my arms before long, when I shall lavish upon you a million kisses, burning as the equatorial sun.

Special occasions

There are some circumstances in which there is a need for a rather more formulaic personal letter. These are often sent to mark the most joyous and the most solemn occasions in a life.

Announcing the birth of a baby

> 15th October 2006
>
> Dear David and Emily,
>
> We are delighted to be writing to let you know that early yesterday morning John Henry was born. He weighed 7lbs 8oz and is to be known as Jack to distinguish him from my father, after whom he is named. He and Sophie are both very well.
>
> Feel free to come and visit and meet Jack whenever you want to, although it would be best to give us a ring first in case lots of people have the same idea at the same time! Give my regards to all your family.
>
> Looking forward very much to seeing you.
>
> Tony

Informal wedding invitation

> 270 Abbott Street
> Lilacfield
> HF27 4AD
> 27 May 2005
>
> Dear Patricia,
>
> Andrew and I are getting married soon after our return from Japan. The date we've set is 30 September. We would like to invite you and Derek to the wedding, which will be a small family affair with only a few friends. The vicar has agreed to marry us in the garden of my parents' house in Greenfield. The ceremony will be at 3 p.m. and there is to be an evening reception at the local hotel.
>
> There's plenty room at Mum and Dad's house if you need to stay the night, although it would help their arrangements if you could let me know in advance should you want to do this.
>
> We hope to see you at the ceremony.
>
> Best wishes,
>
> Harriet

Formal wedding invitations

Formal wedding invitations are always written in the third person and are usually printed on cards with no opening greeting or complimentary close. The letters RSVP are an abbreviation for the French phrase *répondez s'il vouz plaît* meaning, in English, 'Please reply'. When receiving a formal invitation in the third person, you should also reply in the third person. Two samples are given with a slight variation in style between the two.

Formal wedding invitation (1)

Mr and Mrs Hubert Onslow
request the pleasure of your company
at the marriage of their daughter

Harriet

to

Mr Andrew Hetherington-Dashwood
at Lilacfield Parish Church
on Saturday 30th September
at 2.30 p.m.
and afterwards at the reception at
The Jedstreet Hotel, Lilacfield

RSVP
270 Abbott Street
Lilacfield
HF27 4AD

Formal wedding invitation (2)

> Mr and Mrs Hubert Onslow
> request the pleasure of the company of
>
> *Miss Patricia Holsworth*
>
> at
> the marriage of their daughter
> Harriet
> to
> Mr Andrew Hetherington-Dashwood
> at Lilacfield Parish Church
> on Saturday 30th September
> at 2.30 p.m.
> and afterwards at the reception at
> The Jedstreet Hotel, Lilacfield
>
> RSVP
270 Abbott Street
Lilacfield
HF27 4AD

Accepting a formal wedding invitiation

> Miss Patricia Holsworth thanks Mr and Mrs Onslow for their kind invitation to their daughter's wedding, and to the reception afterwards. She has much pleasure in accepting.

Declining a formal wedding invitation

> Miss Patricia Holsworth thanks Mr and Mrs Onslow for their kind invitation to their daughter's wedding, and to the reception afterwards, but regrets that a prior engagement prevents her from attending.

Congratulations

> Sender's Address
> 5 January 2002
>
> Dear Gordon
>
> I was delighted to come across your name in the New Year's Honours List. I would like offer you my hearty congratulations.
>
> The award is a fitting tribute to your work as a long-term member of the community council, and your unstinting and enthusiastic contribution to many charitable and voluntary organizations over the years. I cannot think of anyone who is more worthy of the such an honour.
>
> With very best wishes
>
> Anna

A GUIDE TO LETTER-WRITING

Sympathy

The tone and content of a letter expressing sympathy for an illness or injury will depend very much on whether the illness is serious or not. If the person is very likely to recover and is also someone you know reasonably well, the letter can be lighter in tone.

If the illness is a serious one, be careful about using the 'Get well soon' formula, because this may cause distress to the patient and their close relatives.

Letter expressing sympathy at injury

> Dear Annabel
>
> I was very sorry to hear that you had been injured in an accident. To fall from a moving bus must have been a terrifying experience. I wish I had known earlier and I would have visited you in hospital.
>
> I'm very glad to hear that you are now back home and the plaster cast is coming off your arm next week. I'm sure Harry will make sure that you don't do too much fetching and carrying for the moment.
>
> I'd like to come and visit later in the week. Let me know when would suit and if there is anything you need. I have some magazines that I think you'll enjoy, and those little strawberries you like so much are just about to ripen in the garden, so I shall certainly bring some.
>
> Be sure to take good care of yourself.
> Best wishes,
> Katy

Condolence

Even those people most practised in the art of letter writing find letters of condolence amongst the most challenging to write. It can be very hard to find the right words, and many people shrink from the task for fear of intruding on the bereaved's unhappiness. Obviously the person who is going to receive it is going to be in a distressed state and it is hard to think of anything to say that will bring any kind of comfort. In fact because it is impossible to give real comfort, the bereaved often appreciate very much the fact that people have remembered their relative and thought highly enough of him or her to write. A simple and natural acknowledgement of the loss suffered will always be appreciated and be a positive comfort.

Writing a sensitive letter of condolence

A letter or message of condolence should, if possible, be handwritten.

Try to use straightforward everyday words and phrases.

Be as sensitive as you can to the feelings of the person who will read the letter.

Avoid expressions like 'a blessed release' and 'good innings'.

Only refer to religious matters if you know the recipient is a believer.

It is difficult to avoid clichés in letters of sympathy and condolence, but bereavement is not an area in which striving for originality is especially appropriate. In the circumstances, a few clichés can be quite acceptable. One more thing – it is as well to set aside your typewriter or word processor. Unless your handwriting is completely illegible it is much better to write, rather than type, letters of sympathy. This makes them personal in a way that a word-processed document can never be.

Often people opt to send a card with a short personal message written inside. It is probably better to go for a plain card with no pre-printed message. A message that is not in your own words can often seem a little impersonal. It is nearly always better to avoid those cards that include flowery poems.

Letter of condolence to a business contact

B&P
B& P Industries
Hard Grind House
43 Banks Street
Workton

25 January 2004

Arthur Wilson
Managing Director
Drew, Wilson & Wilson
Great Barrow Lane
Blackfield
BK77 1XY

Dear Mr Wilson,

It was with deep sadness that we read of the sudden death of your chairman, Steven Drew.

My staff join me in sending our sincere condolences and deepest sympathy to you and members of his family.

Yours sincerely,

Kenneth Vernon

Kenneth Vernon
Vernon and Orwell

Personal letter of condolence (informal)

> 15th April 2005
>
> My dear May,
>
> We were terribly sad to hear the tragic news of Tom's death. It was a great shock, and we wanted you and the children to know just how much you are all in our thoughts.
>
> Tom was loved by everyone who knew him, and we will treasure the memory of his warmth, kindness and sense of fun always.
>
> You know that you can call on us at any time, and please don't hesitate if there is anything at all that we can do to help.
>
> With all our love,
>
> Ronald and Katherine

Personal letter of condolence (formal)

> Sender's Address
> 4 February 2004
>
> Dear Mrs Hughes,
>
> I was so sorry to hear of the sudden death of your husband. Please accept my deepest sympathy.
> It is some time since I saw Peter but we were good friends when I worked with him at G& H Law's. I particularly enjoyed his wonderful sense of humour. He could cheer us all up when we were feeling low.
> He will be very much missed by his colleagues at Law's and also by the community in general. He always gave freely and so willingly of his time in raising funds for charity.
> I know that you will have your family around you but if there is anything I can do please do not hesitate to get in touch.
>
> With kind regards,
> Yours sincerely,
>
> Jonathan Brown

Sample Letters

Informing a friend or acquaintance when someone has died

> The Paddocks
>
> 15 June 2005
>
> Dear Mr Peters,
>
> I am very sorry to tell you that my father died at St Anthony's Hospice on Tuesday the 13th of June.
>
> As you know, he had been ill for some time, but fought that long battle very courageously. It was only in the final few days that, at his own request, he was transferred to the local hospice. He died peacefully in his sleep.
>
> I know you and my father had been friends since childhood, and he often talked with great affection of you and your family.
>
> The funeral service is at 2.30 p.m. at Hurtlington Crematorium. If you are able to come, we would be very pleased if you and your wife were also able to join us at my mother's house afterwards.
>
> Yours sincerely,
>
> *Alice Northholt*

Thanks

You should always write to thank someone – especially someone of the older generation – for a gift. Of course, it is often quite appropriate to telephone one's thanks. You have to try and judge the preference of the person to whom you owe thanks and act accordingly.

Just as letters of condolence require a marked degree of sensitivity, so to do letters of thanks, especially those in response to presents. The problem is often one of knowing what to say about the unwanted gift without being excessively enthusiastic and so risk getting a similar gift again! This calls for tact.

It is often difficult to decide how to fill space in a thank-you letter. You can keep the message brief, but you have to do better than a couple of lines. However much or little you choose to write you might think of writing the letter by hand instead of dashing it off on your word processor. Some people prefer the more personal touch of the handwritten note as in the first of the two sample thank you letters that follow.

Informal thank you for a holiday visit

Dear Margaret,

Thank you very much for having me to stay over Easter. It was very kind of you to invite me and to make me so much a part of the family.

It was very pleasant to get away from the bustle of London for a few days. I must say that you live in a very beautiful part of the world and it was good to have time to explore it.

I would love to return your hospitality. If ever any of you, or preferably all of you, feel like a few days in London, just get in touch. You will be very welcome.

With very many thanks,

Yours sincerely,

Joyce Green

Sample Letters

Thank you for a present

> Sender's address
> 12 October 2003
>
> Dear Aunt Madge,
>
> I am writing to thank you very much for the birthday present. It was very kind of you to remember, and to take so much trouble over it.
> The silk scarf is absolutely lovely. The soft lavender colour will go really well with my winter coat.
> I hope that you are in good health and getting out and about a bit despite this grim winter weather. When the weather gets a little warmer and drier you must think of coming up to London. Do let me know if you would like to come and if you might be able to spend a few days with us. We would all love to see you.
>
> With many thanks and best wishes,
> Love,
>
> *Jill*

Appendices

Appendix 1
Some Special Forms of Address

Government, civic, legal and professional

AMBASSADOR (BRITISH)
opening greeting: Dear Sir ——, *or* Your Excellency, *or* Sir, *or* Dear Mr —
name on envelope: His Excellency The British Ambassador and Plenipotentiary, *or* His Excellency, Sir —— KCMG, *or* His Excellency —— KCMG, *or* His Excellency, H.B.M's Ambassador to — (i.e. *name of relevant country*)

CHANCELLOR OF THE EXCHEQUER
opening greeting: Dear Chancellor
name on envelope: The Rt Hon. —— MP

CONSUL GENERAL, CONSUL & VICE CONSUL
opening greeting: Sir
name on envelope: —— Esq. H.B.M's Consul General *or* Consul *or* Vice Consul

COUNCILLOR (LOCAL GOVERNMENT)
opening greeting: Dear Councillor —, *or* Dear Councillor Mrs/Ms/Miss —, *or* Dear Mr/Mrs/Ms/Miss —
name on envelope: Councillor ——, *or* Councillor Mrs/Ms/Miss ——

DOCTOR OF MEDICINE (*see also* SURGEON)
opening greeting: Dear Dr *or* Doctor —
name on envelope: Dr *or* Doctor —

DOCTORATE, HOLDER OF
opening greeting: Dear Dr —, *or* Dear Sir/Madam
name on envelope: (*forename*) — (*surname*) — *followed by the initials* LLD, MusD, *or whichever is applicable*

MINISTER OF STATE (*see also* SECRETARY OF STATE)
opening greeting: Dear Minister
name on envelope: —— MP, *or by appointment* (e.g. The Minister for Housing and Planning)

A GUIDE TO LETTER-WRITING

JUDGE (CIRCUIT)
opening greeting: Dear Judge, *or* Dear Sir /Dear Madam
name on envelope: His Honour the Judge/Her Honour the Judge

JUDGE (HIGH COURT) (Note that in the UK a female High Court Judge is conventionally addressed as *Mrs* even if she is unmarried.)
opening greeting: Dear Sir/Dear Madam
name on envelope: The Hon. Mr Justice — /The Hon. Mrs Justice —

LORD MAYOR (Note the different greeting and form of address for the Lord Mayors of London, York, Cardiff, Belfast and Dublin.)
opening greeting: My Lord Mayor
opening greeting for Lord Mayors of London, York, Cardiff, Belfast and Dublin: My Lord Mayor, *or* Dear Lord Mayor
name on envelope: The Right Worshipful the Lord Mayor
name on envelope for Lord Mayors of London, York, Cardiff, Belfast and Dublin: The Rt Hon. the Lord Mayor of London/York/Cardiff/Belfast/Dublin

MAYOR (UNITED KINGDOM & IRELAND)
opening greeting: Dear Mr Mayor
name on envelope: The Right Worshipful the Mayor of — (*for some towns and cities*), *or* The Worshipful the Mayor of — (*for some cities, towns and boroughs*)

MAYOR (UNITED STATES)
opening greeting: Dear Sir/Madam, *or* Dear Mr/Madam Mayor
name on envelope: The Honorable — — Mayor of —

MEMBERS OF PARLIAMENT
opening greeting: Dear Mr — *or* Dear Mrs/Ms/Miss—
name on envelope: — — MP

PRESIDENT OF THE UNITED STATES
opening greeting: Dear Mr President/Dear Madam President, *or* Sir/Madam
name on envelope: The President of the United States

PRIME MINISTER
opening greeting: Dear Prime Minister, *or* Dear Mr—/Dear Mrs/Ms/Miss —
name on envelope: The Rt Hon. — — PC, MP

PROFESSOR
opening greeting: Dear Sir/Madam
name on envelope: Professor — —

Appendices

SECRETARY OF STATE (*see also* **MINISTER OF STATE**)
opening greeting: Dear Secretary of State, *or* Dear —— (*giving appointment, not personal name,* e.g. Home Secretary, Foreign Secretary)
name on envelope: The Rt Hon. —— PC, MP, *or address by appointment* (e.g. The Home Secretary, The Foreign Secretary, etc.)

SURGEON (Note that surgeons are not addressed as 'Doctor'. Note also that, in England and Wales, gynaecologists and obstetricians are addressed as for a surgeon, not as a doctor of medicine.)
opening greeting: Dear Mr/Mrs/Ms/Miss —
name on envelope: Mrs/Mrs/Ms/Miss ——

US CONGRESSMAN & CONGRESSWOMAN
opening greeting: Dear Congressman/Congresswoman —, *or* Dear Sir/Madam
name on envelope: The Honorable ——

US GOVERNOR
opening greeting: Dear Governor —
name on envelope: The Honorable ——, Governor of —

US MEMBER OF THE HOUSE OF REPRESENTATIVES
opening greeting: Dear Representative —, *or* Dear Sir/Madam
name on envelope: The Honorable ——

US SENATOR
opening greeting: Dear Senator —, *or* Dear Sir/Madam
name on envelope: The Honorable ——

Royalty, Aristocracy and Peers

BARON (*see also* **LIFE PEER**)
opening greeting: Dear Lord — (i.e. *name/placename*)
name on envelope: The Rt Hon. the Lord — (i.e. *name/placename*), *or* The Lord — (i.e. *name/placename*)

BARONESS (*wife of a* **BARON**; *see also* **LIFE PEERESS**)
opening greeting: Dear Lady — (i.e. *name/placename*)
name on envelope: The Lady — (i.e. *name/placename*)

BARONET
opening greeting: Dear Sir, *or* Dear Sir —
name on envelope: Sir ——, Bt, *or* Sir ——, Bart.

A Guide to Letter-Writing

BARONET'S WIFE
opening greeting: Dear Lady —
name on envelope: Lady —

COUNTESS
opening greeting: Dear Countess of —, *or* Dear Lady —
name on envelope: The Countess of —

DAME
opening greeting: Dear Dame —
name on envelope: Dame — — (*with appropriate decoration*)

DUCHESS (*see also* **ROYAL DUCHESS**)
opening greeting: Dear Duchess of —, *or* Dear Duchess
name on envelope: Her Grace The Duchess of —, *or* The Duchess of —

DUKE (*see also* **ROYAL DUKE**)
opening greeting: Dear Duke of —, *or* Dear Duke
name on envelope: His Grace the Duke of —, *or* The Duke of —

DUKE OF EDINBURGH
opening greeting: Your Royal Highness, *or* (*when sent to his private secretary*) Dear Sir/Madam
name on envelope: His Royal Highness the Duke of Edinburgh, *or more usually* The Private Secretary to His Royal Highness The Duke of Edinburgh

EARL
opening greeting: My Lord, *or* Dear Lord —
name on envelope: The Rt Hon. the Earl of —, *or* The Earl of —

HONOURABLES (*the children of the aristocracy*)
opening greeting: Dear Mr/Mrs/Miss —
name on envelope: The Honourable *or* The Hon. Mr/Mrs/Miss —

KNIGHT (Note KBE = Knight of the British Empire, KCB = Knight of the Bath, KCMG = Knight of St Michael and St George, KG = Knight of the Garter, KT = Knight of the Thistle)
opening greeting: Dear Sir
name on envelope: Sir — — KBE, *or* KCB, *or* KCMG, *or* KG, *or* KT *as applicable*

KNIGHT'S WIFE
opening greeting: Dear Lady —
name on envelope: Lady —

Appendices

LIFE PEER (Note that the full title, e.g. *Lord Middlebank of Squireshire*, should not be used on letters. Use only *Lord Middlebank*.)
opening greeting: Dear Lord —
name on envelope: The Rt Hon. the Lord —

LIFE PEERESS (Note that the full title, e.g. *Baroness Appletree of Fairfield*, should not be used on letters. Use only *Baroness Appletree*.)
opening greeting: Dear Baroness —
name on envelope: The Right Hon. the Baroness — , *or* Baroness —

MARCHIONESS
opening greeting: Dear Marchioness of — , *or* Dear Lady —
name on envelope: The Marchioness of —

MARQUESS
opening greeting: Dear Marquess of — , *or* Dear Lord —
name on envelope: The Marquess of —

PRINCE OF WALES
opening greeting: Your Royal Highness, *or* (*when sent to his private secretary*) Dear Sir/Madam
name on envelope: His Royal Highness the Prince of Wales, *or more usually* The Private Secretary to His Royal Highness The Prince of Wales

QUEEN (Note that letters to the reigning monarch should always be addressed to her/his private secretary.)
opening greeting: Dear Sir/Madam (i.e. *the Queen's private secretary*)
name on envelope: The Private Secretary to Her Majesty the Queen

ROYAL DUCHESS
opening greeting: Your Royal Highness
name on envelope: Her Royal Highness The Duchess of —

ROYAL DUKE
opening greeting: Your Royal Highness
name on envelope: His Royal Highness The Duke of —

ROYAL PRINCES AND PRINCESSES
opening greeting: Your Royal Highness
name on envelope: His/Her Royal Highness, The Prince/Princess —

UNMARRIED DAUGHTER OF A DUKE, MARQUESS OR EARL
opening greeting: Dear Lady — —
name on envelope: Lady — —

A GUIDE TO LETTER-WRITING

VISCOUNT
opening greeting: Dear Viscount —, *or* Dear Lord —
name on envelope: The Rt Hon. the Viscount —, *or* The Viscount —

VISCOUNTESS
opening greeting: Dear Viscountess —, *or* Dear Lady —
name on envelope: The Viscountess —

Religious leaders and clergy

ARCHBISHOP (ANGLICAN)
opening greeting: Your Grace, *or* Dear Lord Archbishop, *or* Dear Archbishop
name on envelope: His Grace the Lord Archbishop of —, *or* The Most Rev. and Rt Hon. the Lord Archbishop of —

ARCHBISHOP (ROMAN CATHOLIC)
opening greeting: Your Grace, *or* Dear Archbishop —
name on envelope: His Grace the Archbishop of —

ARCHDEACON (ANGLICAN)
opening greeting: Dear Archdeacon, *or* Mr Archdeacon, *or* Venerable Sir
name on envelope: The Venerable the Archdeacon of —

BISHOP (ANGLICAN)
opening greeting: Dear Lord Bishop, *or* Dear Bishop
name on envelope: The Rt Rev. the Lord Bishop of —

BISHOP (ROMAN CATHOLIC)
opening greeting: My Lord Bishop, *or* Dear Bishop —
name on envelope: The Rt Rev. — —, Bishop of —

BISHOP OF LONDON (ANGLICAN)
opening greeting: Dear Lord Bishop
name on envelope: The Rt Rev. and Rt Hon. The Lord Bishop of London

CANON
opening greeting: Dear Canon, *or* Reverend Sir
name on envelope: The Rev. Canon —

CARDINAL (ROMAN CATHOLIC)
opening greeting: Dear Cardinal —, *or* Cardinal —
name on envelope: His Eminence the Cardinal Archbishop of —, *or* (*if not an archbishop*) His Eminence Cardinal —

Appendices

CHIEF RABBI
opening greeting: Dear Chief Rabbi, *or* Dear Rabbi —
name on envelope: The Chief Rabbi Dr —

CHRISTIAN CLERGY (ROMAN CATHOLIC)
opening greeting: Dear Reverend Father
name on envelope: The Reverend — (*followed by the initials of the religious order, if applicable*)

CHRISTIAN CLERGY (PROTESTANT AND ANGLICAN)
opening greeting: Dear Reverend — , *or* Dear Sir/Madam, *or* Dear Mr/Mrs —
name on envelope: The Reverend — —

DEAN
opening greeting: Very Reverend Sir, *or* Dear Dean, *or* Dear Mr Dean
name on envelope: The Very Rev. the Dean of —

MINISTER OF THE CHURCH OF SCOTLAND
opening greeting: Dear Mr/Mrs/Ms/Miss — , *or* Dear Minister
name on envelope: The Reverend — —

MONSIGNOR (ROMAN CATHOLIC)
opening greeting: Dear Monsignor —
name on envelope: The Reverend Monsignor — — , *or* The Reverend Monsignor

POPE
opening greeting: Your Holiness, *or* Most Holy Father
name on envelope: His Holiness the Pope — — (i.e. *name and number*)

VICAR, RECTOR *and* **RURAL DEAN**
opening greeting: Dear Mr — , *or where relevant* Dear Father —
name on envelope: The Reverend — —

Armed Forces

SERVING OFFICERS
opening greeting: Dear (*rank*) — (*surname*) —
name on envelope: (*rank*) — (*forename*) — (*surname*) —
(Note that the professional rank always comes before any other title.)

RETIRED OFFICERS
(Note that after retirement from the forces, army officers above the rank of Captain, naval officers above the rank of Lieutenant, and airforce officers

above the rank of Flight Lieutenant may continue to use their armed forces rank. Not all retired officers choose to do this.)

opening greeting: Dear *(rank)* — *(surname)* —
name on envelope: *(rank)* — *(forename)* — *(surname)* —

Appendix 2
United States Guidance on Addressing Mail

Addresses

RETURN ADDRESS
Print or type your address in the upper left corner on the front of the envelope.

EXTRA SERVICES
Place labels for extra services, such as Certified Mail, to the left of the postage.

POSTAGE
Use a stamp, postage meter, or a PC Postage Program to affix the correct amount.

PLACEMENT
Print the delivery and return addresses on the same side of your envelope or card. The addresses should be written parallel to the longest side.

ADDRESSING LETTERS
Print or type clearly with a pen or permanent marker so the address is legible from an arm's length away. Do not use commas or full stops.

MILITARY MAIL
Military addresses must show the grade, full name with middle name or initial, and PSC number, unit number, or ship name. Replace the city name with 'APO ' or 'FPO', and the state with 'AA', 'AE', or 'AP', and use a special ZIP code.

STREET ADDRESS
Use a post office box or street address, but not both. If the address also has a directional (e.g. 'NW' for Northwest), be sure to use it. Remember there may be more than one Main Street.

APARTMENT *or* SUITE NUMBER
The correct apartment or suite number helps to ensure delivery to the right location.

A GUIDE TO LETTER-WRITING

CITY, STATE *and* ZIP CODE
Using the correct ZIP code helps to direct your mail more efficiently and accurately. To check the correct spelling of a city name or to find a ZIP code, visit the United States Postal Service website at www.usps.com.

ENVELOPES
Letters, bills, greeting cards, and other documents can be sent in standard white, manila, or recycled paper envelopes. Items needing extra protection can be sent in bubble-lined, padded paper, or waterproof envelopes.

US Postal Service: Approved Abbreviations for US States

State	Abbreviation	State	Abbreviation
Alabama	AL	Montana	MT
Alaska	AK	Nebraska	NE
Arizona	AZ	Nevada	NV
Arkansas	AR	New Hampshire	NH
California	CA	New Jersey	NJ
Colorado	CO	New Mexico	NM
Connecticut	CT	New York	NY
Delaware	DE	North Carolina	NC
District of Columbia	DC	North Dakota	ND
Florida	FL	Ohio	OH
Georgia	GA	Oklahoma	OK
Hawaii	HI	Oregon	OR
Idaho	ID	Pennsylvania	PA
Illinois	IL	Rhode Island	RI
Indiana	IN	South Carolina	SC
Iowa	IA	South Dakota	SD
Kansas	KS	Tennessee	TN
Kentucky	KY	Texas	TX
Louisiana	LA	Utah	UT
Maine	ME	Vermont	VT
Maryland	MD	Virginia	VA
Massachusetts	MA	Washington	WA
Michigan	MI	West Virginia	WV
Minnesota	MN	Wisconsin	WI
Mississippi	MS	Wyoming	WY
Missouri	MO		

US Postal Service: Street Names and the Standard Abbreviations

Name	Abbreviation	Name	Abbreviation
Alley	**ALY**	Creek	**CRK**
Annex	**ANX**	Crescent	**CRES**
Arcade	**ARC**	Crest	**CRST**
Avenue	**AVE**	Crossing	**XING**
Bayoo	**BYU**	Crossroad	**XRD**
Beach	**BCH**	Curve	**CURV**
Bend	**BND**	Dale	**DL**
Bluff	**BLF**	Dam	**DM**
Bluffs	**BLFS**	Divide	**DV**
Bottom	**BTM**	Drive	**DR**
Boulevard	**BLVD**	Drives	**DRS**
Branch	**BR**	Estate	**EST**
Bridge	**BRG**	Estates	**ESTS**
Brook	**BRK**	Expressway	**EXPY**
Brooks	**BRKS**	Extension	**EXT**
Burg	**BG**	Extensions	**EXTS**
Bypass	**BYP**	Fall	**FALL**
Camp	**CP**	Falls	**FLS**
Canyon	**CYN**	Ferry	**FRY**
Cape	**CPE**	Field	**FLD**
Causeway	**CSWY**	Fields	**FLDS**
Center	**CTR**	Flat	**FLT**
Centers	**CTRS**	Flats	**FLTS**
Circle	**CIR**	Ford	**FRD**
Circles	**CIRS**	Fords	**FRDS**
Cliff	**CLF**	Forest	**FRST**
Cliffs	**CLFS**	Forge	**FRG**
Club	**CLB**	Forges	**FRGS**
Common	**CMN**	Fork	**FRK**
Corner	**COR**	Forks	**FRKS**
Corners	**CORS**	Fort	**FT**
Course	**CRSE**	Freeway	**FWY**
Court	**CT**	Garden	**GDN**
Courts	**CTS**	Gardens	**GDNS**
Cove	**CV**	Gateway	**GTWY**
Coves	**CVS**	Glen	**GLN**

Appendices

A GUIDE TO LETTER-WRITING

Name	Abbreviation	Name	Abbreviation
Glens	GLNS	Mill	ML
Green	GRN	Mills	MLS
Greens	GRNS	Mission	MSN
Grove	GRV	Motorway	MTWY
Groves	GRVS	Mount	MT
Harbor	HBR	Mountain	MTN
Harbors	HBRS	Mountains	MTNS
Haven	HVN	Neck	NCK
Heights	HTS	Orchard	ORCH
Highway	HWY	Oval	OVAL
Hill	HL	Overpass	OPAS
Hills	HLS	Park	PARK
Hollow	HOLW	Parks	PARK
Inlet	INLT	Parkway	PKWY
Island	IS	Parkways	PKWY
Islands	ISS	Pass	PASS
Isle	ISLE	Passage	PSGE
Junction	JCT	Path	PATH
Junctions	JCTS	Pike	PIKE
Key	KY	Pine	PNE
Keys	KYS	Pines	PNES
Knoll	KNL	Place	PL
Knolls	KNLS	Plain	PLN
Lake	LK	Plains	PLNS
Lakes	LKS	Plaza	PLZ
Land	LAND	Point	PT
Landing	LNDG	Points	PTS
Lane	LN	Port	PRT
Light	LGT	Ports	PRTS
Lights	LGTS	Prairie	PR
Loaf	LF	Radial	RADL
Lock	LCK	Ramp	RAMP
Locks	LCKS	Ranch	RNCH
Lodge	LDG	Rapid	RPD
Loop	LOOP	Rapids	RPDS
Mall	MALL	Rest	RST
Manor	MNR	Ridge	RDG
Manors	MNRS	Ridges	RDGS
Meadow	MDW	River	RIV
Meadows	MDWS	Road	RD
Mews	MEWS	Roads	RDS

Appendices

Name	Abbreviation	Name	Abbreviation
Route	**RTE**	Trafficway	**TRFY**
Row	**ROW**	Trail	**TRL**
Rue	**RUE**	Tunnel	**TUNL**
Run	**RUN**	Turnpike	**TPKE**
Shoal	**SHL**	Underpass	**UPAS**
Shoals	**SHLS**	Union	**UN**
Shore	**SHR**	Unions	**UNS**
Shores	**SHRS**	Valley	**VLY**
Skyway	**SKWY**	Valleys	**VLYS**
Spring	**SPG**	Viaduct	**VIA**
Springs	**SPGS**	View	**VW**
Spur	**SPUR**	Views	**VWS**
Spurs	**SPUR**	Villages	**VLGS**
Squares	**SQS**	Ville	**VL**
Station	**STA**	Vista	**VIS**
Stravenue	**STRA**	Walk	**WALK**
Stream	**STRM**	Walks	**WALK**
Street	**ST**	Wall	**WALL**
Streets	**STS**	Way	**WAY**
Summit	**SMT**	Ways	**WAYS**
Terrace	**TER**	Well	**WL**
Throughway	**TRWY**	Wells	**WLS**
Trace	**TRCE**		

Appendix 3

Abbreviations for English and Welsh Postal Counties

County	Abbreviation
Bedfordshire	**BEDS**
Berkshire	**BERKS**
Buckinghamshire	**BUCKS**
Cambridgeshire	**CAMBS**
Cumbria	**CUMB**
Derbyshire	**DERBYS**
East Sussex	**E SUSS**
Gloucestershire	**GLOUC, GLOS**
Hampshire	**HANTS**
Hertfordshire	**HERTS**
Lancashire	**LANCS**
Leicestershire	**LEICS**
Lincolnshire	**LINCS**
Mid Glamorgan	**M GLAM**
North Yorkshire	**N YORKS**
Northamptonshire	**NORTHANTS, NHANTS**
Northumberland	**NORTHD**
Nottinghamshire	**NOTTS**
Oxfordshire	**OXON**
Shropshire	**SHROPS**
South Glamorgan	**S GLAM**
South Yorkshire	**S YORKS**
Staffordshire	**STAFFS**
Warwickshire	**WARKS**
West Glamorgan	**W GLAM**
West Sussex	**W SUSS**
West Yorkshire	**W YORKS**
Wiltshire	**WILTS**

Appendix 4

Irregular Verbs

A regular verb is one in which the past tense and past participle is formed by adding -*ed* to the infinitive, as in:

Infinitive	Past tense	Past participle
ask	asked	asked
grin	grinned	grinned
point	pointed	pointed
talk	talked	talked

An irregular verb is one that does not conform to this pattern of adding -*ed* to the past tense and past participle.

Irregular verbs fall into several categories:

- Verbs whose past tense and past participle forms are the same as the infinitive form (also known as the base form) of the verb, and which do not end in -*ed*. These include:

Infinitive/base form	Past tense	Past participle
bet	bet	bet
burst	burst	burst
cast	cast	cast
cost	cost	cost
cut	cut	cut
hit	hit	hit
hurt	hurt	hurt
let	let	let
put	put	put
set	set	set
shed	shed	shed
shut	shut	shut

slit	slit	slit
split	split	split
spread	spread	spread

- Some verbs have two past tense forms and the same two past participle forms, one regular and formed with -*ed* and the other irregular, as in:

Infinitive/base form	Past tense	Past participle
burn	burned, burnt	burned, burnt
dream	dreamed, dreamt	dreamed, dreamt
dwell	dwelled, dwelt	dwelled, dwelt
hang	hanged, hung,	hanged, hung
kneel	kneeled, knelt,	kneeled, knelt
lean	leaned, leant	leaned, leant
leap	leaped, leapt,	leaped, leapt
learn	learned, learnt	learned, learnt
light	lighted, lit	lighted, lit
smell	smelled, smelt	smelled, smelt
speed	speeded, sped	speeded, sped
spill	spilled, spilt	spilled, spilt
spoil	spoiled, spoilt	spoiled, spoilt
weave	weaved, woven	weaved, woven
wet	wetted, wet	wetted, wet

- Some verbs have irregular past tenses and *the same* irregular past participle. These include:

Infinitive/base form	Past tense	Past participle
bend	bent	bent
bleed	bled	bled
breed	bred	bred
build	built	built
cling	clung	clung
dig	dug	dug

feel	felt	felt
fight	fought	fought
find	found	found
flee	fled	fled
fling	flung	flung
get	got	got
grind	ground	ground
hear	heard	heard
hold	held	held
keep	kept	kept
lay	laid	laid
lead	led	led
leave	left	left
lend	lent	lent
lose	lost	lost
make	made	made
mean	meant	meant
meet	met	met
pay	paid	paid
rend	rent	rent
say	said	said
seek	sought	sought
sell	sold	sold
send	sent	sent
shine	shone	shone
shoe	shod	shod
sit	sat	sat
sleep	slept	slept
slide	slid	slid
sling	slung	slung
slink	slunk	slunk
spend	spent	spent

stand	stood	stood
stick	stuck	stuck
sting	stung	stung
strike	struck	struck
string	strung	strung
sweep	swept	swept
swing	swung	swung
teach	taught	taught
tell	told	told
think	thought	thought
understand	understood	understood
weep	wept	wept
win	won	won
wring	wrung	wrung

- Some irregular verbs have regular past tense forms but two possible past participles, one of which is regular (ends in -*ed*). These include:

Infinitive/base form	Past tense	Past participle
mow	mowed	mowed, mown
prove	proved	proved, proven
sew	sewed	sewed, sewn
show	showed	showed, shown
sow	sowed	sowed, sown
swell	swelled	swelled, swollen

- In some irregular verbs, the past tense and past participle are different from each other, and also different from the infinitive or base form of the verb, as in:

Infinitive/base form	Past tense	Past participle
arise	arose	arisen
awake	awoke	awoken
bear	bore	borne

Appendices

begin	began	begun
bid	bade	bidden
bite	bit	bitten
blow	blew	blown
break	broke	broken
choose	chose	chosen
do	did	done
draw	drew	drawn
drink	drank	drunk
drive	drove	driven
eat	ate	eaten
fall	fell	fallen
fly	flew	flown
forbear	forbore	forborne
forbid	forbade	forbidden
forgive	forgave	forgiven
forget	forgot	forgotten
forsake	forsook	forsaken
freeze	froze	frozen
forswear	forswore	foresworn
give	gave	given
go	went	gone
grow	grew	grown
hew	hewed	hewn
hide	hid	hidden
know	knew	known
lie	lay	lain
ride	rode	ridden
ring	rang	rung
saw	sawed	sawn
see	saw	seen
rise	rose	risen

shake	shook	shaken
shrink	shrank	shrunk
slay	slew	slain
speak	spoke	spoken
spring	sprang	sprung
steal	stole	stolen
stink	stank	stunk
strew	strewed	strewn
stride	strode	stridden
strive	strove	striven
swear	swore	sworn
swim	swam	swum
take	took	taken
tear	tore	torn
throw	threw	thrown
tread	trod	trodden
wake	woke	woken
wear	wore	worn
write	written	wrote

Appendix 5
Some Abbreviations, Acronyms and Short Forms Used in Text Messaging and Email

2DAY	today
2Hot2Hndle	too hot to handle
2MORO	tomorrow
2NITE	tonight
4EVRYRS	forever yours
A3	anytime, anywhere, anyplace
A&S	all and sundry
AAMOF	as a matter of fact
AB	ah bless!
AbsntMndd	absentminded
ActLIkUMEnIt	act like you mean it
AFAIC	as far as I'm concerned
AFAICS	as far as I can see
AFAICT	as far as I can tell
AFAIK	as far as I know
AFK	away from keyboard
AIUI	as I understand it
AKA	also known as
ALIWanIsU	all I want is you
ALOrO	all or nothing
AML	all my love
ASAP	as soon as possible
A/S?	age, sex?
A/S/L?	age, sex, location?
ATB	all the best
AWGTHTGTATA	are we going to have to go through all this again?
AYOR	at your own risk
AYPI?	and your point is?
B3	blah, blah, blah
B4	before
BAK	back at the keyboard
BBFN	bye bye for now
BBIAB	be back in a bit
BBL	be back later
BCNU	be seeing you
BdBy	bad boy
BF	boyfriend

BFN	bye for now
BICBW	but I could be wrong
BION	believe it or not
BITMT	but in the meantime
BL&	bland
BoTl	bottle
BRB	be right back
BTAIM	be that as it may
BTDT	been there, done that
BthD8?	when were you born?
BTW	by the way
BYKT	but you knew that
CIIYIMFL	could I include you in my friends' list?
c%d	could
Cld	could
CMIIW	correct me if I'm wrong
Cngrtultns	congratulations
C/P/S	city (or country), profession, status
CSThnknAU	can't stop thinking about you
CU	see you
CUIMD	see you in my dreams
CUL8R	see you later
CU2Moro	see you tomorrow
CYA	see ya
CZIN	season
D8	date
DLTBBB	don't let the bed bugs bite
DQMOT	don't quote me on this
EOL	end of lecture
EOM	end of message
EML	evil manic laugh
F2T	free to talk
FITB	fill in the blank
FOC	free of charge
FWIW	for what it's worth
FYEO	for your eyes only
FYI	for your information
GAL	get a life
GAO	glad all over
GAS	greetings and salutations
GF	girlfriend
GFETE	grinning from ear to ear
GG	good game
GMeSumLuvin	gimme some lovin'
GMTA	great minds think alike
Gr8	great
GSOH	good salary own home

Appendices

GSOH	good sense of humour
GTG	got to go
GTSY	glad to see you
H&K	hug and kiss
H8	hate
HAGD	have a good day
HAGN	have a good night
HAND	have a nice day
HITULThtILuvU?	have I told you lately that I love you?
HldMeClse	hold me close
HTH	hope this helps
IAC	in any case
ICLW\YLuv	I can't live without your love
IDK	I don't know
IDntDsrveU	I don't deserve you
IDST	I didn't say that
IDTS	I don't think so
IGotUBbe	I got you babe
IIRC	if I recall correctly
IJC2SalLuvU	I just called to say I love you
ILUVU	I love you
IMHO	in my humble opinion
IMNSHO	in my not so humble opinion
IMO	in my opinion
IOHO	in our humble opinion
IOW	in other words
IYKWIM	if you know what I mean
IYSS	if you say so
JM2p	just my two pennyworth
JstCLMe	just call me
KIT	keep in touch
KOTC	kiss on the cheek
KOTL	kiss on the lips
L8	late
L8R	later
LETA	letter
LetsGt2gtha	let's get together
LOL	laugh out loud
LstinU	lost in you
LTNC	long time no see
LtsGt2gthr	let's get together
LuvU	love you
MkeMyDaSa+!	make my day say yes
M$ULkeCraZ	miss you like crazy
MO	moment
Mob	mobile
MYOB	mind your own business

NE	any
NE1	anyone
NO1	no one
NRN	no reply necessary
NW	no way!
OIC	oh I see
OTOH	on the other hand
PCM	please call me
PLS	please
PPL	people
QT	cutie
R	are/our
RB@u	right back at you
ReCv	receive
ResQMe	rescue me
Rkive	archive
RmbaYaMne	remember you're mine
ROFL	rolling on the floor laughing
RTM	read the manual
RU?	are you?
RUOK?	are you okay
RUTLKN2ME	are you talking to me?
Salt&ILDoIT	say it & I'll do it
SETE	smiling ear to ear
SIT	stay in touch
SITD	still in the dark
SOH	sense of humour
SOHF	sense of humour failure
SOME1	someone
SOPA*	superstar
SRy	sorry
StckOnU	stuck on you
SvnALMyLuv4U	saving all my love for you
SWG	scientific wild guess
SYS	see you soon
TBDF	to be discussed further
TDTU	totally devoted to you
THNQ	thank you
Thx	thanks
Ti2GO	time to go
TIA	thanks in advance
TIC	tongue in cheek
TLMeImDrmn	tell me I'm dreaming
TNX	thanks
TPTB	the powers that be
TTFN	ta ta for now
TTYL8R	talk to you later

Appendices

TWIMC	to whom it may concern
U	you
U+Me=Luv	you + me = love
UCnDoMgic	you can do magic
UdoSumthn2Me	you do something to me
UR	you are
WAN2	want to
WAN2TLK?	want to talk
WenCnICUAgn?	when can I see you again?
WER R U?	where are you?
WLUMRyMe?	will you marry me?
WRT	with respect/regard to
WTTW	word to the wise
WUWH	wish you were here
X	kiss
Xclusvly Yas	exclusively yours
XLNT	excellent
Xoxoxoxo	hugs and kisses
Y?	why?
YBS	you'll be sorry
YYSSW	yeah, yeah, sure, sure, whatever